For the Gooleys.
Present, past and future.

Tristan Gooley is a writer, navigator and explorer. He has worked in travel most of his life, led expeditions on five continents and pioneered a renaissance in the very rare art of natural navigation. Tristan is the only living person to have both flown solo and sailed single-handed across the Atlantic. He is a Fellow of the Royal Geographical Society and the Royal Institute of Navigation and Vice Chairman of the UK's largest independent travel company, Trailfinders.

Also by Tristan Gooley

The Natural Navigator

THE NATURAL
EXPLORER

TRISTAN GOOLEY
Illustrations by Neil Gower

First published in Great Britain in 2012 by Sceptre
An imprint of Hodder & Stoughton
An Hachette UK company

First published in paperback in 2013

3

Copyright © Tristan Gooley 2012

'Sylva Anathema' from *Tales from the Woods* by Felix Dennis, published by Ebury
Press (2010). Reprinted by permission of Felix Dennis.

Every reasonable effort has been made to contact any copyright holders of
material reproduced in this book. But if there are any errors or omissions,
Hodder & Stoughton will be pleased to insert the appropriate acknowledgement
in any subsequent printing of this publication.

A CIP catalogue record for this title is available from the British Library

ISBN 978 1 444 72032 7
eBook ISBN 978 1 444 720 334

Typeset in New Baskerville by Palimpsest Book Production Limited,
Falkirk, Stirlingshire

Printed and bound by Clays Ltd, St Ives plc

Hodder & Stoughton policy is to use papers that are natural,
renewable and recyclable products and made from wood grown in
sustainable forests. The logging and manufacturing processes are expected to
conform to the environmental regulations of the country of origin.

Hodder & Stoughton Ltd
338 Euston Road
London NW1 3BH

www.hodder.co.uk

© The Royal Society/portrait of James Holman by George Ghinnery: page 24
Maps and Illustrations © Neil Gower

Contents

The Lost Explorer:
An Introduction

And that, in brief, is all there is to tell about the South
Pole. One gets there, and that is about all there is for
the telling. It is the effort to get there that counts. We
put the Pole behind us and raced for home.

Richard Byrd

The explorer has taken a wrong turn.

In the National Gallery of Ireland there hangs a
painting of a tall, dark-skinned and well-built man. He is
dressed in flowing robes and a turban, clothes he is unlikely to
have chosen. The portrait was painted by Sir Joshua Reynolds and
in 2001 it sold for a record £10.3 million.

The man in the picture had travelled from the other side of
the world and appeared at the heart of London society in the
autumn of 1774. The handsome visitor wore a Manchester velvet
suit lined with white satin and lace ruffles; an elegant sword hung
by his side. News of his arrival caused a sensation and spread
across the city; he was quickly introduced to the elite of the day.
The stranger met King George III three days after setting foot on
English soil.

Omai was the first Polynesian to visit London and had arrived
aboard HMS *Adventure*, one of Captain Cook's two ships from his
second great exploratory voyage. He had been adopted by the
expedition for both good and bad reasons, but he was not coerced.
Omai cannot be held accountable for what happened next.

The Noble Savage, as he was labelled at the time, was eagerly chaperoned by Sir Joseph Banks. Banks had sailed with Cook on his first voyage, as a self-sponsored gentleman botanist, and met Omai in his homeland of Tahiti during this journey. Banks had been quick to capitalise on the success of Cook's previous circumnavigation. In the months after Cook and his crew returned from that voyage it was Banks who positioned himself as the righteous feeder of public curiosity. (He walked away from the second expedition before it departed, in a sulk after being told that the extra cabins he had insisted on having built on top of an otherwise excellent vessel had made Cook's ship unseaworthy and dangerous.)

Banks, Omai and Cook, three men from three very different worlds, gave us some of the golden moments in the history of exploration and in turn the opportunity for us to build a picture of what it means to be an explorer.

Banks, for all his self-aggrandising, was a formidable naturalist. Discovery was his business – he brought back 30,000 plant specimens from his travels, including 1,400 never seen before, which increased the number of the world's known plants by a quarter. He also vividly embodied both gallivanting hero, fighting to push back the frontiers of human knowledge, and fame-crazed egotist. He was able to draw from impressive reserves in each department when the occasion demanded and coming across Omai for the second time, it was the latter resource that he reached for.

Banks was ahead of his time in having an eye for what the public wanted and the chutzpah and means to deliver it. He took Omai under his wing and began a campaign to grab the attention of the British public, or to be more accurate, the public that mattered to him: high society.

It was Banks' interest that pushed Omai to the centre of attention. The noble man, who had left the comforts of home to travel half way around the world in arduous conditions, had metamorphosed into someone who enjoyed the attention, perhaps a little too much. Omai had become a celebrity. His visit was not without controversy, he was criticised for joining a rakish circle, for playing cards and kissing a lady's handkerchief.

The scientist, the discoverer, the navigator, the conquistador, the hero, the celebrity . . . The explorer wears many masks. But behind them all lies a simple philosophy. The explorer must do two things: make discoveries and communicate these to others.

Omai gratefully accepted a lift with Cook's third great voyage and returned to his life in the Pacific. Unfortunately we know little about his time after settling back there. He doubtless regaled the islanders with rich tales of the people and customs in London and the discoveries he had made on the other side of the world. In this way he was as much an explorer as Cook or Banks and he did us a great service by illustrating that it was possible to discover a place that regarded itself as the political and cultural centre of the known world. He died two and a half years after his return, possibly from a disease contracted in England.

It has been more than two centuries since this trio came together and helped to increase knowledge and fire imaginations. The masks available to the explorer have not changed much, but as time passed, two proved more popular than the others: hero and celebrity. This was a gradual process but there are moments when we are able to get a front-row seat to observe it.

By the first half of the nineteenth century existential angst had crept into the thoughts of the more conscientious explorers. The Prussian explorer of Australia, Ludwig Leichhardt, wonders, in a breathlessly-long sentence, which mask people will see him wearing.

Others considered the undertaking exceedingly dangerous, and even . . . madness on my part; and the consequence of a blind enthusiasm, nourished either by a deep devotion to science, or by an unreasonable craving for fame: whilst others did not feel themselves justified in assisting a man who they considered was setting out with an intention of committing suicide.

Almost a century after Leichhardt's journey the change was gathering pace, but it took a boy from County Kildare, Ireland, to act out the tipping point. On Sunday, 7 March 1912 a cable arrived from Hobart, Tasmania. In it the Norwegian explorer Roald Amundsen informed his brother and, in turn, the world, that he had reached the South Pole.

In an article published four days later in the *New York Times*, Sir Ernest Shackleton analysed Amundsen's victorious cable. In the Anglo-Irishman's choice of words it is easy to sense his mildly begrudging respect for his rival's achievement: in the short piece he describes Amundsen as fortunate on four separate occasions. However, if there is the slightest hint of bitterness it is almost certainly brought on by a weightier problem than one man's achievement, however envy-inducing.

The South Pole had stood as one of the greatest goals in the imagination of explorers and the public for centuries and was the only one left after the North Pole had apparently succumbed in 1909. (The American explorer, Robert Peary, claimed to have reached the geographic North Pole on 6 April 1909. He was given credit for it at the time and for many years afterwards, although the balance of opinion has now shifted against him. The debate as to whether he reached it or not rumbles on.) Both Poles had now been trampled and therefore sullied as goals of the highest kind for polar explorers. To a man as finely tuned to the market-ability of large expeditions as Shackleton, this news was as cold a wind as he would have felt in Antarctica.

Shackleton was acutely aware that the business of exploration required a delicate balance and clever packaging. Now that the race to the South Pole was over, he would need to offset its neat-ness of goal with the scale of his new venture, and the danger it promised. This was a raising of the polar exploration stakes that he had forecast exactly one year to the day before. Writing in the *Daily Mail* on 11 March 1911 Shackleton attempted to explain, and perhaps plead, that the game that he had given his life to, must go on. 'The discovery of the South Pole will not be the end of Antarctic exploration. The next work [would be] a transcontinental journey from sea to sea, crossing the Pole.'

Therein lay the rub. If it was not before, it had most definitely now become a game. Previously it had been easy to argue that the human race needed to know what lay at the Poles. Now it transpired that there was nothing to differentiate the geographic Poles from the ice that lay all around them, but we only know that because explorers, like Amundsen, reached them and reported back.

It might sound risible now, but nobody could actually prove that these places were not marked by pots of gold or being patrolled by icy dragons. While any doubts lingered, however small, discovery of more of the same was every bit as valid in geographical terms as the discovery of a smoking and thundering waterfall on the Zambezi river.

The problem with Shackleton's new trans-Antarctic proposal was that the aims of exploration had shifted. The crux of his new expedition was not that it would make discoveries, but that it would be physically, technically and mentally at the limits of human potential. It promised to deliver a great narrative, but it did not offer to teach us much that was new about the world we live in. The geographer and explorer, Sir Clements Markham, wrote that he was 'astounded at the absurdity of Shackleton's plan' and added that it was, 'designed solely for self-advertisement.' Markham was certainly no fan of Shackleton's, but he was not alone in holding reservations. Even *The Times*' upbeat assessment was that Shackleton's aim was to restore Britain's prestige by putting it back at the top of polar exploration – prestige, not discovery. The Royal Geographical Society limited its support to an aloof £1,000 and then showed some regret for even that level.

By both design and then accident, the story that emerged from Shackleton's now famous Endurance epic, or the 'Imperial Trans-Antarctic Expedition' to give it its formal title, was extraordinary. The boat, *Endurance* herself, became trapped and then crushed in the southern ice, after which the expedition unravelled completely. As Shackleton fought to protect his team, he led his men over ice, onto the elements-torn Elephant Island, across the Southern ocean in a small boat and then over the dangerous land of South Georgia to the refuge of a whaling station.

With each stage there followed another chapter in a tale of hardship, leadership, courage, sacrifice, navigation, bad and good luck that has possibly never been exceeded in the history of exploration. This story has been told often, the point here is that its power has played a significant part in re-shaping the image of the explorer in the minds of the public and consequently in the minds of explorers themselves.

It is no coincidence that before the expedition set off, Winston Churchill referred to Shackleton as, 'this adventurer' and not 'this explorer'. The crossing of Antarctica was not conceived as a voyage of discovery, even before it went horribly wrong, and by the time each person had miraculously survived the ordeal, discovery had been dramatically expunged from the popular picture of the explorer altogether. Who would be so greedy as to cry out for greater insight into our world, when such a feast of the human spirit prevailing over nature's cold wrath was being served up for all to enjoy?

The Trans-Antarctic expedition was conceived as a 'pitch', something Shackleton knew would stand a good chance of lighting the interest of the public, media and sponsors, although not necessarily in that order. This triad of interest had now completed its move from the background of expedition ambitions to the foreground. Science had been trumped, it lacked the public appeal of adventure, and it took its seat at the back.

Shackleton was by no means the only one responsible for the switch of emphasis from discovery about the world we travel through to the travails, danger and, not least, glory of the individual explorers themselves. However, he personified this shift well and played his part with vigour.

The trend continued throughout the twentieth century and now, sadly, in the second decade of the twenty-first it feels as though we might have reached a point where it is difficult to find a good home for the word 'explorer'. The word 'exploration' now feels equally moribund, and is most commonly used when companies look for oil, gold or other precious minerals.

The physical goals have been steadily mastered and it becomes increasingly obvious that the rewards to humanity of driving harder in this area are diminishing. There is talk of learning more about what we are capable of, mentally and physically, but this is not a convincing argument. There might not have been an expedition since Shackleton's *Endurance* voyage one hundred years ago that has taught us much more about what our species can achieve in extremis.

What explorers moulded in the old style so often mean, but do not say, when they use this argument is that we will learn what they *as individuals* are capable of. The results are often undeniably impressive journeys, but might they be of greater service to the individual than the species?

Before this philosophy dominated, there was a golden age of exploration. More than one in fact, and they were not golden because places on the map had not been walked upon by white men, but golden because these were times when to explore meant to discover and share. We have fallen into the trap of believing that territory needs to be virgin for exploration to be possible or, failing this, an explorer must risk their life and dance with the extremes of physical endurance. Neither of these notions is true.

We must collectively share responsibility for allowing the concept of exploration to be monopolised by those who have been consumed by these ideas. It is time to wrest it back, time to forge a new explorer by reaching back to the many who had the spirit in years gone by and out to the few who have held on to it.

For a new age of exploration to be worthwhile, the aim must be to return to celebrating the acts of discovering and sharing, on however modest a scale. We can take our inspiration from the most curious of those that have gone before and go further, as we are not limited by the boundaries of knowledge or communication of their era. An ardent spirit of inquisitiveness married with the opportunity to connect more deeply and share more widely with the world around us than ever before: this is where the joys lie.

The person who brings greater understanding of the role a wild flower plays in the universe and the impact it might have on our thoughts and emotions, serves us better than the person who finds some novel way to punish themselves by exercising in remote places. In the future there will be two types of explorer, but only one will be happy to settle for quiet enlightenment, shared.

The great German explorer of South America, Alexander von Humboldt, who relished the interconnections that the natural world offered two centuries ago, holds a light for the new explorer. Humboldt was an inspiration at a time when a spirit of inquiry was treasured – Charles Darwin took his *Personal Narrative* with him on his travels and knew passages by heart. We should not be surprised to learn that Humboldt can hint at paths ahead for us.

It is the task of the explorer (and it is this which distinguishes them from the traveller) to make discoveries and to share them with the world. The latter part of the role offers exciting new possibilities for the next generation of explorers. When Humboldt wrote about his travels he did so in a way that conveyed his sense of wonder. He clearly viewed the opportunity to share his discoveries with as much zeal and ambition as the journey itself. His writing is entrancing and drew all who read it into the moments he had experienced. It is no coincidence that he was admired by French literary giants including Balzac, Hugo, Chateaubriand and Flaubert. He was friends with many luminaries of the German Romantic movement too, including Schiller and Goethe, who told his biographer, 'What a man he is! I have known him so long and yet he amazes me all over again.'

The opportunity to share the joys of discoveries with others through creativity has always been with us, it is part of being human, but we are especially fortunate that we live in a time when the potential to both create and share is growing exponentially.

Human beings have always marvelled at novelty, but we also find much to love in things that emerge from the dialectic course of our past. Deciding to see exploration as a challenge to make discoveries in lands that have been mapped many times and then share this experience in creative ways, marries tradition and novelty.

The experience of witnessing a deer move across white slopes as the intricate lattice of a snowflake cracks the light of a low sun into a perfect spectrum, can bring exaltation of a few seconds to an aware observer. The experience can also be wrought into a painting, a poem, book, song or sculpture and the whole journey of a few seconds or many years, shared with the world via the exploding potential of a digital age. Somewhere along this path the observer becomes an explorer. The opportunity is there for a new golden era.

It took a lot of courage for men to haul sleds across icy crevasses or to risk dropping down dead for want of a drop of water. It takes a different courage to attempt to make discoveries in a world that is so self-consciously drowning in knowledge and then to share this through creative expression. This is the gauntlet that the Natural Explorer runs.

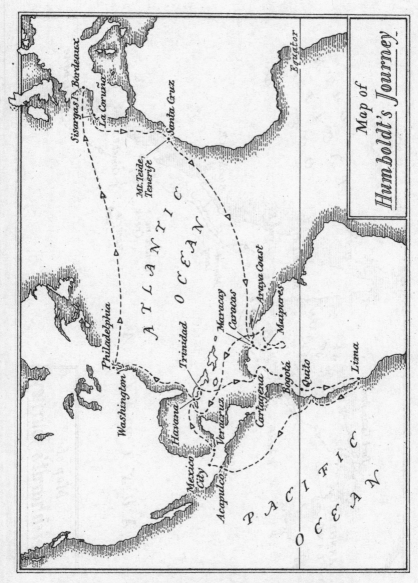

Alexander von Humboldt's American Expedition 1799–1804

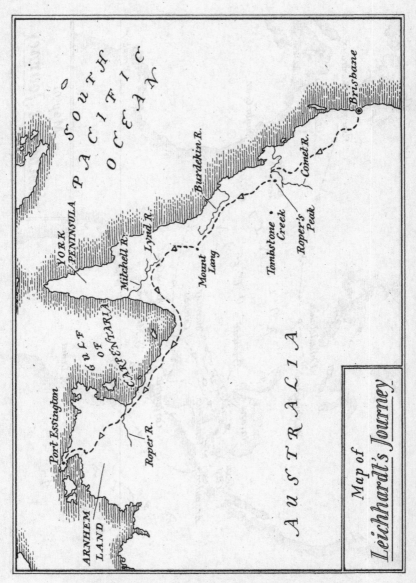

Ludwig Leichhardt's Australian Expedition 1844–1845

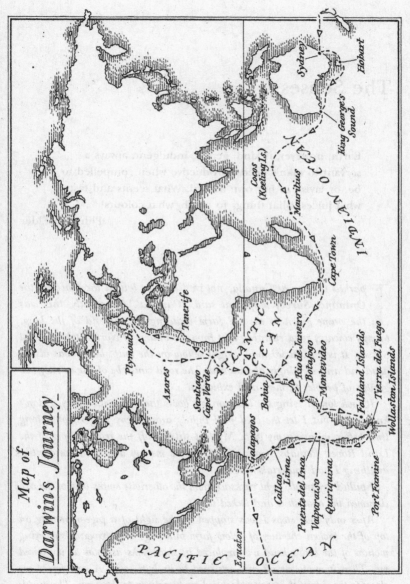

Charles Darwin's Beagle Expedition 1831–1836

The Senses

Earth, however, is kind, gentle, indulgent, always a
servant to man's needs, productive when compelled to
be, or lavish of her own accord. What scents and tastes,
what juices, what things to touch, what colours!

Pliny the Elder

I parked the car at Canada; not in Canada, but at the place on the
Ordnance Survey map that said, 'Canada'. Apparently, this was
the name given to the old farm buildings at the end of the long,
bumpy country road running east from the village of North Stoke in West
Sussex. It is an official road, bright yellow on the map, but it was also a
dead-end and seemingly abandoned. The road could be of use to only two
groups of people: farmers and explorers.

It took longer tying the laces on my boots than was necessary. I don't
know why, but I let the cord pull tightly around my fingers for a long
time before releasing my grip. My foot slipped off the rear bumper of the
Land Rover. Perhaps I was afraid. Before me lay an expedition unlike
anything I had undertaken before.

I pulled my small, light rucksack from the otherwise empty boot of the car,
slammed the door shut and locked it.

After only four steps I was stopped by the sight of a pigeon resting on
top of the broken chimney of a low farm building. The arrogant surveying
motion of the bird's head was replaced by short jerks as soon as it noticed
me. Then it wrote me off and returned to its lofty scan. A gate forced me
closer to the side of the track, which led my eyes down to the verge. The purple

head of a thistle bowed and bobbed and a bramble tugged at my arm. I reached down past the thorns to a perfectly ripe blackberry and let it roll in my mouth, feeling each demisphere on the tip of my tongue, before giving in and letting my teeth force a juicy explosion.

Ahead, I could see many hues in the path: a pale dust dominated but there were darker dry patches too. In the depressions the track grew darker still, with the wetness from the rains of a couple of days before.

I lifted my gaze to the greens, golds, purples and browns of the fields that rolled all the way down to the sea. The sea appeared to be blending with the sky, as it so often does on hot days, but I could just distinguish it between the haze of the horizon and a line of dark forest. Arundel Castle interrupted the smooth roll of a hill, its juts throwing brown stone up towards the sky.

A few steps further on I paused again, my ears directing my eyes upwards, to where a tug-aircraft was working hard to pull a glider up into the sky. Behind this sound, the wind was combing the trees and long grasses and a distant dog gave an occasional yelp. Under it all there was a comforting hum of crickets, their chirps so evocative of warmer places. I continued and these sounds were half-buried in the dusty crunch of my boots landing in the chalk and flint.

I took the northerly fork in the path and found myself ambushed by wild-flowers. The sky-blue chicory was first to emerge from the thousand greens of the long grass. Then the radiant yellow of the hawksbit, followed by the mauve of some wild basil. Halting my slow walk, I stepped off the path and bent down to the smell of public lavatories in the flowers of hogweed and then offset this masochism by revelling in the vanilla hay scent of some Lady bedstraw. My fingers ran up over the tickling softness of some Timothy-grass and then I stopped and felt the sun warm the backs of my calves and the wind cool my neck. I felt a need to sit down on the grass. I was exhilarated, but also daunted. I had walked about three hundred metres.

• • •

The sound of the dogs barking woke the slaughterhouse workers on the morning of 29 August 1911. When the butchers went outside to see what had excited the dogs they were shocked by what they saw. They called the local sheriff, J. B. Webber, and asked him to come over from the town of Oroville. The sheriff set out with his deputies, armed and ready, and arrived to find a man who was starving, naked except for an old canvas poncho and with hair that had been burned off short. They were looking at the last Native American in California.

The emaciated man was from the Yahi, a southern group of the Yana people. There had been as many as 3000 Yana until miners and prospectors systematically slaughtered them in the 1860s. Only about 50 survived this genocide and they were forced into hiding along the creeks of the surrounding country.

Three years before Ishi, as he became known, surrendered to the Oroville sheriff, he had been forced to flee once more when two engineers who were returning to their camp stumbled upon his family's village. Ishi, his sister and an old man fled the scene, leaving Ishi's mother, who was bedridden, under some blankets and hides. Ishi ran one way, his sister and the old man headed in a different direction.

When he felt it was safe, Ishi returned to care for his mother. Neither he nor anyone else ever saw his sister or the old man again. He presumed they had died, either drowning in the dangerous creek or victims of a bear attack. His mother died soon afterwards, leaving Ishi as the last of the Yana. He lived all alone until he stumbled, apathetically but deliberately into the corral of the slaughterhouse that August morning in 1911.

From that moment, however terrifying and bewildering it must have been at times, Ishi's fortunes improved. He was cared for and then employed by anthropologists at the University of California, Berkeley. For five years he helped the researchers piece together an understanding of the Yana lifestyle.

The Yana were hunter-gatherers and Ishi explained and then demonstrated to his new friends that this method of survival depended on being able to sense an animal before it became aware of the hunter's presence. His sight, hearing and smell all needed to be employed as effectively as possible. Having found a clearing, Ishi made sure that he was downwind of it, concealing his scent from the animals, but also giving him the opportunity to smell prey as small as a rabbit. He would press two fingers against his lips and emulate the kissing sound of a rabbit in distress, drawing them close enough for him to kill with his bow and arrow. He could also impersonate quails, squirrels, geese and other animals as the prey demanded.

Ishi explained that prior to hunting it was essential for the hunter to remain pure. The decontamination ritual before a deer hunt included abstaining from sex, eating fish or smoking tobacco, sometimes for several days. On the morning of the hunt he abstained from all food and sweated himself. He refused to hunt with smokers. Sometimes Ishi would complete his immersion into the world of the animals by putting a stuffed deer's head over his own, using it to peep over rocks and to lure the curious animals towards him.

Ishi's ability to sense the presence of smaller animals and remain finely tuned to his surroundings was not the result of any inherent differences. He did not possess any biological advantages or strange powers. It was the result of cultural and anthropological differences driven by necessity. Most people have the potential to do what Ishi did, even if they have lived in a city all their life, if they choose to give their full attention to their senses and practise using them.

Ishi had lived his life away from the bombardment of unnatural sensations to which modern life subjected most Californians, even at the end of the nineteenth century. Sadly, Ishi's sensitivity to the world extended to an immune system that had not been exposed to the prevalent illnesses of the time. He caught his first ever common cold within a few weeks of arriving in San Francisco and pneumonia that same winter. Ishi developed a bad cough in December 1914, one that never fully left him. He lost his life to tuberculosis on 25 March 1916, aged, it was best guessed, 49.

Ishi had depended for survival on tuning all his senses, but it is the sense of sight that will dominate if allowed to. Ludwig

Leichhardt was impressed by his Aboriginal companions' ability to notice the smallest details on their travels and he always fell short in any contest to spot something inconspicuous.

> Every new moon also was hailed with an almost superstitious devotion, and my Blackfellows vied with each other to discover its thin crescent, and would be almost angry with me when I strained my duller eyes in vain to catch a glimpse of its faint light in the brilliant sky which succeeds the setting of the sun.

It is more likely that Leichhardt lacked practice than that his eyesight was not up to the job. Wilfred Thesiger had similar experiences in the Arabian deserts, where the Bedouin would point out camels on the horizon that he had failed to notice. As he strained his eyes to detect them, the Bedouin would be debating whether they were 'in milk' or not, their eyesight having been so perfectly honed that they could make out the shape of the animals' udders where even a seasoned desert traveller, such as Thesiger, struggled to see more than a dot. Thesiger was later reprimanded by the Bedouin when he failed to notice some oryx in the distance. Thesiger could make out the white dots on the plain when they were pointed out to him, but *he had not seen them*. He was being admonished for his lack of awareness, not his eyesight, 'If they had been Arabs you would have sat there, without seeing them, until they came and cut your throat.'

Practice improves our awareness, but awareness is also a state of mind, one that develops from a need or desire to register details. Having noticed something in our environment, we need to make a decision about how keen we are to think about it and consequently to remember it. Awareness and memory form two parts of our conscious experience, both of which are fed initially by our senses, but which then depend on our choice to hone them. Leichhardt witnessed this coming together of awareness and memory in the way the Aboriginals experienced the land.

The impressions on their retina seem to be naturally more intense than on that of the European; and their recollections are remarkably exact, even to the most minute details. Trees peculiarly formed or grouped, broken branches, slight elevations of the ground – in fact a hundred things, which we should remark only when paying great attention to a place – seem to form a kind of Daguerreotype impression on their minds, every part of which is readily recollected.

A state of heightened awareness is not the same as familiarity: it is a habit that is transferable. At a village in the Kalahari, Laurens Van Der Post learnt that the Europeans that lived there would gather to study an aircraft as it came in to land, but they were always outdone by the locals. The local villagers could tell from the style of flying who the pilot was that day. They were never wrong.

Eyes are formidable organs capable of recognising between 150 and 200 colours. Their position at the front of the head, the predator's alignment, allows us to focus on an object with both eyes simultaneously, bringing it into sharp focus. Faint stars, clouds or very distant objects can disappear into the background when we close one eye. Pilots and other professionals that depend heavily on their vision are taught to understand the peculiarities of the eye's geography. Our muscles align the eyeballs so that the light from the point we are interested in falls on the fovea, the only area with a dense concentration of sensitive cells. This allows focused vision. If we hold a book up in front of us we can read its words, but moving it even a few centimetres to one side will blur the words if our eyes, and therefore our foveas, do not follow the text.

The point at which the optic nerve enters the eyeball contains none of the necessary cells for vision and so it creates a blind spot. Although usually compensated for by the other eye, there is a spot that each eye cannot see at all.

Finding Your Blind Spot.
Close your left eye and hold this page about 20cm from your right eye.
Look at the cross and slowly move the page forward and backward until the black circle disappears.

When we enjoy looking at something outdoors we are seeing it as a mix of perfect focus, imperfect peripheral vision and blindspots. Pilots are taught to scan the sky when looking for other aircraft, by moving the eyes in short hops from one spot to the next. We can use the same techniques when appreciating the outdoors as it will bring different points into sharp focus and allow discoveries that would otherwise pass unnoticed. Our eyes tend to be drawn to certain things: landmarks such as buildings, dominant trees or unusual landscape features. If there is anything interesting but inconspicuous to either side of these features it will go unnoticed by the majority who allow their focus to settle on one spot.

It helps to scan an outdoors scene in the opposite direction to the way we read. When we look at the world from left to right we have a tendency to skip from one thing to the next, our eyes jumping forward to find the next meaningful 'word' or object. If we reverse this direction, and look from right to left, then we become more observant.

The latest research is showing that we do not all see colours in the same way. Or, to be more precise, we do not all see greens and reds in the same way. Sensitivity to blues and yellows is hard-wired into all of us, since our earliest ancestors in the sea needed to be able to detect these colours to regulate their depth. However, experiments have shown that some monkeys are not sensitive to reds and greens, and scientists now believe that this is a very late evolutionary development. Experiments have shown that we 'learn' our responses to reds and greens, in a way that we do not need to with blues and yellows. This means that our upbringing and culture will influence the way we see reds and greens.

The most dramatic cultural effect on the way we see colours can be demonstrated through language. People who grow up speaking a language that has a small number of words for colour are less sensitive to differences in those colours. The nomadic Himba people of northern Namibia have only five words to describe all the colours they see. The word 'burou' groups green with blues and purples and experiments have shown that the

Himba find it incredibly difficult to tell many blues from greens. This link between language and perception appears to be universal. It can be seen in a very different context in the fact that the words for pink and brown had to be imported into Welsh.

It is testament to the power of our eyes that loss of vision is feared so greatly. Blindness was used as a punishment for the mythical Tiresias and inflicted by the Persian ruler, Abbas the Great, upon members of his own family he felt threatened by. In the film by Luis Buñuel and Salvador Dali, *Un Chien Andalou*, terror is struck into the audience by the sight of the heroine's eyeball being sliced with a razor blade. The power of sight is a gift for those who have it, but it is a dominant one. If we think of the sensory experience as an ecosystem then vision is the alpha-beast that gobbles up all the resources, to the detriment of the other senses.

Since the Renaissance, vision has been seen as the highest sense and this is only being reinforced by the current trends in technology. The hours of television we watch, the number of photographs we take and websites we view is growing irresistibly. It is not a harmless trend.

'The fundamental event of the modern age is the conquest of the world as picture.' Heidegger's words should be a call to arms for those who value the power of the other senses. The man to turn to for leadership at this point is James Holman.

James Holman, who lived from 1786 to 1857, was a British adventurer known as the 'The Blind Traveller'. The son of an apothecary, Holman was serving in the Royal Navy when he was seized by an illness that reduced his mobility and left him blind at the age of 25. From that moment he rose from obscurity to fame via a circumnavigation of the world and other great journeys, before slipping back to obscurity again and dying at the fair age of 70. His legacy was an inspiration to many, including Charles Darwin and Sir Richard Burton, but perhaps of greater interest is the inspiration he remains to those who have lost their sight and those who are trying to make fuller use of their other senses.

I am constantly asked, and I may as well answer the question here once for all, what is the use of travelling to one who cannot see?. . . The picturesque in nature, it is true, is shut out from me, and works of art are to me mere outlines of beauty, accessible only to one sense; but perhaps this very circumstance affords a stronger zest to curiosity, which is thus impelled to a more close and searching examination of details than would be considered necessary to a traveller who might satisfy himself by the superficial view.

Holman's biographer, Jason Roberts, gives a beautiful analogy to explain one of the ways Holman and other blind people manage to overcome this disability. Just as a spark in a dark wood supplies those with sight a fleeting chance to build a picture of their surroundings, so the metallic click from the tip of a walking stick hitting the ground gave blind people the opportunity to interpret the echoes around them 'as a compressed definition of ambient space'. Holman learned to use sound in every way that he could to build a more detailed picture. He differentiated between the sounds of a carriage and a cart approaching, he learned to distinguish types of footwear from the sounds they made and connected these to the different social classes and even professions of their wearers – he chose to salute some as he passed them on the street and not others.

Holman also found himself building a picture of the beauty of a woman through her voice and he was popular with the opposite sex, not despite of his blindness and not because of it, but partly as a consequence of it. Holman's blindness robbed him of his sexuality in the eyes of other men, sometimes reducing him to the status of a eunuch. He was a handsome man who was given the opportunity to spend more time in the private company of women than sighted men would have been allowed. This access combined with his true fascination in a companion's every sound, movement and intonation gave him a sensitivity that women found refreshing and very attractive. Holman is a role model for the suitor as well as the explorer.

James Holman, 'The Blind Traveller'

Natural Explorers follow their nose. Our five [sensory] sensory cells are capable of detecting 10,000 different [smells,] one is able to transport us across space and time, from [a smell] that conjures up an old school and has us checking that we [have] washed our hands properly to the jasmine thick in the cooling air of a Spanish dusk. Smell has a reputation for being primal, we can smell emotions that other senses fail to pick up. As Margaret Atwood noted, 'fear has a smell, as love does.' It is this potential for detection that invites smell to become a metaphor for sensing something hidden in each other: we smell a rat when we think we are being deceived and we smell blood if an opponent shows any sign of weakness.

There is no right or wrong in the sense of smell, but the spectrum is broad, the fashions eclectic and the cocktails that nature provides, diverse. The opportunity for delights and shocks is always there and they often stick in the memory. When we remember smells, we inevitably make associations and the world of smell becomes a complex tapestry, squares of familiarity mixed with surprise, nostalgia and intrigue.

The thousands of individual smells are rarely found in isolation and if they were it would quickly become confusing. The smells we recognise are collections of individual notes that we tend to group together in bunches, minty ones, floral ones, pears, musk, camphor, rotting and acrid ones. The most delightful and shocking smells rarely escape us and they garner a disproportionate amount of attention. It is the notes that lie behind or away from the wafting beacons of freshly cut grass, excrement, rotting herbage and flesh, flowers, the sea and body odour, that offer the finest enhancements to a journey. The sweet smell of pine resin on a fire cheered Ludwig Leichhardt, but there are joys to be found in less pretty sources, like rain and earth.

Humboldt believed that the musky smell of earth after rain could be compared to the smells given off by the jaguar, the capybara, the gallinazo vulture and the viper. He thought it must be emanating from a mould that contained worms and insect

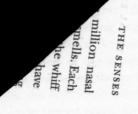

THE SENSES

million nasal
mells. Each
he whiff
have

rong, the smell of the earth after rain
ms, but much smaller than Humboldt
a in the mud. There are some bacteria,
cetes family, that thrive in warm damp
dries out these bacteria produce spores
churns the spores into the air and the
g us a rich musty smell.

slightly acidic, especially in or near urban
chemical reactions take place as soon as
it comes into contact with chemicals in the soil, on the ground
or on buildings. The rain reacts with the oils and resins that plants
and trees release, giving another different and appealing scent,
or with any petrol on the surface of roads, accentuating its odour.
The potential for a rich and bizarre mix of smells after rain in
the suburbs is great.

Places smell and smells anchor places in the mind. Smells
are the silent rope and pulley system that writers use to haul
readers into their settings and moments. We can enjoy the scent
of a cup of lime-flower tea with Proust before appearing in bed
next to melancholy Lawrence Durrell, as he breathes in the
musty smell of Arabia on the Levantine wind. Gore Vidal found
Mongolia smelled of mutton fat, but the Mongols themselves
did not smell at all, even though the Russians complained of
their lack of ablutions. People do smell differently, the amount
of body hair varies with genes and therefore regions. Sweat
lingers and feeds bacteria in body hair and so hairy people will
smell more if they do not wash regularly. On top of genetic
differences there are differences in preferences and cultures.
Napoleon famously once asked Josephine not to bathe for the
whole fortnight before they next met.

• • •

James Holman felt drawn to attempt an ascent of the active volcano
Vesuvius, picking his way through beds of hot lava in June 1821.

When he was offered a lift on a mule he declined, explaining, 'I see things better with my feet.' He reached the summit, something that was considered a great achievement even for someone with all their senses.

To walk barefoot on any surface is to know it through its texture, its temperature and ability to draw heat from us. A cold marble floor exacts a very different sensation to a wooden floor at the same temperature: the heat in our blood is drawn greedily through the skin of our feet into the stone. Most of us spend a far greater proportion of our childhood without shoes than we do as adults, with the result that walking with bare feet can bring back feelings of innocence, the responsibilities of adulthood cast off with our shoes – it sometimes seems a shame to have to put them back on. Shoes are a choice, a very sensible one, but a choice nonetheless, as countless indigenous tribes and the poor Helen Walker might testify.

Ms Walker lived up to her name by walking barefoot from Scotland to London in the first half of the eighteenth century. In a moving precursor to countless contemporary charity adventures, Helen's aim was to plead with the Duke of Argyll in a bid to spare her sister's life after she had been accused of murdering her baby. She arrived with blisters, a pardon was granted and her sister spared.

Touching enables a relationship with the natural world that the other senses fail to achieve. A pebble in a stream or on a beach may look smooth, it may even sound smooth if it is dragged across other pebbles by a retreating water, but nothing can give us smoothness like that moment of holding and caressing a smooth pebble in our hands.

Touching allows us to verify. On coming across a still body, those trained in first aid begin with a series of checks; feeling for a pulse will confirm or deny the biggest of questions. Another of the great questions was tackled with touch in Caravaggio's 'The Incredulity of Saint Thomas'. The doubter can see Jesus and the wound in his side and yet Jesus still needs to pull his hand towards him, forcing Thomas to use his sense of touch to confirm what his eyes have already shown him to be true. And so it is with the less grand questions.

Does an oak's bark feel as it looks? Are those fructicose lichens that hang in aerial gardens from the sycamore worth a moment's touch? Those who only allow their eyes and ears to sample the fountain in the town square on a hot day walk away poorer than those that take with them the electric sensation of fingers that are colder than their arms. Our hands warm up, sometimes with a faint throb and always with the lightest tickle at the fingertips as the water drops onto the paving below.

Vision can reach out miles, but touch is intimate. There is no escaping that it brings us within arm's length. There are thrills to be found in touching anything that ought not be touched. Is this the same thrill that James Holman felt when he asked other visitors to let him know when the soldiers' backs were turned so that he could reach out and break the rules by touching and feeling the sculptures in the Vatican?

The sense of taste only ever shakes off its label of poor cousin of smell when we sit down to eat and even then smell tries to take the credit for everything that isn't salty, sour, bitter or sweet. Taste makes the most of honey and lemons, of salt and bitter rocket leaves, but it is left to one side in most travel experiences, barged out of the way by sight, smell, touch and hearing. It is only when we get our tongues onto something that the usually modest taste buds elbow their way to the front.

Taste is the most intimate of all the senses. Sight allows us to sample something many miles away and hearing can take us into a storm rumbling over a distant horizon. Smell forces us closer into air that has mingled with our target and touch closer still, but with the sense of taste we must take an object into one of the most sensitive areas of our body. Humboldt encountered Indians who could identify a wood type by chewing it. This reflects both the Indians' finely tuned sense of taste and also their close relationship with the forest that sustained them.

It is worth considering the possibility that if a place fails to excite our senses, that might be more a reflection of us than our location. Dylan Thomas' sentiments serve us well at such times.

> Everything is very ordinary in Llangollen; everything is nicely dull, except the summer world of wind and feathers, leaves and water. There is, if you are deaf, blind and dumb, with a heart like cold bread pudding, nothing to remark or surprise.

The Plants

Flower in the crannied wall,
I pluck you out of the crannies;—
Hold you here, root and all, in my hand,
Little flower — but if I could understand
What you are, root and all, and all in all,
I should know what God and man is.

Alfred, Lord Tennyson

*T*he plants surged from the verges of the path. They pulled me closer, like Sirens. There were poppies still in their prime and those past it, lining the edge of the path. The breeze was squeezing the red petals of one, flattening the flower, but it bounced back into a fuller shape with each lull in the wind.

The car was no longer in sight, it was hidden behind a tree. I took the left branch of the two paths ahead. It led gently uphill past an area called The Burgh. I continued until a valley opened up to the north. On the higher ground near the top of the ridge there was a modest colony of gorse. The flowers of this bush had passed, which was a pity, as I adore their coconut scent. I always admire gorse, choosing to grow on the exposed, rocky, unloved parts that other plants deem unsuitable.

The track led me down into the small valley, the home of Stoke Hazel Wood, and the plants changed as the soils grew deeper and richer. The lowest point was marked by a distinct triangle of mugwort or Artemisia, the plant standing out as the light caught the silvery undersides of the leaves. It is this silver colour that gives the plant its lunar associations and in turn a feminine identity. Artemis was the Greek goddess of the moon. Mugwort oil has been used by herbalists to enhance fertility and help with all aspects of the female reproductive system.

The track was worn and clear, but at either side there was a carpet of the broad rosettes of plantains. They are swift to colonise and happy to invade compacted soil. They tolerate more than their neighbours, being undeterred by the odd heavy tyre or boot. They, like the gorse, are survivors.

I reached the mugwort triangle and passed through a gate into a density and variety of plant life that surprised me. On a bank there was St John's Wort and Viper's Bugloss. Then wild carrot, wild oregano, wild parsnip . . . I plucked a sprig of wild mint and put it into my water bottle, dispelling the scent of manufactured plastic with something more uplifting.

• • •

The African Association was founded in London in 1788 'for promoting the discovery of the inland parts' of Africa. In 1790 it dispatched a retired army officer, Daniel Houghton, to sail up the Gambia river and make for Timbuktu. He lasted less than a year. Sir Joseph Banks, who was a member of the Association, suggested the medically trained and marvellously named Scottish botanist, Mungo Park, as his successor. Park accepted the commission and set off for the Gambia in May 1795, with a brief to learn as much as possible about the course of the Niger.

In August the following year, Mungo Park was travelling from Kooma, accompanied by a pair of shepherds who were heading the same way. The shepherds went on ahead and Park held back with his tired horse, which was struggling to negotiate a steep and rocky road. Park heard a commotion ahead and fearing that a lion had taken one of the shepherds, he went 'to have a better view of what had happened.' He found one of the shepherds prostrated and apparently dead. The man was not dead, he managed to speak and whispered to Park that he had been attacked. Before Park had time to consider a retreat he was ambushed, released and then ambushed for a second time by the same gang, who were clearly of a fickle and dangerous mind. The armed banditti began by cutting the metal buttons from Park's waistcoat, then stealing the whole waistcoat and then taking the second waistcoat below that. They eventually stole every one of his possessions, leaving him naked, before throwing him his hat and an old shirt and pair of trousers. The thieves made their escape, leaving Park to contemplate his situation. He sat for a while and looked around in amazement and terror.

Whichever way I turned, nothing appeared but danger and difficulty. I saw myself in the midst of a vast wilderness, in the depth of the rainy season, naked and alone; surrounded by savage animals, and men still more savage. I was five hundred miles from the nearest European settlement . . . I confess my spirits began to fail me. I considered my fate as certain, and that I had no alternative but to lie down and perish.

The fact that we have this firsthand account is evidence that something changed Mungo Park's mind. Whilst in the depths of a terminal gloom he noticed a detail that gave him the strength to continue.

At this moment, painful as my reflections were, the extraordinary beauty of a small moss, in fructification, irresistibly caught my eye. I mention this to show from what trifling circumstances the mind will sometimes derive consolation; for though the whole plant was not larger than the top of one of my fingers, I could not contemplate the delicate conformation of its roots, leaves, and capsula, without admiration.

The sight of this delicate moss gave Mungo Park a renewed sense of purpose and he walked until he found a nearby village and two very surprised shepherds. Park had experienced a moment of divine wonder, he felt that any God that had 'brought to perfection' such a small plant in such an obscure part of the world would surely have some concern for him, and so he roused himself.

The beauty of life in plants hints tantalisingly at something profound. Carl Jung once likened the experience of looking at plants to that of peering over the shoulder of the Creator as he made toys and decorations. Compared to humans or other animals, plants are biologically simple yet they still suggest something wonderful, beyond chemical reactions. It does not matter if modern evolutionary theory can account for alpine plants that keep warm using fuzzy stems that trap air for insulation, or for the ones that produce high levels of salts that act as anti-freeze, or those that actually generate heat to help them melt the snow they are growing through. No theory, however prosaic, will ever dispel the wonder. Some scientists see that wonder despite the explanation and some because of it, but we must pity anyone who thinks such theories diminish a plant's beauty, as if a painting's beauty could be diminished by explaining the composition of its oils.

The lack of a central nervous system makes plants less complex than animals, but no less beguiling. Somehow these organisms manage extraordinary feats without a brain, and without the motives and tarnishing guilt that go with it. They have a purity we lack and crave in our lives. A plant grows towards the light because of a process it does not think about. But it is not a passive bystander. The lichens devour rocks, and a young ailanthus teases open the crack in a pavement and reclaims the hard grey asphalt for the softer green. A witch hazel hurls its ballistic seeds across the ground as the sundews feast on insects among the bogs. All without an apparent thought.

Witch Hazel seeds exploding out of their capsules

The challenge arrives not in persuading ourselves of the joys to be had in studying the plants we encounter on our travels, but in deciding where to begin. There are more than 25,000 species of orchid alone and a life dedicated to their study will leave many mysteries in that one species.

With the poppy we get a taste of how intricately connected our lives are with plants, quite literally when we use its oil for cooking, but more laterally when we consider what this flower means to us. The poppy reminds us of opium wars, heroin and Afghanistan, but also the fields of Giverny that Monet painted. Poppy seeds need light to germinate and so grow best in worked soil. They are symbolic of the extreme upheavals of the earth during the First World War and have come to symbolise remembrance in modern times, but they stood for sleep and death long before that. The small gold and violet silken flowers of one poppy in Tibet behaved like an altimeter for the botanist Frank Kingdon-Ward, who found they only grew between 15,000 and 17,000 feet.

It is tempting to concede defeat to the tangled green masses before their diversity overwhelms us. This emotion is brought on by a desire for total knowledge; it is a controlling instinct. The yearning for control might lead to better-regimented gardens, but it does little good among nature's bigger canvasses. Any exploratory journey will take us out of the arena we know, this is surely the point, and then the desire to know all can be replaced with a celebration of noticing any small detail that brings a sense of connection.

As with the first gaze at a large painting, we notice the broad brushstrokes first. Each plant has its ideal conditions and tolerance levels. Plant habitats are connected to the climate, which in turn is shaped by the relief of the land and the Earth's position relative to the sun.

Humboldt explained that the Befaria will grow at lower altitudes as the latitude increases. They 'descend towards the plains in proportion as their distance from the equator increases'. Each region has its characteristic species. For Humboldt, the American west coast was made distinct by the cacti that grew there. He was also aware that two regions with similar climates will not necessarily share the same species. 'The pines of Mexico are absent in the Peruvian Andes. The Caracas La Silla is not covered with the same oaks that flourish in New Granada at the same height.' It is a jigsaw puzzle. One observation is of little value on its own, but an awareness of climate, topography and geology combined with an eye for the species of plant that are thriving, quickly build a picture that is greater than any plant studied in isolation. The plants become friends and their familiarity brings other benefits: anomalous species draw attention, familiar ones bring comfort when found far from home. The botanist Sir Joseph Dalton Hooker was reminded of the Scottish Highlands by the lichen, L. geographicus, that he found in the Himalayan hills.

Once the broad picture is coming into focus it becomes possible to look for finer details and to relate to the land through the behaviour of the plants we find there. The classical system of the four Elements: Earth, Water, Fire and Air, has fallen from favour, but it remains helpful in understanding the environment of plants. If we think of Fire as the sun, then we have the four major environmental variables of all plants. These are the factors that determine their existence and wellbeing, and each plant is trying to tell us something about these Elements.

In spring and summer, streams can be found by looking for strips of grass that are brighter green. In the winter the presence of water is again an asset to the grass since it moderates cold temperatures. Rushes are another clue to water and soft ground, but the relationship between plants and soil is so close that the land can be read back from the plants themselves. In his book *The Living Landscape*, Patrick Whitefield has drawn up a list of the soil indications from differing plant types in the UK. They range, from the well-known, such as the rhododendrons that indicate acidic soil, to the more obscure clues, like the pineapple weed that indicates compacted soil near paths or gateways. Agrimony will be found on well-drained soil and meadow buttercup on moist. Chickweed occurs in rich soil and common sorrel in poor. Over time the plants come to define the character of the soil as much as the soil determines them and it becomes possible to read the value of the land. Whitefield heard it summed up in an old saying in England and Wales.

> There's gold under bracken,
> Silver under gorse
> And famine under heather.

Plants often give clues about the air as well as the land. Lichens are so sensitive to pollution that they are used by environmental scientists to gauge air quality, and so the more we find the deeper we can happily breathe. There are usually more lichens up in the trees than near the ground, where the heavier pollutants mingle.

A recently felled tree is an excellent place to find a thriving lichen community.

All plants are also very sensitive to salt and salt-laden winds; any journey from the coast inland will show a transition from the most salt-tolerant plants to the least, a typical progression being from grasses to shrubs and finally trees.

Every plant is reacting to the sun on a daily basis. Through processes such as phototropism and heliotropism, hormones shape the growth and movement of the plants. Alpine buttercups track the sun throughout the day and most plants grow more heavily on their sunnier side. Branches on the sunnier side of trees grow more horizontally than on the shaded side.

Plants are great travellers. Millions of tiny seeds are carried for miles on the wind and then there are the big seeds that like to float across oceans, such as the coconut. Mangrove seedlings float horizontally, like a canoe and spread along the coast. The hand of the human traveller can be found behind many plant journeys, too. There is an intimate relationship between the pioneers and the migration of certain species around the planet.

Sugar cane was not native to Venezuela and so the sugar plantations stood out to Humboldt. During his visit to a farm he learned the provenance of the three different types of sugar cane, each recognisable from the varying colour of their leaves; one had arrived from the West Indies, one came with Bougainville, Cook and Bligh and a third from Java. The pasture grasses of North America have nearly all been brought over from Europe, they are better suited to grazing than the indigenous species. This earned the plantain grass the nickname of 'white man's footprint' among the Native Americans.

Grasses, with help from man, have become some of the most successful plants on the planet. They paint the United States with their different hues and strokes, tall bluestem grasses in the wet east, wheat grass as it dries a little to the west and, further west still, the short grasses that can tolerate the drier conditions, like the blue grama and buffalo.

Though they appear innocuous above ground, the lives of the grasses are more complex below the surface. One experiment demonstrated this well: botanists took two cubic feet of soil and grew some winter rye grass in it for a period of four months. Above ground the grass grew to a height of 20 inches, but when the scientists delved into the subterranean world and teased out the roots to measure them they discovered that the main roots were 378 miles long and the minute root hairs added up to a length of 6,000 miles. The roots had grown, on average, three miles *each day*.

In Southern Queensland, Ludwig Leichhardt revelled in the sight of luxuriant grasses, showy red leguminosae and bright yellow compositae, and he found the cattle there in equally rude health. Since grasses provide pasturage of many names, from the steppes of Europe and Asia, to Argentinian pampas and the American prairies, the sight of abundant healthy grasses is nearly always good news for grazing cattle and no less for omnivorous humans.

Plants have long been believed to provide more than sustenance; they maintain and restore life and the ability to pass on life through procreation. It is inevitable that they should have grown beyond food and towards our culture, medicine and broader life.

In ancient times, the appearance of mistletoe in an oak tree triggered an elaborate Druidic ceremony. On the sixth day of the lunar cycle, the Druids would face the moon and greet it with a phrase meaning, 'healing all things'. Then a Druid priest, dressed in a white robe, would climb up into the oak tree with a golden sickle and cut the mistletoe down, allowing it to be caught in a white cloak. A sacrifice of two white bulls would then be made beneath the tree. The Druids believed that drinks containing this mistletoe would restore fertility to any barren animals and act as an antidote to any poison.

Every part of our growth, life, sex, birth and death cycle has plants associated with it. Pliny tells us that Helenium was used by ancient women to 'preserve physical charm' and to help them acquire 'a kind of aura of attractiveness and sex appeal'. Moss was used to apply cress and salt-water to treat infections of the female sexual organs. Pliny is less forthcoming with male herbal remedies – although the ancestors of Viagra were abundant – and he is sceptical about the claim that the oil of juniper, rubbed on the penis, would prove an effective contraceptive. Perhaps Pliny would have appreciated the old joke, 'What do you call men who rub juniper oil on their penis as a contraceptive?'

'Fathers.'

• • •

Plants often lose out to animals when it comes to a sense of urgency. 'Quick, look!' we whisper, as a rabbit lifts its head in front of us.

This makes sense – we cannot see an animal after it has fled our heffalumping approach. But we should stay sensitive to the moment in our appreciation of plants, too. There are some that will punish us if we are too casual. One fairly common bamboo, called madake, only flowers once every 120 years, at the same time all over the world, and then dies. It last flowered in 1970 and many of us will never see its blooms. It is not our time. But there are many we can catch. In the Bahamas, Selenicereus cactus flowers come into bloom for one night each year, have sex and then, like blushing furtive teenagers, are gone by morning. Each grass flower opens for only one hour in its life and wheat for only fifteen minutes.

The clock ticks too for fungi aficionados, who need to be ready to rush to the woods when it rains after a dry spell. The tip of these icebergs only pop above the surface for short periods, before retiring back underground where they form some of the longest organisms on Earth. In folklore, the mushrooms are brought out by lightning. Each moment we have to enjoy plants lasts a little longer than lightning, but it will never be repeated exactly or strike us the same way twice.

The Changing Mountain

The wilderness has a mysterious tongue
Which teaches awful doubt, or faith so mild,
So solemn, so serene, that man may be
But for such faith with nature reconciled;
Thou hast a voice, great Mountain, to repeal
Large codes of fraud and woe; not understood
By all, but which the wise, and great, and good
Interpret, or make felt, or deeply feel.

Percy Bysshe Shelley

I began the climb out of the valley, past the field labelled 'The Burgh' on my map. The land opened up in all directions. The flat coastal plain to the south emerged from the foothills of the Downs beyond Arundel and the village of Burpham. To the east and west high ground rolled in each direction as far as I could see. To the north the land dropped away.

To the northwest, in the distance, I could make out a very broad hill that looked as though a giant digger had scooped out its centre. This was a section of the Weald, where the rocks have folded up to form high ground. The different rocks have weathered in different ways. The softer impervious clays in the middle section have been eroded by running water, but the harder porous sandstones on either side have survived. The gap in the middle is called the Vale of Fernhurst.

This was a gentle walk, my height above sea level was changing only a few hundred feet, but the land reflected even these small changes. There was no gorse in the valleys and few trees on the modest hill summits. The wind I felt in the valleys was weak and warm compared to the fresh gusts on the summits.

The Vale of Fernhurst

There is a hill in the southern part of Rome called Monte Testaccio. It is not a mighty hill, standing only thirty-five metres tall and a walk to the top will barely ramp the breath. It would be possible to walk all around this small bump in the landscape without having been at all impressed by it.

It is only when we peer below the surface that Monte Testaccio is allowed to leave its mark on our minds: it is a man-made hill, built entirely from the broken fragments of the discarded amphorae that were used to import olive oil to the heart of the Roman Empire. Monte Testaccio is a giant refuse heap, one that would have been even bigger in ancient times, and this knowledge makes the hill play on our minds. It becomes simultaneously fascinating and gently repellent.

Natural hills and mountains hide much of their beauty and intrigue in the same way that Monte Testaccio conceals its secrets. Vaughan Cornish, the prolific British geographer of the late nineteenth and early twentieth centuries, believed that we need to get under the skin of mountains, since 'knowledge of the anatomy of mountains contributes to the recognition of their beauty'. Cornish likened the process of admiring the beauty of mountains to that of taking in the wonder of the Sistine Chapel, which he maintained could only be fully appreciated by those who had studied muscular anatomy.

On the evening of 20 February 1943 a Mexican farmer and his family were ploughing their cornfield in Michoacán when they noticed some smoke coming out of the ground; seconds later they smelt sulphur in the air. Then there was a small eruption of stones and ash from the same spot. One week later there stood a baby volcano in the cornfield, it had already risen to over thirty metres tall.

The volcano kept growing and by the time a year had passed since the family saw its first smoke, it had risen to over 300 metres high. The volcano continued to grow slowly until 1952 when it retired from active life as a 424m-high hill, having buried the two neighbouring villages, after the residents had, very sensibly, moved out. The Paricutin eruption was the first time that scientists had been given the opportunity to study the full life cycle of a volcano, from its gentle birth through its un-malevolent life to its extinction.

An erupting volcano is the only place that any of us can watch a mountain under construction and although it can wreak devastation, it is also an essential part of our story. The steam that can be seen pouring out of volcano vents is the source of much of the Earth's water.

Each volcano erupts according to its own sense of urgency, some are violent, and some, like Paricutin, are gradual. The speed of a volcano's eruption will determine the shape of the mountain that forms: the faster and more violent an eruption the steeper the sides of a volcanic mountain. The explosive Sangay volcano in Ecuador has the steep profile of a violent volcano, whereas the more gentle slopes of Hawaii's mountains speak of more gradual flows of lava to the surface.

The highest point on the island of Hawaii is the summit of Mauna Kea, a dormant volcano that occupies almost a quarter of the land of the island. The mountain is impressive when seen from sea level, but knowing that the base of the volcano that formed it rises from the seabed 6,000 metres below affords this mountain a new respect. Measured from its subaqueous base, Mauna Kea is the tallest mountain in the world, higher than Everest, at over 10,000 metres tall.

All mountains have life cycles. They are formed and then instantly start to wear away to nothing again. The violent movement of molten rocks caused by volcanoes leads to distinctive eruptive landscapes, complete with sharp cones in the case of the young volcanoes and worn rounded domes in the older ones. The aging process is inexorable and can be dramatic. On John Lubbock's second visit to Vesuvius in the late-nineteenth century he found that 200 feet had disappeared from the summit. Beautiful lake-filled calderas are the scars left behind when summits of volcanoes have been blown clear off a mountain-top.

Mount Fuji in Japan, with its broad base and gentle concave slopes has forced its way happily into the consciousness of a nation. Japan cannot help but celebrate this powerful partner, silent since its last eruption in 1707, and its form can be found resurfacing throughout the country: from the art of Hokusai's *Hundred Views of Fuji* to the shape of temple roofs.

Mount Fuji

Volcanic activity explains the history of most conical mountains, but many others have a different story. Charles Darwin found fossils in the rocks of a mountain in the Andes when he was at an altitude of 13,000 feet. The presence of fossils indicates a sedimentary rock and Darwin was looking at sediments that were now nearly two and a half miles above sea level, which proved that this part of the Earth's crust had been forced upwards long ago in its history.

When the plates of the Earth's crust come together the great mountain ranges are formed, like wrinkles in the skin of an apple drying on a windowsill. When the plates are wrenched apart, huge rifts are the result. Leave a bowl of bread sauce out to dry and a skin will form; as the sauce dries and contracts the skin will be pulled apart and rifts form in the surface, grand canyons develop.

Each of these great upheavals in the plates can be traced back to the convective flows in the magma deep below the surface of the crust. Whether the plates are coming together or drifting apart, this very slow motion (think of the speed of fingernail growth to get an idea) will lead to drama at the junctions. Where mountains and rifts are not formed in a slow orderly way, worse things happen.

In Chile Darwin heard accounts of cows rolling off hillsides into the sea and one *mayor-domo* at Quiriquina told him that he only became aware that he was caught up in an earthquake when he found he was rolling on the ground with his horse instead of riding it. Darwin learned about the ensuing aftershocks and the great wave that caused further havoc. In the coastal Chilean town of Coquimbo, the residents were accustomed to the dangers the earth posed and it was here that Darwin heard the curious tale of a precautionary German.

Whilst playing cards in Valparaíso, this man explained to his fellow players that he had nearly lost his life to an earthquake in Chile and so did not like to sit inside with the doors of a building shut. He stood up, walked over and opened the door and at that moment he felt a terrible tremor. 'Here it comes again!' he cried. The entire card-playing party escaped through the door before the building collapsed and credited their survival to the actions of the precautionary German.

But the story of plate tectonics is not restricted to these areas of contemporary geological violence. The whole world's crust has been on the move for billions of years and nowhere has escaped being shaped in some way by land floating and colliding. Five hundred million years ago the northwest of Britain was further from the southeast than Britain now is from the USA. Loch Ness sits along the Great Glen fault line, with tiny tremors still occurring. One Italian geologist, Luigi Piccardi, believes that the story of the Loch Ness monster, whose earliest sightings in the seventh century were accompanied by the Earth shaking as it appeared and disappeared, may be connected to seismic activity.

No mountain is static. From the moment they are created they are vanishing. Water hits the surface and erodes it, then it freezes and breaks open rocks and cracks. Soil with seeds infiltrates fissures and roots begin to mine, worms and insects make their home, lichens devour the surface and the wind carries off pulverised particles. The whole starts to shrink. Just as sandpaper takes off the rough edges and protrusions of a surface, so the more exposed areas of mountains bear the brunt of the erosive forces. Erosion has a smoothing effect and older mountains, like the Urals, lack the sharp edges of their younger siblings, the Himalayas, who are 'adolescents with sharp, punkish ridges'. The slow processes are overtaken by the wild and savage erosion that occurs when glaciers overrun a range; these great ice trains are barely contained by the rocks.

When the softer rocks have been rubbed away, all that will be left is those that are most resistant. Depending on the distribution of the different types of rock, the result might be smooth plateaus or strange shapes, like the eerie Shiprock in New Mexico.

Anyone who has enjoyed the dark dramatic landscapes of Lanzarote in the Canary Islands will have sampled the pleasures of a volcanic terrain that is sharp and young. The equally impressive but very different Cairngorm mountains in Scotland are a place where great buckets of time – the mountains were formed

40 million years ago – have failed to remove the mountains altogether but have worn them down to smoother plateaus. The
Cairngorms were once as mighty as the Himalayas, but now have
low curved backs, like the old ladies they are.

Mountains hold court over many levels. There are different
climates at each one, and the mountain will influence them all.
For every 300 metres or 1000 feet in altitude gained the air
temperature will drop on average by two degrees Celsius. This
temperature gradient leads to the familiar, gently undulating lower
limits of the snow on a mountain.

The gradual change in temperature with altitude, combined
with the differences in local climate can lead to wild differences
in environment. Mount Everest is at the same latitude as southern
Florida, they both receive the same amount of solar energy, but
their climates are riotously different as a consequence of altitude
and the influence of landforms on weather systems.

The island of Tenerife lies on the same latitude as the Sahara
desert. It is dominated by the impressive volcanic mountain of
Teide, which rises through warm moist tropical airs to a snow-
capped summit of 3,718 metres, the highest point in the Atlantic
Ocean. The mountain's influence on the island's climate is
dramatic and it is not a coincidence that the main tourist resorts
are in the hotter and drier southern parts. Long before the air
of these coastlines was filled with the rich smells of tanning oils
and the sounds of glasses chinking together, Humboldt had
noticed the climatic contrasts to be found on the island.

It is easy to see why the inhabitants of beautiful climates of
Greece and Italy thought they had discovered one of the
Fortunate Isles on the western part of Tenerife. The eastern
Santa Cruz side is everywhere marked with sterility.

It is typical of Humboldt that he notices something on the
ground that contemporary travellers can appreciate with the help
of satellite images: from space the island appears in rich green

shades on its northwestern sides and a thirsty brown on its south-eastern flanks.

There was one aerial perspective that Humboldt could avail himself of and it was an experience that inspired countless subsequent travellers, not least Darwin. Humboldt climbed Mount Teide and revelled in the views from the summit and the contrasts in the landscape. The eruptions of the volcano had left their mark and as Humboldt tripped over enormous blocks of stone that had been ejected by the volcano, he remarked, 'From up here the island becomes an immense heap of burned matter surrounded by a narrow fringe of vegetation.'

The changes and contrasts that Humboldt passed through on his ascent are of even greater interest than the imprints of the volcano's eruptions, as these are the sliding transformations that can be witnessed on all mountains of sufficient scale, volcanic or otherwise. Humboldt climbed up through brambles, laurels and arboreal heaths with masses of flowers, but these give way to a region of ferns and above the ferns he reached a juniper and pine wood, which had been battered by storms. These were typical of the zones that might be expected on ascending: grass, deciduous trees, evergreen trees, alpine meadow and then the snow line. When Humboldt emerged from the junipers and pines, though, he lamented finding a plain strewn with pumice and obsidian stones rather than an alpine meadow. There was no life excepting a few goats and rabbits. 'Everything here betrays a deep solitude.'

The effects of altitude on the flora of a mountain lead to the equivalent of the snow line: the tree line, above which trees fail to grow because of the cold, and to a lesser extent the air pressure and dryness. Since places near the equator tend to be warmer than higher latitudes, all other things being equal, the tree line for each species will descend as you move away from the equator. Later in his travels, once on the South American continent, Humboldt noticed this effect with other plants. 'There is a saying that a mountain is high enough to reach the rhododendron and befaria limit.' This is an elegant way of describing the altitude of a mountain, once we accept that it is a scale that needs adjusting for the mountain's latitude.

The sliding scale of temperature and climate allows for a perfect band for agriculture somewhere on a mountain's slopes. If the soils are not forbidding determined farmers will cut into the steep sides and work on the terraces, as they do in Nepal. The paddy fields across southern and eastern Asia rely on the climate but also the waters and minerals that flow down from the higher slopes in rivers.

The natural irrigation effect of the water running off mountains was noticed by Marco Polo in Armenia, in the area where Noah's Ark was said to have come to rest (he was shown a dark patch on the hillside, which was reputed to be the final resting place of the Ark itself). Marco Polo found the lower slopes of Mount Ararat were filled with lush and luxuriant vegetation, thanks to the water from the melting snows higher up. The animals noticed this too and flocked to these slopes in the summer. Animals like the Alpine ibex, a mountain goat, use the higher altitudes to remain out of reach of predators, only venturing lower to feed briefly.

In the highest parts of the mountains, where the plants and animals lose their foothold, myths swarm in to fill the gap. According to the thirteenth-century Italian friar and chronicler Salimbene of Parma, Pedro III of Aragon came face to face with a dragon at the summit of Pic Canogou in the Catalonian Pyrenees. Later, more secular-minded scholars were not immune to the power of visitations, either. Johann Scheuchzer was a Swiss poly-math of the early Enlightenment, a professor of maths and physics and author of a paper on grasses that gave birth to the branch of botany called agrostology. He also made an extensive collection of dragon sightings in each Swiss canton.

• • •

Knowledge of the formation of mountains is an excellent fence, it breaks the skipping gaze and reminds us to pause and consider before moving on. Understanding the life of a mountain even allows us to see beneath its skin, but this dry knowledge on its own serves us best by encouraging us to stop and think. Anything that provokes this pause is worthwhile, because it is from this moment that the true potential of our relationship with these peaks grows.

Dragons no longer divide opinion, but reverence for the mountains does. George Mallory famously answered the question, 'Why do you want to climb Everest?' with, 'Because it's there.' Mallory's response has achieved a myth-like status in the world of Western mountaineering, but from a traditional Eastern perspective his words may seem crude as well as flippant.

Dominant mountains have long been worshipped. The sacred mountains like Fuji in Japan, Taishan in China and Uluru in Australia are hugely important for these cultures. Mountains inspire devotion all over the world, although the form this takes varies from one society to another. Marco Polo reported that a very high mountain with steep cliffs in Ceylon was revered as the birthplace of Adam, but that the Saracens disagreed and believed it to be Adam's grave. Meanwhile the 'idolaters' maintained that it was the Buddhist monument of Sakyamuni Burkhan. The only thing that was not in doubt was that this was a place of great religious significance.

The Japanese scholar of Zen Buddhism, D.T. Suzuki, described the Western habit and phrase of 'conquering mountains' as a desecration.

We of the Orient have never conceived Nature in the form of an opposing power. On the contrary, Nature has been our constant friend and companion, who is to be absolutely trusted in spite of the frequent earthquakes assailing this land of ours. The idea of conquest is abhorrent. If we succeed in climbing a high mountain, why not say, 'We have made a good friend of it?'

Suzuki's philosophy was sorely tested in March 2011 as Japan struggled to recover from the worst earthquake in its history. But the deepest beliefs are resistant even to such seismic shocks.

The contrasting Western view was not formed in the absence of religion, but from an anthropocentric view of nature within that religion. Comparing Suzuki's sentiments with those of the nineteenth-century British soldier, statesman and traveller Francis Bond Head as he arrives at the summit of the San Pedro Nolasco mountain in the Andes, reveals a very different philosophy.

> The whole scene around us in every direction was devoid of vegetation, and was a picture of desolation, on a scale of magnificence which made it peculiarly awful; and the knowledge that this vast mass of snow, so cheerless in appearance, was created for the use, and comfort, and happiness, and even luxury of man; that it was the inexhaustible reservoir from which the plains were supplied with water, made us feel that there is no spot in creation which man should term barren, though there are many which Nature never intended for his residence.

Labels such as 'Eastern' and 'Western' will necessarily oversimplify or obfuscate the wonderfully complex relationship between humans and a mighty landform. Spiritual and humble views of mountain summits can be found in every corner, not just the East, but they might be more common among those who have tasted fear and experienced gratitude. Norgay Tenzing made a small snow cave near the summit of Everest and left some food offerings to the God of Chomolungma, the Buddhist divinity who inhabits the mountain. Sir Edmund Hillary left a small cross there, too.

For many others a deep bond with a mountain is possible without either spirituality or summits. The Scottish writer, Nan Shepherd, found that 'the mountain gives itself most completely when I have no destination, when I reach nowhere in particular, but have gone out merely to be with the mountain as one visits a friend with no intention but to be with him.' It is likely that D.T. Suzuki and Nan Shepherd would have enjoyed a walk together.

• • •

From a creek near Roper's Peak in Queensland, Leichhardt observed that the mountains changed as he moved. They meta-morphosed in shape from a series of cones that reminded him of the Auvergne region to a succession of tent-like forms. Henry David Thoreau, the great American philosopher of nature, wrote that a mountain's outline changes each time we take a step. At the start of the sixteenth century a legendary Japanese Samurai and renowned general called Date Masamune felt the same way about Mount Fuji.

> Each time I see Fuji
> It appears changed
> And I feel I view it
> Ever for the first time.
>
> How shall I describe Fuji
> To those who have not yet seen it?
> It is never seen twice alike,
> And I know no one way
> Of describing the sight.

Perspective will change the mountain, but mountains also bring a change in perspective that is internal. Is it the air, the solitude, the sublime magnificence of the views or some heady mixture of all three that triggers visceral responses? The emotional shift that can be experienced on mountains is unlikely to yield to attempts at objective analysis, but that is not to say that it is not very real. Far from being a realm belonging only to those led by physical ambition or religious aspiration, the mountain is a place that finds its way into the core of the cerebral and the creative and sets it alight.

Wordsworth embarked on a rebellious journey to escape from Cambridge University exams in 1790, crossing France with his friend Robert Jones and heading into the Alps. This was a turning point in his life as we discover in his philosophical poem, *The Prelude*. We can feel Wordsworth's gratitude for a metamorphosis from sensible undergraduate to Romantic poet, intoxicated and euphoric with the freedom and licence he feels he has been granted by the wonder he has experienced in the mountains.

> The blessing of my life—the gift is yours,
> Ye winds and sounding cataracts! 'tis yours,
> Ye mountains! thine, O Nature! Thou hast fed
> My lofty speculations; and in thee,
> For this uneasy heart of ours, I find
> A never-failing principle of joy
> And purest passion.

This is the point at which we realise that mountains are neither passive objects to be rendered by artists, nor divorced from the creative process. Keats found time spent among the mountains of the Scottish Highlands better preparation for writing poetry than staying at home and reading books, 'even though I should read Homer'. As environmental and political writer Rebecca Solnit has pointed out, the arrival of the Romantic poet established the process of climbing mountains as a cultural act in its own right.

The mountain has the power to transform our perspectives and emotions about the world, which is exactly what we ask of art. What starts as an appreciation of rifts and curves in rock can lead us far away. For those who have that certain vexing constitution, the mountain is a narcotic. It can tip a person away from the pedestrian life, towards reckless, joyous and creative abandon.

The Coast

The reflections in the water were more beautiful than the
sky itself, purple waves brighter than precious stones for
ever melting away upon the sands. The fort, a wooden
building, at the entrance of the harbour of Calais, when
the evening twilight was coming on, and we could not
see anything of the building but its shape which was far
more distinct than in perfect daylight, seemed to reared
upon pillars of ebony, between which pillars the sea was
seen in the most beautiful colours that can be conceived.
Nothing in romance was ever half so beautiful.

Dorothy Wordsworth

*T*urning around, the coast was clearly visible. The sea rolled
out behind the haze and beyond Arundel Castle, beyond the
dark chunks of the coastal town of Littlehampton. I cannot
be the only walker who finds it impossible to continue in the same
rhythm after the first good sighting of the sea. The legs are keen to
continue, but something deeper slows me down, a visceral brake is
applied.

Why is that? I wondered. Is it something primeval? Does my brain feel
a hangover from evolution, the sea calling us back home? If so, then do
other animals react similarly? I looked around me. The distant cows did
not appear caught in this moment of coastal pensiveness.

The coastline tried to hide in the haze, but it was clear enough. At
night it is far from shy. After the sun sets there is no missing the loud

contrast between the bright lights of coastal towns and the darker than wine nighttime sea.

On this occasion, as on every other one that I can recall, the ocean arrested my progress. The summit of my walk was pulling me too, but the allure of the sea was too great. I stayed, still and silent for a minute, hunting for the scent of the sea. I thought I picked up a trace. I may have imagined it. No, I definitely smelled something.

● ● ●

On the northern Araya coast of Venezuela, Humboldt and his colleagues were repeatedly offered small stones that the locals found in the sand. The stones were flat on one side and curved on the other. Humboldt was eagerly informed that these objects were called 'eye stones' (piedras de los ojos) and had special powers, including the ability to cure any ailments of the eyes. The locals tried to prove the stones' effectiveness by suggesting that Humboldt rub sand in his eyes and then offering to use the stone to solve the problem. Humboldt declined this kind offer.

The eye stones, which appeared to be made of a calcareous substance, were of obsessive interest to the locals, who believed that they were both animals and stones at the same time. To prove the animal nature of the stones, they placed one of them on the flat surface of a plate and then dripped some lemon juice onto it. The stone did indeed spring to life and moved about on the plate. Although Humboldt found these demonstrations intriguing, he placed the romantic's hat to one side at this point and picked up the scientist's hat once more as he sought an alternative explanation of events.

Very quickly we saw that these 'stones' are the thin and porous valves of diminutive univalve shells . . . These calcareous coverings effervesce with lemon juice and start moving as the carbonic acid is formed. When placed in the eyes, these eye stones act as tiny round pearls and seeds, used by the Indians of America to stimulate the flow of tears.

When Humboldt offered this explanation to his Venezuelan friends they rejected it but he remained philosophical. 'For man, nature seems more grand the more it is mysterious, and the physics of the people rejects any simple explanation.'

The fizzing shell that scooted about on the plate before Humboldt was one member of a cast of organisms that act out a turbulent play of life and death on every coastline. The fine sandy beaches that hog our memories of many journeys are vast graveyards of rocks and animals that have lived and then died in company with the waves. The waves break down the rocks along the shore and work them into smaller particles until they are small enough to remain suspended in the water.

Sand varies from country to country and beach to beach. The sand of most temperate beaches is dominated by small rock particles such as quartz and feldspar, whereas the beaches of the tropics contain a higher proportion of the tiny skeletons of marine organisms. Most coarse light-coloured sand is made of small particles of granite, white sand comes from coral reefs and black beaches are often found near the igneous rocks of volcanoes.

The waves bring these tiny fragments to the shore, pushing and pulling at them until the patterns of wind, water and coastline together determine where they should come to rest. The wind will decide the direction that waves wash onto a shore, but gravity dictates the more direct return route for the water. This asymmetric movement of the water leads to sand, pebbles and larger rocks being moved sideways along a beach, in the process known as longshore drift.

The different motions of the waves leave their unique fingerprints on a beach. Receding waves will pick up particles and then deposit them again, marking the sand in beautiful patterns. These are not random decorations but the result of the interplay between the speed of the water and the size of the particles it is running back over. Since the speed of receding waves is governed largely by the gradient of the beach, the patterns will remain constant until the gradient changes. Typically the sand will settle into a dense cross-hatched pattern on shallow beaches, becoming a dimpled orange-skin effect as the beach steepens a little and then overlapping chevrons, like fish scales, on a steeper patch of sand. Other peculiar and beautiful forms occur, like the trunks of trees complete with roots or mountain ranges that stretch into infinity. All of these patterns will be influenced by the motion of the incoming waves too and so every beach becomes a fascinating collection of sandy artworks, perpetually created and then destroyed by the waves.

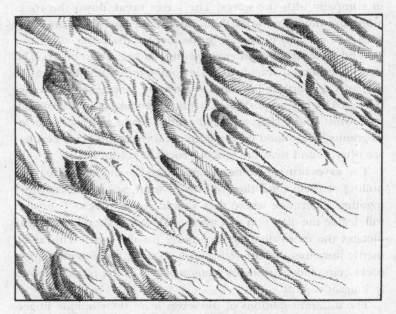

The advancing and retreating waves leave beautiful patterns in the sand of each beach

The inorganic patterns formed by the motion of the waves are very different from the casts of the lugworm. This worm lives under the beach's surface and consumes sand, which it filters for nutrients before excreting the depleted material back up to the surface to form the familiar casts. There is usually also a visible hole, which is a depression formed by the worm's head as it takes in the sand. These lugworms make regular meals for oystercatchers and gulls and also wind up on fishermen's hooks.

The sand is rich in bivalves, creatures with two halves of a shell hinged together. These are the molluscs, with familiar names like the cockle, which opens its shell at high tide to allow the nutritious water in but then shuts the door when the tide falls. The sand is host to more active residents too, not just the passive filterers. At night, crabs scuttle sideways and the starfish hides below the surface where it will seek out and seize a whole cockle or worm, drawing them into its central stomach. Once the starfish has digested the meat it will eject the cockle's shell, leaving it to the pounding waves as raw material for the constant rebuilding of the beach.

Where the waves dash themselves onto rocks we find a microworld beloved by children all over the world. The rock pools play host to a myriad of life and children will happily display levels of patience that seem to escape them during car journeys, as they peer down into this watery biosphere, nets clutched in hand, waiting for a crab to make a move.

Rock pools are not only for children. Charles Darwin enjoyed fishing in rock pools for small creatures as a young man, while a student at Edinburgh University. He would often join the anatomist, Robert Edmond Grant, in this pursuit. There is an irony that later in his life, Darwin's theory of evolution would seek to do away with the view Grant subscribed to. Grant was a Lamarckist; he believed that creatures adapt to their environment and then pass on these new characteristics to their offspring. Darwin's theory explained that the creatures that were suited to an environment survived and procreated, those that were not, did not.

The rocks and their pools contend with the vagaries of tidal heights. The fortnightly extreme high and low tides, known as spring tides, will cover and uncover much more extensive areas of rocks than the more moderate neap tides that occur a week after the springs. This creates distinctly different habitats. At the top is a region known as the splash zone, rocks that get wet indirectly but are not covered even at a high spring tide. This is where we will find a range of coloured lichens, often with a yellow at the highest mark, an orange below that and then a black lichen. Below this is the range that is covered at high water springs but exposed to the air at all other times, just below that is the level covered at all high tides, but no low tides, all the way down to the level that is only exposed to the air at low water springs. These distinct zones occur all over the world, wherever tidal waters meet rocks, and although the range can vary from a dozen metres or more in the Channel Islands to much more modest ranges in other parts of the world, the result will always be layers of different organisms on the rocks and in their pools and corresponding changes in colours, textures and creatures.

The differences in high water marks during the fortnightly cycle of tidal heights can be seen on the sand, too. The strandline is the furthest reach of the waves on the beach at each high water and since this varies, there is often more than one strandline visible on each beach. Strandlines are marked by an accumulation of a wide variety of matter from the sea, anything from bones and dead birds to bottles and boxes, but the main mass of this line is usually a generous helping of seaweed. This rotting seaweed, enriched with other organisms that have found a resting place, will form the basis of a new habitat as sandhoppers, kelp flies, birds and even rodents look for an easy meal. The rich smell of decay and buzz of thousands of small flies make the strandlines an unpopular place for beach towels and in some upmarket beach resorts a lot of time and money is spent removing them altogether.

The sound of waves breaking changes with the tides. It progresses from a soft murmur at low water to a rhythmic boom at high tide. On shingle beaches the retreating water drags the pebbles over each other and makes a sound that simmers between a fizz and a roar. Shingle beaches also rescue beauty from ugliness, when we realise that the dark stains that we at first feared were black tar are in fact the tough early colonists of these beaches, lichens such as the hardy Verrucaria maura.

The wind is always at work on a beach and it helps form another favourite beach haunt for children: sand dunes. Dunes typically form on gently sloping sandy beaches at right angles to the prevailing wind. The dunes are another habitat that is distinct from the beach itself, and they provide a home for species that have adapted to its unique environment. Common terns like to build shallow nests in the sand and amongst the specialist grasses whose roots have firm enough purchase to survive a coastal gale. Flowers, like those of the sea bindweed, that will not be found either inland or on the beach proper, break the greens and beiges.

Behind the smaller worlds of living creatures there is the equally dynamic battle between land and sea. Waves have swept away a Scottish breakwater weighing 2,600 tonnes and hurled a 60kg rock through the window of a 30m-tall lighthouse in North America, but their real power lies in their relentlessness. There is no substance that will withstand an infinite barrage of salt water. The coast is chiselled and harangued into the forms we recognise, each a reflection of the evolving relationship between the profile of the land and its resistance to the erosive power of the water: cliffs, headlands, coves, bays, caves, arches, stacks, spits and bars. It is not always the softest rock that goes first: there is a payoff between the resistance of the rock and its exposure. A hard headland might suffer more than a soft bay, which is all the more incentive to appreciate any stubborn promontory that is resisting destruction, albeit temporarily.

A promontory is a great place to sample the many costumes of a coastline. One single jut might offer opportunities to sample several different beaches, to look inland, out to sea, along a shore, from an elevated position or with wet feet, all in the space of a single walk.

Erosive forces produce coastlines that can look complex, chaotic and random, but erosion actually follows basic principles. One academic in France plugged some simple rules into a computer and set it to follow them as it ate its way into an imaginary coast-line. The result was a fractal pattern that looked a little like the coast of Sardinia.

Erosion is nearly always a destructive process but the material that is broken off can accumulate in new places and create new landforms, such as the tombolo, which forms when currents between two parcels of land such as an island and the mainland, slow to a halt. This allows shingle to be deposited, building to form a bank joining the two together again.

A classic tombolo

The geology of the land and the erosive processes taking place often mirror each other on the opposite sides of bodies of water, even very large ones. The coasts of Cornwall and Brittany are strikingly similar in places and similarities can also be found between Canada and Northern Europe or South Africa and India.

The brine-rich air of the onshore breeze stoops to pick up the moist funk of the strandline and hits our nostrils. They stop dilating and clam up. Looking out across the beach we see the sunlight and clouds take turns to toy with the colours in the sea and we think about a distant shore that mirrors our own.

Coastlines rival mountains for their ability to inspire. Each pebble, shell and grain of sand add up to a whole that is infinitely more powerful in our minds than the sum of its components. How else can we explain the fertile pockets of creativity that we find in coastal enclaves like St Ives in Cornwall and Cadaqués in Catalonia?

Valleys of Ice

A glacier may be considered as a vast instrument of
friction, a white sand-paper, applied slowly but irresistibly
to all the roughnesses of the hill which it covers.

John Ruskin

The great glaciers of the last ice age had not reached this far south,
but the effects of the cold had. This land was once frozen solid
in permafrost, making it impermeable and allowing surface water
to collect and then carve the land in wild torrents. The valleys were steep-
sided and the sinuous path of a long-dried river was so clearly visible at
their bottom that it made me yearn to catch sight of the water, to hear it
flow. But long ago the land had thawed and the water had seeped down
through the porous rock.

Looking down from the high ground north of the Burgh, the walls
descended towards the bottom of the valley with a steady gradient. A glacier
would never have allowed these gradients to survive. The ice sheets preferred
not to negotiate, they would have pressed the proud rocks away, leaving
submissive curves in the hillside.

Instead a river had sliced deep into this land, through the frozen earth.
It was easy to see the perfect V-shape the river had tried hard to leave
behind. It was now softened by the earth that gravity had carried and left
to accumulate at the bottom.

The path crossed down through the contours in a manageable slide. I
paused for a moment to consider how painful it would have been to attempt
to cross this land against the grain of the long-departed river. A descent

*that would turn my ankles, followed by a climb that would sear my lungs
and swamp my legs in lactic acid. It was better to respect and follow the
valley.*

• • •

The work of Louis Agassiz in the first half of the nineteenth
century exemplifies the impact that travel can have on our minds
and understanding. Agassiz was born in Switzerland, moved to
Paris, spent time in Britain and emigrated to the USA. Influenced
by the extraordinary and at this time ubiquitous, Humboldt,
Agassiz developed an interest in fish, became a professor of natural
history and then found himself at the forefront of the battle
between two great ideas.

The diluvial theory maintained that the valleys, caves, boulders
and other geological forms of the land could be accounted for
by a catastrophic flood. One of its keen proponents was the Very
Reverend Dr William Buckland, an eminent English geologist and
Dean of Westminster whose reverence and keenness on this theory
were no coincidence. The great flood was a key event in the
Judaeo-Christian history of the world, and the biblical story of
Noah and his ark formed part of the conventional archaeological
view during Dr Buckland's time.

Buckland was a methodical and thorough scientist even if he
subscribed to a theory we now think of as naïve, and despite his
colourful reputation for subjecting his dinner guests to such deli-
cacies as crocodile steaks, snails and puppy. One night he was
trying to solve a puzzling problem that concerned some fossil
footprints and woke his wife up to insist she make some dough
for him. He then placed his pet tortoise on the dough and watched
it walk across the surface. The results convinced him of the link
between his pet and its ancestors.

Buckland's scientific instincts were sound but he was hampered
by his initial unwillingness to question the orthodoxy of his time.
Inevitably not all the pieces of geological evidence would fit into

the diluvian theory, but Buckland, like so many others, was determined to accommodate them. If bones appeared where they ought not, such as in a cave in Yorkshire, then this was clearly the work of hyenas, long since vanished from Britain.

It is too easy to scoff at the determination of our predecessors to stick to theories that time has blown away, but Buckland deserves lauding not lampooning, because he achieved something that few scientists manage, then or now.

By 1838 William Buckland was fifty-four years old, he was famous and he moved in the highest circles. He could count the Prime Minister, Sir Robert Peel, among his friends. It would probably be fair to say that he felt he knew his own mind. It was at this point in his life that he decided to travel to Switzerland to meet Louis Agassiz, a geologist who was the main proponent of the theory that contradicted Buckland's favoured one. Agassiz showed Buckland evidence that it was ice in the form of glaciers and not a great deluge that could best account for the shape of the land. He demonstrated that Switzerland and most of northern Europe had at one time lain under a great sheet of ice. Buckland returned home having achieved the extraordinary: he had changed his mind.

In 1840 Buckland and Agassiz toured Scotland and looked at the evidence for an ice age together. There they found the trademarks that Agassiz had seen across Europe and would also find when he landed in Halifax, Nova Scotia in 1846. Together this unlikely duo introduced the sceptical British academic establishment to the revolutionary glacial theory.

The reason for the occurrence of the ice ages was beyond the science of the nineteenth century and research continues to this day, but one current theory is that of Milankovitch cycles. The familiar orbit of the Earth around the sun each year gives us our seasons, thanks to the fact that the Earth is tilted and so the north pole points towards the sun for half the year and away from it for the other half. There are however quite a few other cycles taking place that do not influence our climate on a daily or even annual basis, but over much greater periods of time. The Earth's tilt actually varies, it oscillates between 22.1 degrees and 24.5 degrees over a period of 41,000 years. It currently stands near 23.5 degrees and is decreasing.

The shape of the Earth's orbit around the sun also changes very slowly from elliptical to nearer a circle and back again. This cycle is measured in hundreds of thousands of years.

The third cycle takes 26,000 years and is called the 'precession of the equinoxes'. If you think of the Earth as a spinning top (each spin being a day), then this spinning top wobbles like a child's one, as it slows. If we imagine for a moment that the north and south poles do actually have long poles sticking out of them, then rather than spinning steadily in one spot, we would see them trace a small circle in the night sky.

It is difficult to fathom these great Milankovitch cycles, our minds have not evolved to view our surroundings in these ways, but bringing these three long, slow, cyclical motions together does at least offer one logical explanation for why parts of the Earth have been buried under hundreds of metres of ice at certain times and under jungles at others.

Even if an understanding of these issues was beyond Buckland and Agassiz, a solid grasp of the mechanics of glaciers and their effects on the landscape was not. Their pioneering discoveries were the foundation of glaciology.

When a glacier is 300 metres deep, the rock underneath the ice will experience pressures of 1,000 tonnes per square foot. If ice moves over a rock surface it will polish it, but if it drags another small rock over that same surface it will leave striations, the rock 'scratches its own face'. Glaciers leave moraines, accumulations of rocks of various sizes.

A terminal moraine is that pile of debris that amasses at the furthest reach of the glacier. Imagine that it falls to you to clean up after a large family has eaten a meal of bread and cheese at a long table. Having removed the plates you wipe a damp cloth from one end of the table to the other. The cloth is the glacier and the generous pile of bread and cheese crumbs that have amassed in front of the cloth are the rocks and boulders of the terminal moraine. These mounds of rocks can be found wherever glaciers have advanced and then retreated and most of the northern countries of the world have examples. Since the ice receded long ago, the rocks will often have supported new life, such as the conifer-forested bumps in the Swiss valleys.

The glaciers did not merely polish and scratch, they gouged and barged. Rivers may follow a sinuous path but glaciers have no patience for twists and turns, despite their lethargic pace. Glacial valleys tend to be straight and therefore afford excellent views. They are also U-shaped, with flat bottoms and steep walls, unlike the V-shaped walls of a river-carved valley. A classic U-shaped valley can be found at Honister in the Lake District, where the glacier eroded the volcanic rock in a broad sweep, rather than cut into it with a scalpel the way a river would have done.

Glacial valleys are often blessed with treats for the lover of waterfalls. Minor tributaries of ice that once ran from the sides of a valley to join the top of the main glacier now host streams of water that reach the valley's edge to find the glacier long-departed and a steep drop to the bottom of the valley. The water plummets down, to the delight of walkers, poets and painters.

Glaciers like to leave one more fingerprint on a landscape: the rocks that should not be there. 'Erratics' are boulders made from a different material to the underlying rock of an area and whose existence in a location is hard to explain unless they have been carried there. These anomalous lumps are clues to the locomotive power of glaciers.

The ice fists of glaciers have beaten their marks into the land in the least likely places (there are grooves in rocks in the Sahara desert caused by glaciers) but their legacy stretches well beyond geology.

In Tweedsmuir Kirkhead there stands a gravestone with the inscription:

Here lyes
The body of John Hunter
Martyr who was cruelly
Murdered at Corehead
by Col James Douglas and
his party for his adherance
To the Word of God and
Scotland's covenanted
Work of Reformation
1685

John Hunter was a Covenanter, a Scottish Presbyterian rebel, and on 12 August 1685 he was pursued by an English Dragoon officer up the depression in the land known as the Devil's Beeftub. From a flat bottom, the walls of this basin, formed by a glacier, rise to be very steep. Hunter could not escape. He was shot, fell against the valley's walls and died there.

Glaciers shape our walks, our views and our history. Identity and experience continue to be nudged by long-melted ploughs of ice.

The Earth

> Though these two forests are only parted by a narrow
> range of enclosures, yet no two soils can be more
> different: for the Holt consists of a strong loam, of a
> miry nature, carrying a good turf, and abounding with
> oaks that grow to be large timber; while Wolmer is
> nothing but a hungry, sandy, barren waste.
>
> Gilbert White

*L*ooking north towards Amberley, I noticed that the hill ahead of
me was bare in one patch. The grass and earth appeared to have
fallen away, revealing a small sore escarpment of chalk. The
colours changed from a very dark brown near the surface through to a
lighter redder colour, just above the white of the chalk. On the southern
side of the valley the grass had formed long horizontal ridges where the
soil was creeping downhill and tugging at the grass above it. This pasture
gave way to Stoke Hazel Wood and its mixed deciduous woodland spoke
of good alkaline soil. There were only a few hardy conifers, screaming of
sand or acid among their roots.

At the top of the hill the lumps of chalk and flint lay beneath a thin
carpet. Over time the wind and rain had robbed the summit of its soil.
Some of it had clearly washed down into the valley bottom. On my way
down the track I paused by the moist remnants of a puddle and bent
down. Hands must be dirtied to know the earth and I revelled in the
opportunity to rub the brown goo between my fingers. There's clay among
these chalk hills, I thought.

*I reached the bottom of the valley. Here the thick soil was being supple-
mented by something rich in phosphates and nitrogen, and the nettles were
out in force, among the dock. Their profusion hinted that an animal feed
or perhaps animal dung had joined the already fertile soil. This patch of
abundant and varied plant life was like another world compared to the
sparse gorse that I had stood next to quarter of an hour earlier. There
were only yards between the two areas and yet in habitat terms they were
a million miles apart.*

● ● ●

In the middle of the nineteenth century, the English traveller and
writer George Borrow came across an extraordinary roaring white
foam near a 'hog-backed' hill in the Welsh county of Powys. He
described the Pistyll Rhaeadr as the most beautiful waterfall in
Britain. He likened it to 'an immense skein of silk agitated and
disturbed by tempestuous blasts', and said it had, 'the long tail
of a grey courser at furious speed.' Through the waterfall's silvery
threads Borrow could make out the black rocky crag, over which
the booming water was being channelled.

It is not surprising that Borrow's attention was stolen by the light,
movement and sounds of the water, but it is disappointing that he
gives no credit at all to the supporting cast that allowed the water to
star. Not only does Borrow overlook the important role of the rock
in the scene before him, he actually goes on to accuse an unusual
and striking rock arch of detracting from the beauty of the waterfall
itself. The 'ugly black bridge' marred the loveliness of the cataract
for Borrow and he felt the whole scene would be better without it.

This unsightly object has stood where it now stands since the
day of creation, and will probably remain there to the day
of judgement. It would be a desecration of nature to remove
it by art, but no one could regret if nature in one of her
floods were to sweep it away.

The rock that Borrow abuses is as much the waterfall as the water itself. The clues are there, the hill with the 'hog's back', the black rock, but they are not given their due. The hard, dark, igneous dolerite has resisted erosion with more vigour than the neighbouring rocks that carry the Afon Disgynfa river and its stubbornness has created the high cradle for the water to dance through and then leap down in great bursts over two hundred feet. The waterfall's story begins in the eruption of a volcano, the flow and then setting of glowing lava, as much as it does in flowing water.

In their many textures, colours and shades of durability, rocks do us the great service of preventing us from falling to the centre of the Earth. They also set the stage for every landscape we find and yet they so often go without credit. It is only when we are denied rock's comforts that we start to appreciate its crucial role. Ocean sailors pine for rock and Robert Falcon Scott, the great Antarctic explorer, delighted in the sensation of stepping on rock after fourteen weeks of snow and ice. He liked the ability of rocks to give a homely feeling to an otherwise wild and alien landscape.

The relationship between stone and home is deep. Grand and arrogant buildings will source their stone from far away, but the most popular dwellings are proof of what lies below them. We see the rocks rise up and claim a territory, from the honey-coloured limestones that give the Cotswold homes their stamp to the solemn volcanic tufa that is used in Nasu-cho in Ashino, Japan. In parts of the world that have poor building stones, like chalk, the materials have to be brought in from afar and this leads to much greater variety in the constructions and the need for more detective work.

• • •

In January 1832 Charles Darwin was struck by the 'perfectly horizontal white band' of rock that greeted him as the *Beagle* entered the harbour of Santiago, on the largest of the Cape Verde islands. On closer inspection Darwin found the white rock to be embedded with shells and realised that most of these shells could still be

The Pistyll Rhaeadr Waterfall

found on the neighbouring coast. He soon noticed that more layers of rock were also exposed and these strata allowed Darwin to identify three clear and distinct phases in the formation of the land.

On top of the chalk was a basaltic layer of rock, which he deduced must have been formed by lava that had flowed out into the sea and then settled on top of the 'shelly bed'. Both these layers, the basalt and chalk, lay on top of a different layer of yet older volcanic rocks. Before the lava had set solid it must have come into contact with the chalk below it and changed the nature of the chalk layer. It converted it into crystalline limestone in some places and a compact spotted stone in others. In one single location, Darwin had found evidence of the main processes that help make sense of our world of rocks.

The rock family is large and diverse, but it can be greatly simplified by grouping the rocks according to the processes that form them. There are three main types of rock: igneous, sedimentary and metamorphic.

Igneous rocks have formed from the hot molten rock or magma in the Earth's core. They will have either been ejected in liquid form by a volcano or cooled and solidified deep underground. Either way, they form very hard crystalline and erosion-resistant rocks and make excellent materials for building mountains and resisting waterfalls. Granite is a classic igneous rock. Igneous rocks are the patriarchs of the rock family, because they form the basis of the Earth's crust and most other rocks owe their existence to them.

The next major group, the sedimentary rocks, form when deposits are lain down over long periods, typically under oceans but also in lakes, rivers and deserts, where sandstone will form. Sedimentary rocks contain trademark layers and their slow building at the Earth's surface means that they also contain the remains of the animals and plants that lived in these areas at the time: sedimentary rocks are full of fossils.

The soft white rock that punctuates green hills by jutting up as cliffs in the distance or which turns our boots over as awkward lumps in paths and fields is a resting place for billions. Chalk is made up of the sediment of tiny marine organisms, creatures that died about one hundred million years ago and settled on the seabed. The foraminifera, coccoliths and rhabdoliths that formed chalk live on as they wrestle with our tongues and threaten to shipwreck any careless sailors who pass those petite white monoliths, The Needles, at the western edge of the Solent in the English Channel.

Metamorphic rocks are the third group, a subsidiary group that have undergone change from one type to another as the result of great temperatures and pressures. When engineers began making tunnels through mountains for roads they were often greeted with violent explosions as they released the rocks from the very high pressures deep in the mountains. When these extreme pressures are combined with the heat from within the earth's crust, the rocks can undergo structural change. Metamorphic rocks are the kids in the family because they are born from either igneous or sedimentary rocks. Marble can form from limestone, granite can turn into gneiss, and shale will become slate if the conditions are right – the temperatures and pressures needed are normally only found deep underground.

• • •

We are all familiar with the great landscape features of mountains and valleys but the elevation and depression of land, when combined with erosion, can create more unusual forms, often on a much smaller scale. The landscape may be punctuated by the honeycombed rock of the pock-like tafoni in sandstone or the aerodynamic forms of the wind-blasted and sculpted yardangs in the desert.

Bold isolated rocks will become the dominant feature in a landscape in the same way as do isolated trees and can inspire awe, but sometimes it is the absence of rock that catches the eye. The Bullers of Buchan in northeast Scotland formed from a collapsed cave, leaving an imposing juxtaposition of a rock arch and rushing sea below. It left a lasting impression on Samuel Johnson when he visited in 1773; he felt that nobody could look at this cave with indifference, 'who has either sense of danger or delight in rarity.'

The direct impact of the rock's form on a landscape is important and can be dramatic, but it is in some of the secondary effects that we start to uncover the connections between the rocks and the fuller character of a place.

Water is hurled at rocks from the sky and higher land continuously as liquid rain and rivers and as solid ice in glaciers. The rocks will be eroded, but some will also hold on to the water. Rocks are more or less porous, and this has a huge impact on the appearance of an area. Igneous rocks, like basalt, tend not to be porous, sedimentary rocks, like limestone, can be very porous and metamorphic rocks can be either.

In England's Lake District there is a mixture of impervious hard volcanic rocks like granite, cohabiting with softer porous rocks like sandstone. The large lakes are found in areas that have experienced significant erosion – they are lower than the peaks – but the lakes also sit on top of rocks that will not allow the water to seep away, such as the slates in the central areas. There are no substantial lakes in the porous sandstone and limestone that can be found around the edges of the Lake District.

Ludwig Leichhardt noticed a very similar contrast in Australia. 'The difference between the sandstone country and the basaltic plains and ridges, is very striking in respect to the quantity of water they contain.'

Chalk is another porous rock and little standing water will be found in chalk country. In places where porous rocks dominate but where standing water is needed, man has to intervene and borrow nature's geological tricks. In the South Downs in southern England the rainwater seeps down through the chalk hills and escapes. However, the South Downs' farmers needed to provide some standing water for their sheep, so they dug out pits and lined them with impervious clay to form 'dew ponds', which collect rainwater for the sheep to drink. A few of these dew ponds survive to this day, but the clay has usually been replaced by a plastic lining.

The most significant secondary effect of the rocks is on the soil. The rock that lies under a landscape will dictate the type and depth of soil that lies over it. The soil will in turn determine the types of plants that can prosper, and this vegetation will have a strong bearing on the animals and humans that can survive there. The relationship between a pale wild saxifrage flower and a menacing dark rock outcrop might seem tenuous at first glance, but the flower is sensitive to its relationship with the rock and dependent on it.

Rocks contain a staggering variety of minerals. As the geologist Jan Zalasiewicz has demonstrated, a 50 gramme pebble contains about one million million million million atoms and so, inevitably, it contains a smorgasbord of elements. There will be a lot more of the usual suspects like oxygen and silicon than the rare elements, but a random pebble will also contain some colourful characters like gold, silver and platinum to go with the less popular rubidium, yttrium and niobium. It will even host some nefarious and unstable colleagues, like uranium.

It is not necessary to know the exact chemical composition of the rocks that underpin a landscape to connect with that area. A much broader approach can be used; in fact we need only split the rocks into two groups initially: those that contain predominantly acidic minerals and those that are alkaline. This division is so critical because soils based on acidic rocks support far fewer and sparser plants than their alkaline counterparts.

Granite is rich in the mineral silica, a compound of silicon and oxygen, which forms very acidic soils. Granite is also non-porous, the combination of acidic soil and the water-logging that is inevitable above such rocks leads to the wild landscapes of peat bogs and moors. Dartmoor in Devon is classic granite country. The sedimentary rock, sandstone, is much softer than granite, but it also contains large amounts of silica and so it too forms acidic soil, although usually much drier. Basalt is a very different chemical cake, it is typically low in the acidic silica and high in base compounds like magnesium and calcium oxides that form alkaline soils. Basalt country can host a rich and diverse ecosystem. We can witness the dramatic effects of the geological foundations on the vegetation of the land by accompanying Leichhardt as he explores another patch of Queensland, moving from a rich alkaline environment, via an acidic spur, to emerge into another lush alkaline setting.

> We were encamped in the shade of a fine Erythrina; and the Corypha-palm, Tristania, the flooded-gum, the silver-leaved Ironbark, Tripetelus, and a species of Croton, grew around us . . . In the afternoon I went with Brown up the range, following the bed of our creek; and, having ascended a spur of sandstone, with gullies on each side, we came to a large basaltic mountain, clothed with fine open timber, and a great number of arborescent Zamias.

There are general trends to be found all over the world, such as the thin Podzol acidic soils that are bad for farming but support northern coniferous forests happily. And there are smaller pockets of anomalous underlying rock that mark a place out as different. Ben Lawers, a mountain in the Scottish Highlands that is a National Nature Reserve, is home to a rich selection of alpine flora rare in the UK, flowers such as Alpine mouse-ear and a moss found nowhere else in Britain. This rich ecological island owes its existence in large part to the schist rocks that form the mountain, as these rocks provide the right elements and alkaline compounds in the right ratios to create the perfect home.

Gilbert White found that the underlying stone affected not only the types of trees that would grow in his area, but the character of the timber too.

The oaks of Temple and Blackmoor stand high in the esti-
mation of purveyors and have furnished much naval timber;
while the trees on the freestone grow large, but are what
workmen call *shakey*, and so brittle as often to fall to pieces
in sawing.

Minerals regularly have a more specific effect on plant life than
the broad effects of acid or alkaline. Although this often goes
undetected, the effects are sometimes vivid and the wood of trees
may be coloured by minerals in a soil: blue or green from nickel,
red or black from iron. The sensitivity of plants to the minerals
in rocks has led to prospectors using some plants as indicators
for the presence of certain metals. *Thlaspi caerulescens* is prized for
its affinity with zinc and nickel; the small white flowers of this wild
herb mark the ground in the Rockies, like a pirate's X on a
crinkled yellowing map.

The acidic or alkaline nature of soil is governed by the underlying rocks, but there is more to a soil's full character. Soil is a
mixture of rock particles and biological mass in differing ratios
at each depth. At the bottom is the bedrock, above that there will
be loose, weathered and broken rock, above this is the subsoil
which is a mix of rock particles, humus – that is, decaying plants
and animals – and minerals that have been washed down by rain.
Finally, above this lies the topsoil, rich in humus, animal life and
much more influenced by the weather. A handful of topsoil can
contain one billion bacteria and as many as 30 million fungi. One
acre of healthy topsoil might contain as much as 40 tonnes of
plants and animals living in it.

The bedrock that breaks down into smaller particles influences
the character of the soil in one other critical way. Each rock breaks
down differently and, most significantly, will break down into
varying size particles. The largest particles in soil are grains of
sand and individual grains can be seen by rubbing a little sandy
soil between your thumb and fingers. Silt is smaller than sand and
the finest grade is clay which is close to powder. Soil will tend to

be a mix of all three types, but will be dominated by one or sometimes two types, and this will be heavily influenced by the type of bedrock, thus giving it a specific character. Clay soils tend to be heavy because the fine particles become easily compacted and the soil holds a lot of water. Sandy soils are much lighter, contain fewer nutrients and are prone to drying out. The ideal soils for plants therefore have a mixed nature, avoiding each extreme. Each soil has its own character and consequently its own flora, which is why gardeners become familiar with the character of soils, however little they care for the rocks that have sired this earth from below.

Sometimes the behaviour of the tectonic plates, the rocks and the soil of an area work together in an unexpected and deadly way. In 1989 an earthquake measuring 6.9 on the Richter scale hit the San Francisco Bay area of California. It killed dozens and caused hundreds of millions of dollars' worth of destruction. The damage was not spread equally however and some districts fared worse than others. Those with the least stable soils were worst affected and in one case, the Marina District, the earth was landfill, rich in sand. When the earthquake struck this sandy earth, the soil liquefied and the buildings above it crumbled.

Leichhardt was always tuned to the geology of the land he travelled through and used it to both unlock the area, and also to predict what lay ahead, 'In the bed of the river, I still found pebbles of pegmatite, granite, quartz, and basalt; indicating that a country of varied character was before us.' Leichhardt also beautifully demonstrated that this awareness of the bonds between plants, soil and bedrock can be used to decipher the country from either direction: the rocks can reveal the likely soil and plants, or the other way around.

The nature of the soil was easily distinguished by its vegetation: the Bastard box, and Poplar gum grew on stiff clay; the narrow-leaved Ironbark, the Bloodwood, and the Moreton

Bay ash on a lighter sandy soil, which was frequently rotten and undermined with numerous holes of the funnel ant. Noble trees of the flooded-gum grew along the banks of the creeks, and around the hollows, depending rather upon moisture, than upon the creeks; and the forest oak (Casuarina torulosa), together with rusty gum, were frequent on the sandy ridges.

The flooded-gum trees that Leichhardt refers to here were betraying the high moisture levels in the ground, much in the way that alder trees and rushes do for walkers in temperate climates.

The ability of rocks to reveal so much explains why so many of the formidable explorers were on the look out for these clues. Even in lands so harsh that survival was constantly threatened and plant life was scarce, we find the most sensitive explorers remain alert to the life of rocks. Wilfred Thesiger recognised pieces of porphyry, granite, rhyolite, jasper and limestone in the scorched and barren Empty Quarter of the Arabian Peninsula.

In the less forbidding Blawith Common in the Lake District, the permaculturalist, Patrick Whitefield, outlined how he reads the relationship between the rocks and the soil. The shape of the land and the rock formations will have a profound impact on the depth of the soil, with the soil growing thinner close to the rocky outcrops. Whitefield found three soil types were faithfully mapped out for him by bracken, which dominated, heather, which out-competed the bracken where the soil was particularly shallow and grass where water was accumulating and the soil was consistently wet.

Heather also gives clues to the chemical balance of the soil as it is able to tolerate acidic soil whereas bracken and grasses need more alkaline soils. The presence of heather identifies the granite mountains in places like the Scottish Highlands, whereas the mountains formed of base minerals will support brackens and grasses.

Misreading or misunderstanding this relationship between plants and soil leads to a poorer experience for all of us, but for some people in the past this paucity was life-threatening. Pine trees are very hardy specimens that have adapted to inhospitable soils as well as extremes of climate, but this fact had to be discovered the hard way by some miserable pioneers. After the Pilgrim Fathers had shown the way, the early Europeans settled on Cape Cod and tried to tame the land. Seeing great forests they assumed that rich soils would lie underneath and began felling the trees. The unfamiliar pine's tolerance of poor sandy soils was discovered as the cleared land revealed only sand dunes. It was totally unable to support agriculture and the pioneers nearly starved.

Rocks and soils shape the land through economic activity as well as through its plants. There is one sedimentary rock that has done more than any other to shape the economics of Britain: coal. Even long after the glory days of the British coal mining industry, when the link was obvious, a map of defunct coal mines and urban areas outside of London shows some striking correlations. Service industries and in particular, call centres, have sprung up to replace the mines as sources of local employment. This has led to one of the more unusual connections with the rocks. The likelihood of encountering a particular accent when we speak to someone on the phone to query a household bill, has been influenced by a black sedimentary rock.

Soil types can influence politics, too. In areas with poor sandy soils the potential gain from farming is less and so the desire to own the land is weaker. The county of Surrey has sandy soils and it is not a coincidence that it also has more commons than any other southern English county: the land has been abandoned to common use by previous generations of frustrated landowners.

Conversely, rich soils are credited not just with an ability to sustain diverse plant life, but to imbue these plants with particular qualities emblematic of their nations of origin. Al-Masudi, the great Arab geographer and historian wrote in the tenth century

**There is a strong correlation between the location of coal mines and
cities in the UK**

that oranges and lemons were transported from India to be grown in Oman, Iraq and Syria but none of these displaced citrus trees could produce fruit with 'the penetrating sweet smell and beautiful colour they had in India, because they lacked the air, soil and water of their native land.'

• • •

In the world borne from rocks, even the least dramatic scenes contain stories that have emerged slowly from the stones below. A patch of nondescript mud is wet soil, it is still a window to the past and an opportunity for the future. Mud contains the particles of the rocks that have been attacked over millions of years by wind and rain, then chiselled at by ancient plants until these small particles could be washed away and accumulate in resting places as the gloop we know today.

The mud is unlikely to stay still for long – if natural forces do not set to work on it, then a human hand might. In the City of Djenné, in Mali, there stands the finest mud building in the world. There has been a mosque on this site since the thirteenth century, and the current structure was built using sun-dried mud bricks and is protected from the seasonal rains with fresh layers of mud each year.

If the mud does somehow manage to stay in one place for long enough it may be crushed over time, thus forming a new layer of sedimentary rock and the starting point for another rock story.

Soil covers almost the whole land surface of our planet, with the exceptions of rocky promontories or beneath thick icecaps. The more we are able to fathom this soil the better our chances of connecting with a landscape. It might remain dirt to some, but for the aware traveller, rocks and their soil become master keys. William Blake felt the exciting potential for gaining powerful insights from humble earth when he began his poem, 'Auguries of Innocence', with the line, 'To see a world in a grain of sand'.

When we rest for a moment from the dizzying and intensely

rich clues that are offered up all around us by the rocks, we might decide to get ready for a night out by enjoying a hot bath. As Gilbert White discovered in Selborne in 1788, our experience in the bath will be shaped by rocks deep below it: soap does not lather well in hard water, that is water which has picked up calcium from the rocks it passes through.

Fleeing from the rocks that have climbed into the bath with us, we make it to a restaurant and finally unwind. The waiter pours a glass of water. This water will have been given its taste by the rocks and soil. The minerals from the rocks find their way over waterfalls, meander through the process of bottling into beautifully designed receptacles and then penetrate the restaurants of the world. There is no hiding place. The earth makes its way inside us, wherever we are.

The Animals

> The essential quality of an animal is that it seeks its own
> living, whereas a vegetable has its living brought to it.
>
> Henry Mayhew

*N*ear *Stoke Hazel Wood, the day's peace was shattered for the three sheep. They abandoned their resting place, a mud hollow in the shade of a hawthorn tree, with a gentle stampede because they had sensed my approach down the track. In the rhythmic drum of their footsteps I became aware that I was having an impact on the animals around me, although that was never my intention.*

I felt less sympathy for the fly that broke my unwritten rule. It was fine for the flies to congregate around the rim of my Panama hat and even to buzz in my face. But trying to land on my eyeballs was not something I could tolerate as a passive observer. The transgressor would have felt my hand encourage it on its way.

Who knows how many tiny creatures were less fortunate and fell underfoot for the first and last time? The ones that stayed clear of the ground would be safer from my boots, the bright-striped cinnabar caterpillar on some ragwort and the orange soldier beetle that I found at work on the Hogweed were in no danger from my heavy feet.

I met the flies again on my descent. They buzzed with morbid enthusiasm around the exposed and drying spinal column of a rabbit on the path, one that had been cut in two, presumably by some piece of farm machinery. The rabbit's hind legs were coiled for the jump that it never got to make. Next to the drying half-carcass, there was fresh dung from a sheep, which cared not for the sanctity of death. Not in a rabbit anyway. Would it have left its droppings next to the mutilated carcass of another sheep? Perhaps. Soon, there was more death in the squashed body of a field vole on the track. Did it die from the vehicle, or, more likely, did it fall prey to one of the buzzards that I could hear overhead and was subsequently pressed into the earth by a tyre?

Some of the signs of animals gave me great pleasure: the now-dry prints of a pheasant and a rabbit that had passed over wet mud. The rains of two days before situated these tracks in a time-window, the pheasant and rabbit could not have passed before the rains or after the mud had dried. Knowing this and letting my fingers run over the ridges of their tracks brought me close to these creatures. Strange how touching their impressions can sometimes move me more than a sight of the animal itself.

Closing a gate behind me, I wondered about its purpose. The fence corralled the sheep, which in turn shaped the plants. There was an explosion of wildflowers near the bottom of the valley, but it was only on one side of the gate. Sheep and few wildflowers on one side of the fence. No sheep and copious wildflowers on the other.

The sound of an invisible farmer calling 'Come on! Come on!' rolled towards me from Downs Farm on the ridge ahead. The cows made their way up the steep slope; the reward for their exertion would be the relief of milking time. I felt hungry and pressed on, just one more mammal marching to the beat of a biological drum.

• • •

The diversity of wildlife that Marco Polo encountered in Abyssinia made him weary. 'They have the prettiest hens to be seen anywhere, and enormous ostriches scarcely smaller than a donkey. In short the diversity of animals is such that it would be tedious to enumerate them.'

There are 750 different species of fig tree in the world and each one is pollinated by its own individual wasp. In 1995 one study of 19 trees in Panama counted 1,200 different beetle species in the trees and eighty per cent of these were new to science.

Unless we are scientists or spotters, the joys of appreciating animals are not to be found in classification, since the scale of the task is overwhelming, but in the connections we come to recognise between the animal kingdom and the spaces we share. Animals colour the places we know, they shape its appearance and its time.

The naturalist Richard Mabey has described how for him, the pink-footed goose dominated Holkham in Norfolk. Norfolk is home to half the world's pink-footed goose population with up to 150,000 birds, but these dry facts do nothing for our emotions. Mabey wrote about the moments when, near the March equinox and in the early evening, the birds were migrating so high overhead that they caught the last of the sun's pink on their bellies, matching the pinks of their feet. 'I've more than once involuntarily dropped to my knees under them.'

Some of the richest differences we find on our travels are in the varying ways humans have forged a relationship with animals and have encouraged different interactions between those animals. Most farming involves a keen interest in this, but there are more colourful examples too. In India domesticated female elephants are given a fragrant musk-oil rub-down to make them more sexually attractive to the bull elephants. This is a practice that was likely borrowed directly from the human Ayurvedic tradition and Abhyanga practice, where oils are used, and the Tantric sexual ceremonies.

Watching any animal's routines, from defecating to courtship will provoke a response in us, from repulsion through curiosity to giggling. It is hard for us to remain unmoved by the way the animals remind us that, beneath our layers of elaborate clothing and honed protocols, we eat, sleep, breathe, sweat, fart, shit, have sex and die.

Leichhardt took some live bullocks on his Australian expedition, to supplement the dry rations. When supplies were low or the remaining meat had turned bad, they would slaughter another of the animals and dry the meat. Leichhardt noticed how the surviving bullocks would always return to the place where one of their kind had been slaughtered. The last bullock left, named

Redmond, returned mournfully and frequently to the spot where his last friend had been killed.

Sexual displays and reminders of death produce primal responses in us, but there are subtler, more interesting ones. In the Kalahari, Laurens van der Post learned about the honey-diviner bird from the bushmen. He was told that the bird would lead a man to a gorgeous brown honey, but that its offer of assistance was part of a bargain. The bird would help, but in return it expected to receive some of the honey. If a person was too greedy to share the bounty with the bird, then the honey-diviner would punish that selfishness. Van Der Post learned how one greedy man from the Bapedi tribe followed the bird to the honey but then guzzled it all himself. The next day he followed the same honey-diviner, only this time it led him to a hole in the ground. The Bapedi tribesman looked in and was greeted by an angry female puff-adder, who bit him. He coiled in pain and died from the venom.

The honey-diviner bird

We come to recognise traits in animals and then we project these back on to ourselves. As Ralph Waldo Emerson wrote, a 'lamb is innocence' and a 'snake is subtle spite', but 'an enraged man is a lion, a cunning man is a fox . . .'

Like all relationships, that between humans and animals evolves and this can be seen in the way travellers recount their experiences. Almost all these encounters come to seem dated. Leichhardt is sensitive to the curiosity of the animals he encounters, he writes of being watched by an emu and bronze-winged pigeons, but then seems disappointed that he can't learn much about the teeth of a snake, because he has bludgeoned its head beyond recognition.

One of the biggest shifts in Western attitudes towards animals is a sharp movement away from the belief that animals have been placed on the planet for the sole purpose of serving humans. This is a belief that makes the perspectives of earlier travellers almost comical. The Scottish explorer of New Zealand, Charles Douglas, became known as Mr Explorer Douglas thanks to his extensive surveying of the country towards the end of the nineteenth century. His account of his irritation with the mosquitoes there is an amusing reminder of the broader anthropocentric attitude to animals of the Victorian era.

> I am perfectly aware that the mosquito and sandfly have a purpose in this world, but why don't they attend to it? Their destiny is to keep down microscopic insects, who I believe would otherwise taint the air, and give us fevers instead of the present bad temper, so science says, but their sphere of use is when they are in the grub state. Why don't they stick at that and not trouble innocent unoffending prospectors who can't carry a curtain?

If our ancestor's perspective of the animals' place in this world seems quaint or amusing, we should pause for a second to reflect that our own views will seem as naïve to someone in a century's time. Part of the human arrogance is for each generation to believe that they are perfectly enlightened, but that all who went before were deluded, barbaric or both. It is hard to know exactly how or why contemporary attitudes will seem ludicrous to future generations, all we know is that they surely will.

A kinder treatment of animals may be a reflection of an enlightened society, but it is also the product of one that has developed from hardship to relative ease. The treatment of animals has always been harsh in places where human life is hard. Darwin reports one Argentinian medical remedy of cutting two puppies in half and then binding each of these half-puppies around a broken limb to aid its healing.

One of the traps we can fall into is that of a patronising view of nature. Kindness and understanding are not the same as condescension and it does us good to occasionally be reminded by an insect or larger animal that we are not lords over all we see. In the parts of the world where it is harsh for all, then the animals are less inclined to live and let live. The Danish navigator, Vitus Bering, served in the Russian navy and explored the eastern boundary of Russia, finally reaching Alaska in 1741 at the age of sixty. Georg Steller, the brilliant German scientist who accompanied Bering, recounted how the party had to be wary of foxes on Bering Island. If they lay still the foxes would come and sniff their nostrils to check whether they were still alive. The men even discovered, through an experiment that cannot have been repeated often, that if they held their breath the foxes would assume death and bite at their noses. The foxes would gnaw at the fingers and toes of the dead as their graves were being prepared, and on one occasion a fox clamped its teeth around the penis of a man who attempted to urinate out of the door of their hut at night. No amount of keen shouting would get the fox to release its grip.

In more recent times the relationship between most humans and animals has developed according to a mix of economic exploitation and conservation, the blend varying across the world depending on wants, needs and culture – the hunting of whales, for example, is abhorred by many and revered by some. Farming has in many places traditionally tried to sit as close to the middle of this seesaw as it can, although the animals might articulate a different story if they could.

If animals can somehow sense our love of economic gain, the termites are leading their remonstrations. In April 2011, staff at a bank in Uttar Pradesh in India were disciplined after failing to prevent termites from devouring ten million rupees' worth of banknotes. Their protest is not a twenty-first century phenomenon. In the first years of the nineteenth century, Humboldt found that whole areas of South America had no paper that was more than one hundred years old, the termites having devoured every scrap of paper they could find. At the risk of anthropomorphising, the insects appear to be bent on a world without money or bureau-cracy: a utopian creature if ever there was one.

In the instances where a harmonious relationship between humans and animals is reached it often provides a beautiful scene. In the Moroccan city of Fez, leather of an exceptionally high quality is produced thanks to the traditional techniques of leather tanning. The tanners in Fez use the excrement of pigeons and it helps them to achieve a softness in the leather that is prized internationally. It is unsurprising that pigeons are welcomed in Fez and they have excellent houses built for them all over the city.

Pigeons are less welcome where they fail to contribute to the economics and nowhere has been designed with the pigeon less in mind than the sprawling mirror-glass empire that is Dubai. In the land of seven-star hotels they have chosen to fight fire with fire and a full-time falconer is employed to use his falcons to deter the pigeons from the towering glass of the hotels.

Even the pigeons of Dubai may be happier than the bird that can lay one dubious claim to success, as a result of having endeared itself to humans. The human appetite for eggs and chicken meat means there are about sixteen billion of the birds on the planet, making the chicken one of the most numerous warm-blooded creatures on Earth. Other animals achieve similar levels of success alongside human development despite being loathed by human beings. Rats match the number of residents in New York, at nine million.

We have always been quicker to admire animals when their superior abilities can assist us. Horse riders who have become separated from their fellow travellers have often been reunited, if they relax the reins and allow their horse to do the navigating. Desert nomads have long relied on their camels' ability to find water.

Animals have qualities, as well as abilities, that draw praise. Pliny admired elephants not just for their physical abilities, but for qualities he found too rare in humans, including 'honesty, good sense, justice and also respect for the stars, sun and moon.' The animal kingdom's penchant for hard work and its frugal habits have drawn lots of admirers. Darwin was impressed with the cows and goats that eked out an existence on the lava-strewn landscape of the Cape Verde islands, where 'a single green leaf can scarcely be discovered.' He also admired the diligent way a wasp searched for a spider that it was hunting and had temporarily lost, using a semicircular search pattern until it found its prey.

The spider spinning its web is thrifty; it spins two spirals, the second in the opposite direction to the first and as it spins the second, it devours the first. Hibernating animals manage an economy of resources that could inspire a generation of climate-conscious humans: the hibernating hedgehog breathes only once every six minutes.

The average bee colony collects over twenty kilogrammes of pollen each year, which requires two million sorties. John Lubbock, a nineteenth-century banker, politician and naturalist, lauded the industry of bees and wasps and commented that Sundays and Bank Holidays were all the same to them. Doubtless this resonated with Lubbock, given that he carried the Bank Holidays Act of 1871 through Parliament. His success gave the satirical magazine

Punch the material it needed for a cartoon and accompanying verse.

> How doth the Banking Busy Bee
> Improve his shining Hours?
> By studying on Bank Holidays
> Strange insects and Wild Flowers!

Lubbock also praised birds' respect for property ownership. 'Their ideas of the rights of property are far stricter than those of some statesmen.' We have all enjoyed one positive consequence of birds' sense of property rights: the competitive song battles that paint the land. Many birds do not restrict their property interests to one place, they like to have a second home. The Arctic Tern combines an extraordinary industry with a thirst for daylight and ranges across the globe, experiencing more daylight than any other creature on Earth.

The interplay between animals and plants is infinitely rich and diverse and any habits we notice are satisfying to see repeated. Flowers that were merely pretty become more interesting as their relationship with animals is revealed. Honeybees prefer blue and yellow flowers, butterflies like red and orange ones and moths, which work more at night, go for light-coloured flowers with stronger scents. Butterflies will alight on a flower whereas moths hover; consequently the moths prefer flowers that hang down and butterflies pick flowers with broader flatter shapes.

So wonderfully are the animals tuned into their surroundings that it is often only when we see an animal move that we notice it. As the land around animals changes, they adapt, evolve or perish. We see only those that succeed. Over the course of fifty years the British pepper moth changed from grey to black to match its habitat; the trees it frequented had become blackened by pollution. Many animals mimic others to improve their chances. Insects that appear on first glance to be wasps are often less-feared flies; the harmless Viceroy butterfly mimics the foul-tasting Monarch and deters even hungry predators.

The animal world is so full of claws and horror that the ability of animals to cooperate is a sight that warms us and perhaps offers us hope. Stories of the plover bird hopping into the mouth of the crocodile, which is grateful for the bird's dental services, date back to Herodotus, but do not lose their charm. Different species of birds will heed each others' warning calls; the Blue Jay is particularly quick to warn of a hawk overhead. The habit of mobbing is used by birds and other animals, like the meerkat, to protect against predators; continual diving by birds to deter the predator is one of the most visible signs that a hawk or owl is in the vicinity. The diving is sometimes accompanied by mobbing calls, where other birds of the same or different species will heed the call and come to aid in the mutual defence. The animals have forged their own United Nations. If a conflict does take place, chimpanzees have astounded researchers by demonstrating a willingness to 'kiss and make up' afterwards. Following a fight, chimpanzees will sometimes extend a hand to each other and then embrace, kiss, pat and groom each other.

As we walk through the land we send the other animals scuttling away, there is a ripple as they take flight. All animals impact on the behaviour of others and we can identify one animal by studying the effects it has on others. Darwin learnt to understand where pumas were hiding through the effect their habits had on the birds. When a puma had made a kill it covered it with foliage and rested. The condors were aware of this and would wheel in the sky above the slain carcass, hopeful of some easy food; the locals would look for the condors as keenly as the pumas themselves.

Learning to read the world around us from the presence and behaviour of animals is the most rewarding part of studying them. This fascination stretches back as far as we can trace it, sometimes appearing as the earliest science and sometimes something closer to myth. Pliny tells us that hedgehogs predict a change in the wind, from north to south in his experience, by burying themselves in their dens.

This relationship of animals with the weather has remained a bulwark of folklore. An old Scottish rhyme finds clues in the behaviour of the gulls. 'Sea-gull, sea-gull sit on the sand/It's never good weather when you're on the land.' Unless the gull is scavenging for food away from the beach (a relatively recent habit) then this holds some truth. Lampyris noctiluca is known as the glow-worm, but is actually a beetle. It has been said that, 'When the glow-worm lights her lamp, the air is always damp.' And there is some truth in this as the beetles like warm, damp conditions.

One of the best-known animals for weather folklore is the swallow, which has been observed to fly lower when bad weather is on the way. When the air pressure drops and moisture levels increase, the insects that the swallow preys on will be found much closer to the ground and it follows them lower. It is unlikely that the Roman poet Virgil knew this, but the wisdom was already formed.

> Wet weather seldom hurts the most unwise;
> So plain the signs, such prophets are the skies . . .
> The swallow skims the river's watery face;
> The frogs renew the croaks of their loquacious race.

Nowhere has animals' influence on the land been more dramatic than in the case of grazing cattle. Sheep and cows do not fell mature trees, but once man has taken his axe to the established woodland these nibblers will keep the growth of new plants close to the ground. This stacks the odds massively in favour of the grasses, as most young plants, including trees, will be killed by grazing. The grasses survive as their buds are below the surface and protected. The question of whether the 'Lamb of God' was seen on 'England's pleasant pastures' is posed in William Blake's poetry, but either way there would have been far fewer of such pastures without the constant mowing of the four-legged lambs.

On a smaller scale the bumps in the land offer clues to life below it. The grassy miniature cairns that can be found across Europe and other parts of the world, are home to the yellow meadow grass ants. The grass cairns betray the presence of the ants in the neighbourhood, but they also suggest relatively dry soil that has been left undisturbed and unploughed for a long time. Ants like warm conditions and their hills will often map out the warmer areas of undulating land, typically south-facing slopes. Molehills tell us not only that moles are about, but that the ground is likely rich in earthworms as these are the moles' staple diet. This in turn also reveals that the soil is not very acidic or water-logged as worms will not tolerate these conditions.

Above ground, horses have a habit of dividing their fields into separate areas: those designated for grazing and others for dunging in. One part of a field will become heavily grazed, shorn down to near the ground, while the other will not be grazed at all and will become wilder-looking, with tall proud weeds and nettles.

If a field contains a few isolated trees then these will offer the only limited shade on a hot day and animals will congregate under these parasols and leave their dung as a rich fertiliser for the soil below the trees. Nettles and other weeds will be quick to colonise. This relationship between animal dung habits and vegetation is global, the animals and patterns change, but the relationship is constant. Al-Masudi noticed these patterns from the behaviour of the hippopotamus in Egypt. 'After having grazed, he returns to the Nile and drinks; then he leaves his droppings in various places and these give rise to a secondary growth of vegetation.'

Animals can give us many clues to the invisible, the inaudible, and perhaps the almost unknowable. Just as condors betrayed the position of invisible pumas for Darwin, so moths can give us clues to the whereabouts of bats. Moths can hear the echo-locating sounds that their predator uses and they react to it. If there are bats nearby the moths zigzag, but if they are further away the moths dive for cover. Pliny seemed convinced that crocodiles were in possession of a knowledge that will forever escape humans. He assures us that Egyptian crocodiles lay their eggs just above the highest line that the Nile would flood to each year, giving warning of these levels.

There are commonsense ways to dissuade many animals from fleeing as we approach, but also some less logical ones. Talking quietly in low tones will dispatch fewer animals than whispering, which emits a deterrent hiss. There are some tricks that draw them closer too: kissing the back of a hand can make some birds curious enough to investigate.

The closer we get to the animal world, the more inspiring we find it and the smaller the division between humans and animals starts to appear. Almost all of the traits and abilities that humans once thought they owned exclusively are now being found in abundance in the animal kingdom. Tools are not reserved for us. Chimpanzees use tools, including spears and rocks to gain food. One gorilla was observed using a stick to test the depth of water that he was walking into (gorillas don't like deep water).

Even crows can use tools. In one experiment the birds proved they could work out how to get food out of a long transparent tube, by picking up a thin stick and poking the food out the other end. Crows are not loved by all and are underappreciated for their intelligence: they have surprisingly large brains. In one test, a crow called Betty demonstrated the ability to both make a tool and then use it. In the test, Betty needed to lift a small pail of food out of a tube that was too deep to reach down into with her beak. She solved the problem by fashioning a hook from a straight piece of wire and then lifting the small pail out by its handle.

The ability to communicate does not mark humans out as special. Two psychologists, Keith and Cathy Hayes, adopted a chimpanzee called Viki and patiently taught her to speak. Viki learnt simple sounds first, 'up' and 'ah', before progressing to using the words 'mama' and 'papa'. Most importantly she understood the meanings of these words. Viki lived with the psychologists at their home and they understandably grew very close to her. They were devastated when she died prematurely, from encephalitis, at the age of six. Those last words must make extraordinary memories.

Viki did not die in vain and her success inspired more research, particularly in the use of sign language. At the age of seven, one chimpanzee called Sarah had demonstrated a working vocabulary of 130 (words).

One of the earliest examples of an animal that was famous for its intelligence became notorious. In 1888, Wilhelm von Osten, a retired teacher from Berlin, announced that he had taught a horse to solve mathematical problems. The horse, Hans, duly amazed onlookers with an ability to perform complex arithmetic, including working out the square root of large numbers. Hans gave answers to mathematical questions by tapping his hoof.

A commission was convened to investigate this extraordinary horse. It included a vet, two zoo directors, a horse trainer, two academics, two military officers, a circus manager and a magician. They watched for trickery, patiently studying both horse and owner. They failed to see how the horse was achieving this spectacle, but all agreed that von Osten was not a charlatan, he was not trying to deceive or even to make money from his extraordinary achievement.

The answer was finally revealed when a graduate student called Oskar Pfungst was given the opportunity to painstakingly investigate every possibility. Pfungst noticed that von Osten's distance from Hans impacted on the results and when he was far enough away the horse failed to get his sums right. Pfungst also noticed that if von Osten did not himself know the answer to a question, then Hans would also fail to get it right.

More investigation revealed that Hans was supremely sensitive to the subtlest clues in body language from von Osten. Unwittingly Wilhelm von Osten was giving cues to Hans when the answer was right, by minutely adjusting his posture. Von Osten was leaning backwards a tiny amount and ever so slightly upwards whenever Hans reached the right number of taps with his hoof.

Far from demonstrating that horses are unintelligent, this story clearly shows something else. Even when we think we are the observers, we are being watched more closely by the animals than we are watching them.

The Shape of Nature

> The most famous of all hexagonal conformations, and one
> of the most beautiful, is the bee's cell.
>
> D'Arcy Wentworth Thompson

For a few minutes I carried in one hand some small white spheres. I had plucked them from the soil of a field near the place called the Burgh. These heavy, hard stones, ideal for catapults, were the flint fossils of sponges. It was their perfect form that drew my eye initially. Further along the path, I noticed one much larger sphere. I picked it up. The mix of smooth curves and jagged protrusions filled my hand, but my head was flooded with other thoughts. Surely this was a skull? The shape screamed of murder most foul. On calmer reflection, it was merely another large sponge fossil. For a moment an innocent shape had conjured scenes of violence, but they evaporated as quickly as they had arrived.

From the high ground, I looked down into the valley. The sinuous bends of the riverbeds were joyous. The way these long-departed rivers swept in from behind a spur and then curved in such a harmonious way until they were out of sight delighted me. There was something about these dry valleys that made them personal and beautiful. Before long they disappeared behind a ridge once more; their past and future was out of reach. Each time I tried to look away, I felt my eyes drawn back to the shape of the curve. It was voluptuous and alluring. It teased a little.

At the bottom of the valley, next to Stoke Hazel Wood, there was a perfect circle in the grass and a shallow depression within it, perhaps fifty feet in diameter. It was thrilling to find this unexplained and unannounced *shape in the grass. It was mysterious and I revelled in the opportunity to decipher it. The circle was too neat, too mathematical, for any natural force that I could think of and I suspected that this circle was all that remained of an old dew pond.*

On one side of the dried pond the curves left by a great grass-cutting machine radiated from the corner of a field. Slicing through these curves, the darker green of a path snaked away along the dry riverbed towards the darker-still line of the woods. I pressed on towards the trees.

● ● ●

Few people can have appreciated the beauty of natural shapes so acutely as Ralph Alger Bagnold, and certainly nobody in the world has done more to help us appreciate the beauty of sand dunes. Born in Devon at the end of the nineteenth century, R.A. Bagnold led a life that would have been uninsurable, had insurers known the challenges that would confront this extraordinary man.

Bagnold fought at the battles of the Somme, Ypres, and Passchendaele during the First World War, spent the inter-war years pioneering desert exploration and research with the help of the Model T Ford, then put this experience to lethal use during the Second World War by setting up the Long Range Desert Group. His legacy is still felt today, in the military and in his unique work to enhance our understanding of the way sand behaves in the desert. Bagnold's book, *The Physics of Blown Sand and Desert Dunes*, is still the foremost book on the subject.

In places vast accumulations of sand weighing millions of tons move inexorably, in regular formation over the surface of the country, growing, retaining their shape, even breeding, in a manner which by its grotesque imitation of life is vaguely disturbing to an imaginative mind.

The analogies with life in something that grows, moves and breeds are clear, but in Bagnold's choice of the word 'shape' he points to something more elusive and intriguing. Whenever we stumble across unexpected shapes in nature, our deductive juices begin to flow. Walking across a field on a hill we might notice two patterns that surprise us. The first is that the line of the lower branches of the trees appears to follow, even to mimic, the contours of the land. They flow in a steady line uphill, perfectly mirroring the gradient of the field. Then, gazing downhill, we notice that the fields on one side of the hill are large and regular in shape, but the fields on the other side are smaller and irregular.

After much head scratching we realise that the trees have been shaped by animals that are no longer in the field, reaching up to a consistent height and so browsing the bottom of the trees in a way that keeps them perfectly in line with the ground. The larger uniform fields are the newer fields better suited to large modern machinery, whereas those on the other side are older, hedged before the combustion engine shaped the land.

Shape can be a clue to the history and activity of the land around us, which is probably why any natural shapes that defy easy explanation cause such curiosity and even wonder.

It is sometimes possible to find patterns and shapes in the way stones appear in fields. Convection causes them to rise up through the soil. As the water in the soil freezes and thaws, the water lower down becomes less dense than the water at the surface and it rises, slowly carrying stones upwards on its journey. In some places this process forms patterns that many have attributed to the hand of man or gods. On sloping ground the process tends to form rows of stones, giving the land stripes, but on flat ground it can form distinct shapes, often hexagons.

Shortly after returning from accompanying James Cook on his first circumnavigation, Joseph Banks was upset at having his proposed alterations to Cook's boat, Resolution, overruled. Banks was not the type of man to wallow for long and he had soon put together a more modest expedition to investigate the geology and natural history of Iceland. He set off in 1772 and on the way there stopped at the island of Staffa in the Scottish Inner Hebrides.

On the island he found a cave that would become famous among geologists all over the world. Banks called it Fingal's Cave and it is filled with numerous basalt columns, which formed from cooling lava. The formation of basalt from lava is commonplace, but the thing that made this cave remarkable was the shape of these pillars. They are near perfect hexagons. Banks' excitement at seeing such ideal forms made him exuberant.

Compared to this what are the cathedrals or palaces built by men! Mere models or playthings, as diminutive as his works will always be when compared with those of nature. What now is the boast of the architect! *Regularity*, the only part in which he fancied himself to exceed his mistress, Nature, is here found in her possession, and here it has been for ages undescribed.

Banks gushes a sentiment that we would all likely share if we had been in his position. Regular shapes, with equal angles and symmetry, strike the eye in a way that makes us think first of some intervention rather than nature. Such shapes conjure up thoughts of design and therefore intelligence, they jar with our experience of seeing so much apparent randomness in the natural world and the tendency of everything to head towards greater disorder. Surely the works of both nature and man become more chaotic: cliffs and great kings' palaces alike fall to dust with time. And cliffs, or basalt pillars for that matter, certainly do not spontaneously organise themselves into elegant and formal shapes.

We are conditioned to seeing symmetry, that is the formation of regular shapes, when a designer of some kind has been at work, typically man. If we had never heard of the Sydney Opera House when we stumbled across its elegant curves for the first time it is unlikely that would we suspect that this was a natural formation.

But man is not the only architect at work and the others have varying levels of intelligence. Birds' nests are round because they have the brain to impose order on the world; birds would have

Hexagonal basalt columns at Fingal's Cave

to wait an infinite amount of time for the wind to blow the twigs together in that shape by chance. Finding one of their circular constructions in a tree is therefore not so mysterious as finding a circular shape in a rock. We become intrigued when nature offers us examples of apparent design that do not seem to be the result of conscious effort or when the level of consciousness appears to be far exceeded by the symmetry and beauty in design. These are the examples that hint at an exterior mind at work.

Nature is full of shapes where no intelligence is inherent. Leichhardt named a place 'Tombstone Creek' after the very regular rectangular blocks of sandstone he found in Queensland and travellers still flock to the 15m high granite Wave Rock near Hyden in south-western Australia. The snowflake is famous for falling in an infinite number of shapes, but why does it always have six points?

The cause of all nature's shapes, whether in rocks or ice, can be uncovered by looking at the forces at work upon them, either inside or outside. A snowflake has six points because of its chemistry: the way water molecules bond causes a hexagon shape to form. Wave Rock was caused by chemicals eroding the surface of the granite underground and this then being exposed by weathering. The hexagons at Fingal's Cave are not the result of the way the rock forms, but the way it cracks apart. Each crack in the basalt develops in a way that relieves the tension in the shrinking rock, and this leads to regular fissures.

There are many examples where a living organism is responsible for making a shape, but the planning process seems beyond the capacities of the creature in question. A bees' honeycomb is hexagon shaped and this has intrigued nature's observers for thousands of years. In the fourth century the Greek mathematician, Pappus, realised that the bee had a limited number of options for cell shape if it wanted these cells to fit together without any gaps. Honey cells will fit together in this neat way if they are triangles, squares or hexagons. The bees 'opted' for the hexagon, which happens to be the most practical and economical shape. The hexagon is the shape that is most efficient, requiring the least wax and work on the part of the bee for the same amount of honey space.

There are echos of the intelligent design versus evolution debate whenever nature creates something that hints at exterior intelligence – a dandelion forms a perfect sphere without any capacity to think of a sphere. The appearance of design is evidence of god to some and nothing of the sort to others. Nature tends to create living organisms that form economical symmetrical shapes by killing off those that create uneconomical asymmetric ones. Birds that spent too long building bizarre trapezium-shaped nests would lose out to those that produced efficient circular ones. Where the processes of natural selection have led to perfect shapes, the appearance of intelligence is seen, from the perspective of evolutionary science, to be a mirage, but that is not necessarily the end of the intrigue.

The close but strange relationship of mathematics with nature can be felt in Galileo's assertion, 'This grand book the universe . . . is written in the language of mathematics'. We encounter another face of the shapes in nature when we use mathematics to describe them.

When Leichhardt was crossing the Australian plains, covered with Bauhinia flowers in full blossom, he was surprised to see some order appearing in the earth below him.

> The stiff soil of these plains was here and there marked by very regular pentagonal, hexagonal, and heptagonal cracks, and, as these cracks retain the moisture of occasional rains better than the intervening space, they were fringed with young grass, which showed these mathematical figures very distinctly.

Leichhardt describes these shapes as mathematical, which of course they are. However, mathematics and the appreciation of nature make awkward bedfellows for a lot of people who see them as incompatible ways of viewing the world. This awkwardness evaporates if we think of mathematics as one way of *describing* what we see and not as an explanation for it. A sunflower remains a sunflower and its seeds occur in a beautiful and orderly pattern regardless of how that pattern is described. The spiralling seeds in the centre of the sunflower are arranged in a way that can be described by the Fibonacci series. This series of numbers begins 0,1,1,2,3,5,8,13,21,34, and although it can appear random on a first visit, it is far from it and is in fact one of the most straightforward numerical series. Each number is generated by adding the two preceding digits together, 1+1 = 2, 1+2 =3 . . . 13+21=34 etc. The patterns it forms are found widely in nature, from pine cones to pineapples.

While this is all true, it does not change the sunflower. We can view the sunflower through the lens of mathematics or not, it is a personal choice. Put another way, looking out onto a Kenyan plain we could describe what we see this way: the fast gazelle is chased by the faster cheetah. Or, we might describe it another way: the gazelle runs at 25 metres per second and the cheetah runs after it at 30 metres per second. Either way the gazelle is probably going to get eaten.

When the Thames meanders along a flood plain, it forms elegant curves, it strikes the eye. The 'S' shapes in a river had a profound impact on the artist Hogarth, who felt they conveyed a sense of liveliness and action. In the case of rivers straight lines are the forms that make us suspect human intervention, nature prefers a curve. Again these forms can be appreciated either through their aesthetic appeal or the curious mathematics that accompany them. The American hydrologist, Luna Leopold, studied more than fifty rivers and arrived at some interesting conclusions, the most beautifully simple being that rivers will not naturally run straight for more than ten times their width, regardless of their size. He also noticed that the radius of the bend in a river is nearly always 2–3 times the width of the river at that point.

Bagnold's book about sand dunes is filled with equations that describe the formation of these dunes with an accuracy that has a beauty of its own, but if Bagnold had never written the book, the dunes would still exist. Sometimes, in describing nature for another observer we add a layer of beauty, and sometimes we detract from it. Our feelings about whether mathematics adds beauty may be expressed in our answer to an infamous question, 'Was mathematics invented or discovered?'

Explanations that involve chemistry, erosion, evolution and mathematics may be excellent at shedding light on processes, but they do not always satisfy a yearning to understand the impact these forms can have on us as observers. It would be a rather one-dimensional scientist who claimed that the physics and chemistry of rocks could account for all the emotions that Banks experienced in Fingal's Cave. It is even harder to know whether the physics of light can account for the vision of a cross in the sky that Emperor Constantine is reported to have seen on the eve of his victory in battle. Perfect circles or halos can indeed form around the sun or moon as the light is refracted through ice crystals in the upper atmosphere. Mock suns, spectre-like shadows and crosses certainly do form as the light refracts, diffracts and reflects off particles in the air. But physics will go little towards explaining the subsequent role Constantine's vision played in his conversion to Christianity and the influence this had on the history of the world.

There is only one concrete conclusion we can come to that applies to all shapes we find and that will unite all parties: something created something beautiful for some reason or no reason at all and either way it can feel wonderful to witness. Scientists and the religious can retire to a room to debate the meaning of the word 'something' until the rocks and animals and plants are all soil and dust, but they cannot take away the wonder from those who experience it.

The Light

As the red disk sank behind the west, the gigantic shadow
of the peak crept up on the foothills, leapt across to the
plains, and climbed at last the far horizon and stood high
in the paling heavens, a vast, shadowy pyramid. It is a
startling thing to see a shadow in the sky. For a few
moments it lingers and then fades in the slow twilight.

Charles Lummis

The sun broke through between the thin leaves of the ash tree. I looked around my feet to see a thousand tiny patches of sunlight appearing and then disappearing, dancing around the ground as the leaves above twisted in the breeze.

Across the valley I could see a pure dark shadow under an oak tree, all light sealed out by the tree's broader leaves and thicker canopy. The oak was at the edge of woodland and I could feel the chill of its shade, I could sense the shiver that would follow a walk into that darkness, even though I was enjoying bright warm light at the time.

• • •

When the English clergyman and author, William Gilpin, was
drawn into a poor woman's hovel at Tintern Abbey he noticed
that there was an aperture at one end which, 'served just to let
in light enough to discover the wretchedness within.' The contrast
between light and darkness mirrored the contrast between wealth

and poverty. In 1827, the German poet and political writer Heinrich Heine, found destitution similarly couched in darkness in London, where vice and crime would only emerge at night, and poverty 'glides from her lair'.

Darkness is so often forced to cohabit with our most negative thoughts and fears, while light is offered the more uplifting roles. Light is good. Light is truth. 'Have you seen the light?' We extend this love of light to be more generous to natural features that support it. Lakes are romantic as they keep the light moving on to us with their reflections. Marshes are seen more favourably than bogs and swamps as there are no trees to keep out the light. In swamps and bogs the sky is occluded by trees, darkness reigns, and we loathe them for it.

Light has the power to transform. George Mallory found in the course of his attempts on Everest that the Himalayan evening light had the power to turn Tibet from ugly to beautiful. For others it is a comfort. On a dark night, the distant light of a fisherman's hut on the Spanish island of Sisarga stirred Humboldt's memories and imagination as he sailed away from the comfort of land and towards the unknown of South America.

Death is darkness. But are we not conceived and nurtured from the egg in darkness? Why does it suffer so greatly from our negative associations? There are practical reasons: as a species we were able to overcome our predators' greater senses of smell and hearing with the use of intelligence and vision, but only in the light of day. Then there are cultural nuances to this relationship, which defy practical explanations. The Japanese author Jun'ichiro Tanizaki, one of the central figures in modern Japanese literature, found this puzzling. Why, he wondered, did Orientals seek beauty in darkness, when Westerners have never delighted in shadows? This contrast is an intriguing idea, but too neat to be universally true. Western writers have found much to celebrate in the lack of light. The Scottish writer, Nan Shepherd, delighted in the clarity of shadows in the clear air of the Cairngorms, watching the shadow of an airplane loom and then slide over a snowy mountain edge. But both Tanizaki and Shepherd agree that light has territorial differences. Shepherd is quick to assert the strength of her local light.

Light in Scotland has a quality I have not met elsewhere. It is luminous without being fierce, penetrating to immense distances with an effortless intensity.

The preference for darkness or light cannot be neatly carved along Occidental and Oriental lines. It is perhaps more true to say that those who connect with a particular area form a bond with the character of both its light, and its absence. Artists and writers dwell on this relationship and mine it for powerful imagery. In a scene in *Heart of Darkness*, Joseph Conrad pulls at every purchase.

We felt meditative, and fit for nothing but placid staring. The day was ending in a serenity of still and exquisite brilliance. The water shone pacifically; the sky, without a speck, was a benign immensity of unstained light; the very mist on the Essex marshes was like a gauzy and radiant fabric, hung from the wooded rises inland, and draping the low shores in diaphanous folds. Only the gloom to the west, brooding over the upper reaches, became more sombre every minute, as if angered by the approach of the sun.

Seven miles from Chepstow, William Gilpin had gazed towards the distant Welsh mountains and contemplated the magical and decisive effect that light can have on a scene. 'Scarcely any landscape will stand the test of different lights.' It is not light or dark that reveals a place's character to us, but the mix, the shift from one to the other and the contrasts between the two. Old towns are more mysterious and their streets more delicious as they mix up areas of darkness and light. They feel warm and welcoming when compared to modern towns, blanched under cold neon lights that stretch away evenly down each street.

The streets of old towns mix areas of darkness and light

The change in light in the east at the beginning of the day signals new movement, it sets our mind and bodies to action, while the darkness of the west stays pitch and still. Before the darkness or light are banished for a turn at the start and the end of each day, there is precious twilight to be enjoyed. Virginia Woolf found that her mind could float away when walking in darkness, but for most, twilight is more nourishing for the imagination. It holds us between being focused and unfocused on our surroundings and this is what allows a deeper contemplation, a meditation. Juhani Pallasmaa, the Finnish architect, has suggested that this is the effect that is being created in Chinese paintings of foggy mountains and in the raked sand of the Ryoan-ji Zen Garden. The gradual shift of twilight is kind on the eyes and the mind – even kinder at high latitudes where sunsets take longer, than low ones where the sun sinks at a precipitous angle.

Sudden changes in light shock. The explosion of the Krakatoa volcano in Indonesia in 1883 threw almost 21 cubic kilometres of rock in the air. It is remembered not just for destruction but also for the effect it had on natural light. Ash blocked out the sun and the region experienced two and a half days of darkness, but this was only the beginning of its toying with the light. The atmosphere was filled with a fine dust, which then dissipated and travelled all the way around the Earth several times. The dust caused spectacular sunsets, which in turn influenced the artists of the time.

Edward Munch is not often labelled an explorer, but in the famous 1893 series of paintings entitled 'The Scream' he explored not just the physical appearance of the sky over Norway, but the terrifying effect it had on him personally. He witnessed and conveyed this with a power that scares to this day.

Unexpected changes in light do not need to frighten, it is not all cowering and squinting. In the autumn of 1985 a hurricane tore through Long Island, New York, tumbling power lines and flicking the electricity switch off. The writer, David Abram, witnessed how a community experienced the night sky for the first time without the bleaching effect of artificial light. 'Many children, their eyes no longer blocked by the glare of the house-lights and streetlamps, saw the Milky Way for the first time, and were astonished.'

The Sky

The moon is at her full, and riding high,
Floods the calm fields with light;
The airs that hover in the summer sky
Are all asleep to-night.

William C. Bryant

The path took me gently up the hill and the sky grew, until, at the top of the hill the horizon completed its bow. The sky was now a full half of all I could see. There were patches of pure blue, although no dark blue. There were also an infinite number of lighter blues, where the sky mixed with the sun's light and the thin veils of cirrus clouds high in the sky. The blues above my head were being scratched by the nails of jet aircraft and they wore these scratches as the straight white lines of contrails. They would heal.

Below the high wisps there was purer white in the fluffy representations of headless, legless sheep, and then a group of three Bakelite telephones made their way unhurriedly across the sky. On a distant hill, below the high sun, the shadows of these clouds seemed to race to keep up with their masters.

Between sky and land there was a white that needed a wash, the dirty cream of haze hung above the land and the sea.

• • •

For those who do not like to see families arguing in public, the Babylonian creation myth, the Enûma Elish, is one to watch through gaps in the fingers.

Once upon a time Apsu, the God of fresh water, and Tiamat, goddess of the ocean, came together and had several children. As a couple they were unable to avoid the universal truths that lurk in most myths and they soon discovered that their children were not perfectly well-behaved. The parents became distraught. The final straw came when Apsu was woken from his sleep and, deciding he had had enough, determined to kill the lot of them. The children, however, got wind of his plans and took pre-emptive action. They drugged and then murdered their father.

Tiamat was not at all impressed by this behaviour. She responded by turning into a fire-breathing monster and enlisting the support of an army of other monsters, vipers, dragons, mad dogs and scorpion-men. One of her sons, Marduk, saw that things were escalating and, not to be outdone, summoned his own army. There ensued, literally, the mother of all battles. Tiamat lost and was killed by her son, Marduk, who then split her in two. He cast one half of her body upwards, forming the sky, and the other half remained at his feet and became the ground.

Whilst a poor model for resolving disputes, this myth does illustrate the ancient view of the sky as a full half of the world, a view that is extinct in the modern world, even among those who like to gaze upwards. The archaeo-astronomer, Anthony Aveni, has pointed out that one of the greatest differences between the contemporary and ancient perspectives on the sky is that we no longer interact with it in the way the ancients did. We may be familiar with constellation names and know that the planets Mars and Venus have an ancestry among the classical gods, but we no longer have a relationship with any of these parts of the sky.

Scientists know more than ever about it, at night or day, but do they *know* the sky in the same way the ancients did? That is debatable, but none of us can contradict one fact that emerges from the non-factual corpse of the Enuma Elish myth: when we are outdoors the sky accounts for half of all we are able to see.

Alexander von Humboldt was, like many eminent figures of his age, influenced by both the spirit of rational enquiry and by more romantic forces such as the poetry of Dante. Today it is rare to find scientists or poets straying from their allotted parking zones into each others', so it is entertaining to look back at what happens when an explorer broaches something that the romantics believe belongs to them and tackles it in a scientific way.

Humboldt took with him on his voyage to South America a contraption that had been invented a decade earlier by the Swiss traveller and physicist, Horace-Bénédict de Saussure. This instrument was called a 'cyanometer' and it was used to measure the 'blueness' of the sky. If ever a subject can have been thought to be safely tucked up in the bed of the poets and out of reach to the avaricious scientists, then the blueness of the sky was surely it. But Saussure and then Humboldt had other ideas, and confidently held this machine up to the sky in a bid to enumerate its blueness. The poet Byron was not going to let that go unpunished and slipped a verse into his wandering epic, *Don Juan*, to chastise Humboldt for his temerity.

> Humboldt, 'the first of travellers,' but not
> The last, if late accounts be accurate,
> Invented, by some name I have forgot,
> As well as the sublime discovery's date,
> An airy instrument, with which he sought
> To ascertain the atmospheric state,
> By measuring 'the intensity of blue:'
> Oh! Lady Daphne! let me measure you!

While Humboldt is ridiculed, Saussure was given the more severe punishment of having his name deliberately and ostentatiously omitted.

The sky's blueness is determined by the transparency of the air and the amount of moisture it contains. It varies from place to place and within each location over time, which leads to advocates of certain areas seizing, often unscientifically, on the blueness of

the sky as one of its charms. Sir Francis Bond Head certainly felt
that the west was best.

> The heavens of America appear infinitely higher, the sky is
> bluer, the air is fresher, the cold is intenser, the moon looks
> larger, the stars are brighter, the thunder is louder, the light-
> ning is vivider, the wind is stronger, the rain is heavier, the
> mountains are higher, the rivers longer, the forests bigger,
> the plains broader.

Others have claimed their patch with the 'delicate china blue
that's unique to the Hebrides' or air in Greece that is 'like some
crystal of an unknown water'.

The blueness of the sky during the day or its blackness at night
will not change as much or as dependably as the real players on
this demisphere, the celestial characters, namely the sun, moon,
planets and stars.

The sun is present in our daily lives, a necessary constant, and
yet there is little that is constant from one day to the next except
its generosity with light and heat. Whichever patch of Earth's land
or sea we choose to roam we see the same sun, but it tailors its
behaviour according to our location. If we travel towards its rising,
east, it rises earlier to greet us. As we travel further from the
equator, its rising and setting points range further from east and
west and its seasonal fluctuations become more pronounced.

Al-Masudi, the Arab traveller who lived near the end of the first
millennium, wandered and wrote extensively and this earned him
the nickname, 'Herodotus of the Arabs'. He tells us that in the
land of the Bulghars there are times when the evenings grow so
short that there is barely time between dusk and dawn to bring
a cooking pot to the boil.

Although imperceptible over very short distances the shape of
the sun's daily passage changes if we take even a small step to the
north or south. Its rising, setting and midday positions and the arc
that it follows to join these points will all shift a tiny amount.

They also change from one day to the next, flexing through curves that repeat themselves over the course of a year, but not from one day to the next. If the light in a place we know well seems subtly different from one visit to the next, despite both days being clear, it is probably because of a combination of the varying moisture in the air and the fact that the sun is at a different point in the sky. The sun will be in a slightly different position if we walk to the same spot at exactly the same time each day for a week.

The way the sun's light is split by droplets and reflects off bodies of water changes by the second not the day. Sun and moon halos appear for a few minutes as the light is bent by many millions of ice crystals many thousands of feet above us, and then they are gone. Nature's 'triumphal arch', the rainbow, notoriously ephemeral, has us seizing each other and pointing urgently before it slips away.

Cézanne painted the view over the fields to Mont Sainte-Victoire in Provence over sixty times. These are the eccentric excesses that a genius is entitled to, some might argue. Those who know the vagaries of the sun's arc, however, are more likely to accuse him of cutting corners. He could have executed twice the number of paintings and not witnessed exactly the same light twice.

The moon, that great ball of rock that borrows the sun's light, teases and flirts, likes to reinterpret the world in contrasts, shadows and mirages. The moon emerges from the sun's dominance then grows to dominate the night, becoming overconfident and trying to steal the day too, until the sun catches up with it and reminds it who is the king of light.

The moon rises in the east and sets in the west, but its exact mark on the horizon takes twenty years' observation from the same place to make good sense of. At sites like Castle Frazer in Scotland the hauling and erection of great stones must have seemed a trifle compared to the patience needed to mark the moon's full routine. Even the moon's more straightforward monthly cycle as it moves from west to east relative to the sun and stars is noticed by few today, but it is quite easy to familiarise ourselves with it.

If the moon is nestled in next to a particular constellation (say Gemini) one night, then the following night it will appear next to the one to the east of it (in this case Cancer). It will also have moved east by the same amount from the sun. It slips to the east by one thirtieth of a circle or twelve degrees each night, allowing it to start the cycle again each month. This is why it appears to rise about fifty minutes later each evening and why the tides, which take their cue from the moon, also slip back by the same amount each day.

The planets, the Greek wanderers, move across the sky with less discipline than the sun or moon. The planets are the flaneurs of the sky. Like a group of foreign students at university, they follow the same rules and yet appear to move in a parallel universe.

Earth is either beaten on the inside track by Mercury and Venus, which hug the sun at dawn and dusk, or it overtakes those of the outer planets that are visible with the naked eye: Mars, Jupiter and Saturn. Either way the planets seem to move across the canvas that is anchored by the stars in a way that refuses to fit neatly into our days, weeks, months or years.

The planets always appear in the same band of night sky, within thirty degrees of the celestial equator, which refers to a line that stretches from east to west via a point overhead if you are on the terrestrial equator and the same line tilted lower in the sky when viewed from higher latitudes.

With the stars, finally there is some order. They rise and set in the same places every evening and although they rise four minutes earlier each night, they do so in a dependable way, catching up with themselves once every 365 days and starting again. This dependability created one of the calendars used by the ancient Egyptians. The rising time of the brightest star, Sirius, was used as a clue to the time of year when the Nile would flood.

The night sky we see changes as we head north or south; an observer at the North Pole will share none of the same stars as one at the South Pole, each being offered only one hemisphere of the night sky to view. However, two people on opposite sides of the world, both standing on the equator will get to see exactly the same stars, albeit at different times. The equator is the only place on Earth where you can see all the stars of the night sky. It takes patience, though, as a full year would be required, given that at certain times of the year many of the stars will be well hidden behind the sun. This 'calendar' is constant and is why some constellations are known as winter ones, like Orion, and others, like Scorpius, are summer ones.

Travelling south from the northern hemisphere, new constellations will be opened up for us, sights that are unavailable from home. For many centuries explorers on land and sea have enjoyed watching a new constellation rise above the horizon for the first time, it was one of the undeniable and treasured hallmarks of progress. Travellers can choose whether to look up and appreciate these rich differences, but it would be remiss of an explorer to miss one half of the differences of a new place, as Humboldt reminds us.

Even those with no inkling of astronomy know they are no longer in Europe when they see the enormous constellation of the Ship or the brilliant Clouds of Magellan rise in the night sky. Everything on earth and in the sky in the tropical countries takes on an exotic note.

The 'long-haired stars' as the Romans called comets were ominous even before their regularity was noted. As the Earth passes through the dust trail of these comets the particles enter our atmosphere and burn brightly, appearing as meteors or shooting stars. Shooting stars lie in the inner sanctum of fascination and at the far reaches of predictability. Comets were used to predict earthly events of import and meteors were thought to presage earthquakes; in the ancient world, neither was ever ignored.

Aurora borealis, the Northern Lights, move over the northern countries 'like a flame in the wind' as charged particles from the sun are deflected by the Earth's magnetic field. The Northern Lights are one of the few of the sky's many characters that have retained their ability to entrance all who see them to this day.

There is not an astronomer on Earth, and there never will be, who can predict exactly what patterns the sun, moon, stars and planets will form in the sky without help from tables. Each moment is a distillation of a dance between these lights that move with a beguiling mixture of order and apparent whimsy. This is probably why the patterns that do repeat themselves are treasured and find their way into our history and culture.

Venus always appears within fifty degrees of the sun, either at dawn or dusk. When the moon is young, three or four days old, it is also near the sun, loitering just above the western horizon after the sun has set. When Venus and the Moon appear together at the end of the day it gives us the partnership known as the 'star and crescent', an image that was popular in ancient times in the Orient and finds its way through the Ottoman Empire into contemporary images such as the Turkish flag.

We have projected heroes, enemies, animals onto the sky, and we have thrown some tin characters up there too. In the post-war era the British historian, W.G. Hoskins, was not enamoured with the burden the nuclear deterrent was placing on the scenery he adored.

And those long gentle lines of the dip-slope of the Cotswolds, those misty uplands of the sheep-grey oolite, how they have lent themselves to the villainous requirements of the new age! Over them drones, day after day, the obscene shape of the atom bomber, laying a trail like a filthy slug upon Constable's and Gainsborough's sky.

If we lower our gaze from the full stretch of the sky to the horizon we are forced to consider in more detail the medium that we are looking through.

The air is the most modest of the sky's characters, filling our scenes and yet happy to go long periods without any consideration. The traveller who wishes to appreciate a place to its fullest will be repaid by giving this humble element some thought. Mountains are the places where the land seems keenest in its bid to merge with the sky and it is here where the air's moods can be most easily dissected.

There is a relationship between the blueness of the sky, the transparency of the air and altitude. As the air cools, the amount of water vapour that it can contain as a gas reduces; this is why steam from hot showers condenses on cool mirrors. The higher up a mountain we go the cooler the air gets, it drops on average by 6.5 degrees centigrade every 1,000 metres of altitude (2 degrees centigrade for every 1,000 feet). So the higher we climb the more likely that the moisture in the air will be condensing to form mist and clouds. For this reason views from the tops of mountains tend to be either excellent – if the air is very dry – or non-existent if the air is moist, as you will be shrouded in cloud. The fog that hugs lower land and the clouds that engulf the mountain climber are the same substance, given different labels out of respect for their altitude.

The combination of dry air and altitude can lead to views through transparent air that are hard to rival, as Humboldt reports from Tenerife.

The Pico de Teide is not situated in the Tropics, but the dryness of the air, which rises continuously above the neighbouring African plains and is rapidly blown over by the eastern winds, gives the atmosphere of the Canary Islands a transparency which not only surpasses that of the air around Naples and Sicily, but also of the air around Quito and Peru. This transparency may be one of the main reasons for the beauty of tropical scenery; it heightens the splendours of the vegetation's colouring, and contributes to the magical effects of its harmonies and contrasts.

Charles Darwin also remembered vividly the coldness of the air, the brilliance of its transparency, the colours and the formidable view, when high up on a pass near Puente del Inca in Argentina.

These experiences lie behind the reason that many mountain trekkers make a start before dawn. This gives the best chance of catching the view before the sun's warmth heats nearby water and the moist air reaches the summit, condensing into droplets and obliterating the view. Mountains that are routinely shrouded by day often enjoy a brief window of nudity shortly after the sun has risen. When the moist air is still low down it leaves the peaks clear to poke their way through clouds and offers the sublime view from high ground of clouds swimming up valleys below.

In the clearest air, free from moisture and dust, the stars' twinkling is muted. The twinkling of stars, or 'scintillation', is caused by their pinpoint light getting gently bounced one way and then another, as it passes through the Earth's atmosphere. This bouncing is caused by temperature fluctuations, moisture and pollution. A star that is bright and steady is a clue that the air is dry, virgin and still. (Or it might be a planet, as the light from planets appears steadier, thanks to their being so much closer to Earth.)

Between clear air and cloud there is mist. Mist is a very fine fog or cloud, forming when water vapour has condensed in cooler air to form droplets, but there is not enough moisture to form a full thick white blanket. Unlike clouds and fog, which draw down curtains, mist plays with scenery and toys with distances. Distant hills can fade away compressing the view and making other hills appear nearer than they are. Heights and distances in cities appear greater, the concrete and steel are stretched. Trees are brought into one dimension, flattened as in some Chinese paintings.

Fresh air is a joyous pleasure that has not diminished over the centuries. Today it is to be contrasted with the artificial urban environments that the poet John Betjeman rebelled against, those 'air-conditioned, bright canteens' and it offers liberation from the 'tinned minds, tinned breath'. In earlier centuries stuffy unhealthy airs were thought to be the harbingers of disease, it was not understood that it was the airborne viruses and bacteria that were spreading infectious diseases, people thought that it was the nature of the air itself that was to blame. We think of fresh air as invigorating, but for many centuries it was even more vital than that.

The cleanest air has by definition no smell and no taste, as its components: nitrogen, oxygen, carbon dioxide et al., are tasteless. However, it is sufficiently rare for air to contain no trace of its environment, no hint of city or sea or decomposing foliage, that this neutral tasteless air can offer an ecstatic contrast. John Muir, the American naturalist who walked from the Middle West to the Gulf of Mexico, left us in no doubt about the rapture that fresh air brought him.

> The sky was perfectly delicious, sweet enough for the breath of angels; every draught of it gave a separate and distinct piece of pleasure. I do not believe that Adam and Eve ever tasted better in their balmiest nook.

Air can be thrillingly refreshing or it can be tasteless, neutral, bland, but it can also be powerful, an integral part of our conscious being. The Navajo see the air as providing awareness, thought and speech. In their world, the divisions between mind and the air cease to exist as we breathe. This beautiful idea is not as alien to science as it first appears. Thoughts can be articulated through speech, which is simply our ability to make the air resonate at certain frequencies. For scientists, each part of the transmission and reception process is compartmentalised, isolated and analysed, but for the Navajo it is all part of one cycle. Our thoughts are not our own, but live within this cycle of air, making our thoughts and mind simultaneously within us and within the air that is part of everyone and everything else.

The sky accounts for half of the world we see, but it is in the places where the sky and earth mix that many find the greatest drama, intrigue and beauty. When the line that separates sky and land, the horizon, is broken it draws our eyes like a magnet. The rays of a rising sun breaking out above a distant hill in perfect radial form will be uplifting to the most downtrodden souls. Even a bird as inglorious as the pigeon can give a majestic feel to a skyline, if, startled by some sudden movement, it rises in a flock that breaks the line together in harmony.

The ground's most persistent intruder into the sky is the tree. Laurens van der Post admired the fantastic Baobab tree in the Kalahari with its 'varicose veins, full of permanganate sap', but it is the image of these trees reaching upwards that best carries across the dry earth to us.

On this hot morning stripped of leaves and tartar fruit they stood out beside our route with their swollen apoplectic columns like the arms of a brood of Titans buried alive, wide open hands protruding from the grave and vainly appealing to the stark blue sky now filled with vultures.

When in 1722 the Dutch explorer Jacob Roggeveen and his crew saw smoke rising above their new discovery, Easter Island, they knew they had found land new to Europeans and evidently a new people, too. Their excitement at the smoke was only a precursor for the astonishment they experienced on finding the giant statues breaking the same skyline.

Stonehenge in England and Rujm el-Hiri near the Sea of Galilee stand as testament to the importance of the sky to our ancestors, by interrupting the line that joins sky and land. Cities from the ancient Teotihuacan in Mexico to the modern Washington DC also testify to the sky's imprint on our minds and lands. Teotihuacan contained the Pyramids of the Sun and Moon. Washington was originally laid out using celestial observations, giving it its orientation along the cardinal lines.

The sky's orbs appear larger when we have the chance to

compare them to more pathetic terrestrial objects like trees and buildings. The sun and moon seem to swell close to bursting as they hang for seconds above the dark chess pieces of a city. The effect grows stronger when the dust of haze scatters out their blue light, leaving these balls cooking gently in their oranges and pinks.

The Weather

> A powerful force was working within this vast assembly,
> urging them ever onwards, but creating discord and
> strife so that they came not in harmony but in seething
> discontent, an angry quarrelsome, agitated mob. There
> was an evil portent in their convulsive moments, in their
> weighty ponderous appearance, in their colour.
>
> Alfred Wainwright, *A Pennine Journey*

*L*ooking *south towards Littlehampton and beyond, it was impossible
not to notice the way the lower cumulus clouds were gathered only
over the land. The sea was being spared their company entirely.
As the sun heated the land more quickly than the sea, warm moist air
was rising and condensing as clouds.*

*Among the seeming chaos of the wispy high cirrus clouds, there was
some order in one corner of the sky. Here the streaks of white appeared to
have been brushed, styled even. Staring up at these mares' tails, I began
to wonder how long the fair weather would hold.*

• • •

On 14 April 1832 Charles Darwin was travelling near Rio de
Janeiro. There was a heavy downpour in the early evening and
then it stopped, abruptly. Looking out over a forest below him,
Darwin felt a chill as he watched the whole tree canopy become
encased in a dense white vapour and saw pillars of steam piling

up from the most densely wooded areas, like columns of smoke. The sun had heated these parts of the forest most ardently during the day and now the trees were passing on their heat to the fresh rainwater and returning it to the cool air as steam, as if the raindrops had fallen on a warm stove.

Over the following weeks Darwin stayed at a house in the coastal area of Botafogo. His temporary home afforded him excellent views of the small but spectacular granite mountain of Corcovado – the mountain that now hosts the statue of Christ the Redeemer. Darwin liked to watch the way clouds formed and then dissipated over this lump. The southerly breeze would bring warm moist air into contact with the sides of the mountain, which was consequently forced up into cooler regions. The vapour would condense into water droplets to form visible clouds, these clouds would roll over the summit and then disappear once more as the droplets returned to vapour in the warmer temperature.

In September of the following year Darwin was in Argentina, where he witnessed a different face of the elements. He was told by the locals that there had been a formidable hailstorm the night before, with hailstones the size of apples. Darwin was incredulous until he was shown the hides of thirteen deer that had been killed by the stones and then the fresh carcasses of seven more. Darwin found ducks, hawks and partridges that had been killed and one of the flattened partridges looked as if it had been struck with a paving stone. He heard reports that about fifteen ostriches had also been killed in the storm.

There are some universal truths that are encapsulated in the weather we experience, the most obvious being, that which goes up must come down – even if it has metamorphosed from harmless vapour to lethal projectiles. Almost every meteorological event finds its roots in the simple concepts of hot and cold, up or down and high or low pressure. Warm air rises and expands, its pressure drops. Cool air sinks and contracts, its pressure rises. Areas of high pressure try to equalise with areas of low pressure, creating winds. Vapour cools to form water droplets, which we know as clouds, these droplets can freeze, forming ice particles that vary in size from microscopic to small boulders.

The sun is the prime mover of the weather and its effects are very regular and dependable, yet we experience such variable conditions. The apparent unpredictability of something that is so fundamental and vital has made forecasting the weather a part of the human experience. This fascination is emphasised on our journeys as we spend more time exposed to the elements and sometimes find ourselves at their mercy.

Explorers develop fine sensitivities to shifts in conditions and become aware of the smallest clues. Ludwig Leichhardt liked to check the wind direction every morning and evening as a way of remaining sensitive to coming change. It is possible to find clues in unlikely places. Darwin discovered that the jaguars roared more than normal at night if bad weather was on its way.

There are many more common and conventional clues than the roar of a jaguar and the easiest to notice are the signs that the weather is going to deteriorate. The clouds that spearhead the arrival of a weather front, which will bring bad weather after good, are normally the wispy high cirrus clouds. These icy clouds can appear as little more than a high thin veil across the sky, which has been interpreted by cultures all over the world as a sign that change is on its way.

When this veil passes in front of the sun or moon, the light refracts in the ice crystals in the cloud and they appear to have a bright ring or halo around them. The Zuni Indians of North America used to interpret this halo as a tepee, which the sun was going into for shelter as rain was on its way.

Another favourite is the rippling of clouds known as a 'mackerel sky', where lines of high altocumulus or cirrocumulus clouds are broken by lines of blue sky. These clouds normally denote strong winds at high altitudes and often presage a change in weather although not always a deterioration, hence the bet-hedging lore, 'Mackerel Sky, Mackerel Sky, Never long wet, never long dry.'

A mackerel sky

The same logic applies to 'mares' tails', which again signal strong winds up high and together these two observations can be used to forecast tricky weather: 'Mares' tails and mackerel scales make tall ships take in their sails.' The clues are usually there, as ever it is a question of awareness.

In the days before meteorology, the ability to predict the weather, even very roughly, elevated the forecaster to the status of magician. It was then only a short step from forecasting what was going to happen to claiming credit for it.

Marco Polo was travelling in a region of Tibet full of brigands when he came across some astrologers who impressed him.

Among other wonders they bring on tempests and thunderstorms when they wish and stop them at any time. They perform the most potent enchantments and greatest marvels to hear and to behold by diabolic arts, which it is better not to relate in our book, or men might marvel overmuch.

There is no need to be overly sceptical here or accuse Mr Polo of being gullible, but it may be fair to say that these astrologers probably knew a good sun halo and mare's tail when they saw one. Marco was perhaps too busy protecting his belongings from the brigands to notice either these clues in the sky above him or that he was possibly being teed up to be robbed in a more entre-preneurial way.

In our bid to understand what it is possible to discern with the senses, the disabled often lead the way. Helen Keller, who was blind and deaf, could still tell a storm was coming.

I notice first a throb of expectancy, a slight quiver, a concen-tration in my nostrils. As the storm draws near, my nostrils dilate, the better to receive the flood of earth odors which seem to multiply and extend, until I feel the splash of rain against my cheek.

Changes in the weather are ferried to us by the wind, which sharpens our relationship with this element. We give it attention not only because it affects the present, but because it can tell us much about what is to come. The wind's fluctuating character gives it a personality and its apparently temperamental habit of bringing good or inflicting havoc allowed that personality to become divine. Vaju, the Hindu god of the winds, worked the same patch as Stribog, the Slavic god, who was grandfather of the eight wind directions. Fujin hopped about ancient Japan with a bag of winds on his back, not unlike the bag of winds provided to Odysseus by Aeolus.

Winds pick up the characteristics of the land and sea they travel over, and spread them wherever they go. Wilfred Thesiger found dew on the ground in the dry world of the Empty Quarter desert, but only when a northerly wind carried a little of the water of the

Persian Gulf over the land. The winds in the UK move broadly and predominantly from west to east (the prevailing wind is a southwesterly) and they bring with them the moisture of the Atlantic. This moisture falls first on the west of the land: the western parts of the British Isles are wetter than the east.

The winds also pick up scents and form sounds as they travel over the surface of the planet. John Muir walked a thousand miles across the US and the greatest change he felt was in the winds that received him in Florida.

They no longer came with the old home music gathered from open prairies and waving fields of oak, but they passed over many a strange string. The leaves of magnolia, smooth like polished steel, the immense inverted forests of tillandsia banks and the princely crowns of palms – upon these the winds made strange music . . .

The wind brings clouds marching overhead and we let them pass without concern until they decide it is time to repay some of the moisture the sky has borrowed from below. We should not underestimate the debt the sky is in: a storm cloud could easily weigh one million kilogrammes.

Very light rains may evaporate before they reach the ground, especially in hotter parts of the world, but the more determined downpours reach down to the earth and fill the air with rich smells and strange sounds. No two people seem to hear the same sounds when it rains. Is it merely a pitter-patter, or a richer chorus? The English writer, George Meredith, heard 'eager gobbling' like swines in a trough. Laurens van der Post exceeded himself when he described the sounds produced when long-awaited rains touched the parched earth of the Kalahari at the end of the dry season.

The deep murmur of the earth taking the rain into her was like the sound of a woman taking a lover into her arms, all the more ardently because secretly she had doubted he would ever come.

John Hull, a professor of religious education at the University of Birmingham, lost his sight gradually and completely in mid-career, but managed to cope. In many ways he did much more than cope. Hull learned to read the contours of a place from the sounds the rain made. 'There is a light cascade as it drips from step to step . . . I can even make out the contours of the lawn, which rises to the right in a little hill.' Obstructions created new echos and interruptions in the sound and added context to his audible landscape.

The elements are not working merely for our audiovisual entertainment, though; they are occupied with shaping the world, chipping away at the ebullient mountains and leaving more distinct footprints. John Muir passed through the 'knob land' of Georgia and witnessed how the rain robbed the soil from the tops of hills, giving it to the lower land.

The rain moves soil downhill to a place where it settles and accumulates. A seed is blown by the wind and falls into this fresh soil. The mature plant looks to the wind again later in life, as it is the wind that helps pollinate many plants, including most of the trees; the oaks, birches and beeches rely on the wind for a sex life.

One of the first things that Darwin found during his *Beagle* travels were acacias in the Cape Verde Islands that had been bent over at right angles by the prevailing wind. Later in the journey Darwin explored the shores of Uruguay where he found 'vitrified, siliceous tubes, which are formed by lightning entering loose sand.' Before this lightning reached the sand it would have been conducting chemistry experiments in the air, 'fixing' nitrogen as ammonia, which could then be washed down into the soil and fertilise the plants.

This is a grand and wild laboratory. There are 1,800 thunderstorms happening around the world at any one moment and over the next twenty minutes there will be about 60,000 lightning strikes. Just as children will remember time spent in a chemistry laboratory, many also remember the first time they worked out how far away a storm is using elephants, that is by counting the time it takes after seeing lightning to hear the thunder. If you count in seconds – one elephant, two elephants, three elephants – then all you do is divide this number by three to get a rough idea in kilometres or by five in miles.

These storms march at the front of change and nature responds to the call. In Australia a storm quenched the parched water-holes around Leichhardt and 'called into life thousands of small frogs, which, by an incessant croaking, testified their satisfaction at the agreeable change.' Long after the storm has passed the land resonates to its stomp, fungi burst forth and the air is filled with the sound of freshly gorged waterfalls pounding the rocks as if for the first time. As the waterfall dies down the storms live on in legends and stories.

The North American planter, William Byrd II, overheard a conversation in 1728 between an Englishman and a Native American on the cause of the rumbling sound in the thunder they heard. The Englishman explained that it was 'the god of the English firing his great guns on the god of the Indians', the lightning fitted neatly into this explanation as the flash of those guns. The Native American saw the humour in this account and joined in, adding that the rain that followed must be a result of 'the Indian god's being so scared he could not hold his water.'

So many of the weather's labours are invisible to us, we can see neither the fixing of the nitrogen or the aerial bacteria that can act as catalysts and trigger the rains to start, although we are enmeshed in the consequences of all these actions. It is a complex and intricate web and a boggler to unravel. There is no perfect method for unlocking the secrets of the weather's influence on an area, but a slide down in scale helps. An interest in the general climate of an area is narrowed to a focus on local weather effects and in turn the microclimate. It is worth looking at an example to see this approach at work.

The sun does not warm the sea as fast as the land, cool air is denser and so high pressure systems regularly form over oceans. One well-known patch is called the Azores High that sits in the mid-Atlantic, drifting north with the sun around June and back south again around December. Winds flow out of this high pressure system in a clockwise direction due to the Coriolis effect, which is caused by the Earth's spin, creating a great clockwise weather system swirling in the Atlantic.

Tenerife lies in the eastern part of the Atlantic and receives dependable strong breezes from this high-pressure system from between the north and northeast. As the wind passes over the ocean it picks up moisture from the sea and when this wet air hits the high ground of Tenerife it is forced upwards, cooling and condensing into rain-bearing clouds. As Humboldt noticed, this creates a more verdant northern side to the island and a drier, more barren, southern side. The same wind will also sculpt the plants, as Darwin spotted on the Cape Verde Islands (which are influenced by the same trade-winds as Tenerife). The shape of the land will dictate the microclimate of the island in dozens of smaller ways: the exposed areas, the sheltered areas, the treeline, the snowline, the places where frosts form. All of these micro-influences form a tapestry of effects on the land. When this tapestry is in turn layered on top of the land's own influence in the form of rock and soil types and altitude, a true picture of a landscape will start to form.

The shape of the land moulds the passage of the low winds and can influence the appearance of the sea as well. The steep volcanic mountains of the Canary Islands act as funnels to the winds and create faster winds in channels between the islands. These fast funnelled winds are known as acceleration zones and bedevil the unwary sailor. The air moving faster as a consequence of this funnelling effect is invisible, but the effects are detectable on the surface of the sea. As the wind is squeezed between two jutting peaks, water that normally appears little more than ruffled by a tame cat's paws looks as though it is being mauled by a tiger.

In the middle of the tenth century when Al-Masudi was in Persepolis, in a southern part of modern-day Iran, he visited a great temple, filled with huge statues of animals and images of prophets. The temple was situated at the foot of a mountain and Al-Masudi listened as winds blew day and night, making a sound like thunder.

> The Muslims say that Solomon imprisoned the wind here, and that he breakfasted in Ba'lbakk in the land of Syria and dined in this mosque, breaking his journey at the city of Palmyra, in the desert between Iraq and Damascus and Homs in the land of Syria.

Solomon's dining habits need not concern us, but it is likely that the winds he is supposed to have imprisoned were 'katabatic' winds. These winds form on a hillside when cool dense air rolls down a mountain, gathering pace and blowing furiously onto the land at the mountain's base. The influences exerted by the shape of the land are the most common form of local weather effect. The town of Llandudno in north Wales cannot escape the moisture hitting the west of Britain, but it does experience very mild winters due to the Fohn effect. When moist air is forced up the high ground to the south of the town, it cools, condenses, loses its moisture and then rolls back down the other side of the mountain and is compressed, which warms the air. This warmer drier air then hits Llandudno town, making it, in the words of one surgeon who wrote about it in the middle of the nineteenth century, 'well fitted for the abode of invalids in winter.'

* * *

Each moment in our travels is also shaped by the weather in more personal ways, as it interacts not with the landscape out there but with our selves: the rain that trickles down the back of our necks or the warmth of a cloud-covered morning after many nights of frost. Perception of a place cannot be divorced from the mood of the observer, which is a subject we will return to, but it is worth acknowledging here that just as the elements shape the hill, they also shape our impressions. Are we not more favourably struck by a winter scene when our faces are hit by the sun at the same time?

When the weather turns against us it can suppress the spirits, there is a temptation to believe that almost every other place in the world is experiencing better weather than the spot we are standing in. No nation has honed this philosophy more ardently than the British. At times when the weather tries us, it can be refreshing and uplifting to think of Francis Bond Head's observations of the inhabitants of Santiago in Chile. Bond Head grew used to the hot clear days and cool clear nights of Santiago, weather that would appear perfect to many Europeans, but he was less than convinced. He thought the locals looked distinctly unhealthy. Bond Head proposed a solution. 'It appeared to me, that a strong dose of British wind, with snow and rain, and a few of what the Scotch call "sour mornings," would do them a great deal of good.'

Still Waters

At that time the idea became fixed in my mind that I
must live near a lake; without water I thought, nobody
could live at all.

Carl Jung

*A*s my boots made contact with the grey brown dust I felt a sadness
in the earth, a melancholy in the dryness of this chalk country.
Where are the lakes? Where are the ponds?

*Water has fallen, plenty of it, but it keeps on falling; there are not
enough impervious rocks to slow its descent to the water table, deep below
my feet. There is a silent deprivation in the dryness of these places. I was
reminded that the theological argument that there could be no Good without
Evil finds its equivalent in the landscape. Whenever we are denied something for long periods we learn to appreciate its true beauty. I suspect the
desert nomad could write a lot more poetry about the beauty of rain than
the British walker.*

*At that moment I yearned to hear the noise of some wet-bottomed ducks
behind rushes, as we surprised each other. The lack of still water made
me cherish the most unloved of all features on the path. The puddles.*

*At the top of the hill, near Downs Farm, there was a junction where
paths from south, east and west met. Here the sun had not yet drawn all
the moisture from the path, and vestiges of the last rains could still be
seen in the darkening shades of the hollows. They could still be felt through
my boots too, in a softened step and sometimes a slip.*

Stumbling across the drying remnants of a small puddle, the desiccating mud at first seemed to offer little of interest. But looking closer there was a beauty in the patterns the cracks formed, order where I had not expected any.

• • •

In the drier parts of the world, pockets of water were always welcomed with relief by the thirsty old explorers. They learned to recognise telltale signs in the landscape from afar and greeted these clues with rapture. Those explorers who maintained an interest that went beyond mere survival were able to build a richer picture around the presence of water.

Ludwig Leichhardt noticed in Australia that lagoons that did not dry out were rich with unio, freshwater mussels, and that the shores of these dependable sources of water, being frequented by the Aboriginals, were littered with the shells of these molluscs. He became tuned to a micro-world whose shapes, colours, motions and sounds were orchestrated by the water. 'A cluster of trees with greener foliage, hollows with luxuriant grass, eagles circling in the air, crows, cockatoos, pigeons (especially before sunset), and the call of the Grallina Australis and flocks of little finches would always attract our attention.'

The same richness can be found all over the world, in very different environments, by those keen to look for it. In Hampshire, Gilbert White noticed that all the kine, that is cows, oxen, calves and heifers, would gather at a pond's edge during the hottest part of the day, between ten in the morning and four in the afternoon. During this cattle social, a bovine version of the gathering around the office water-cooler, the animals would drop their dung (which is where this particular analogy should fail). The insects would in turn gather to feed on the dung and the pond's fish would prosper from the presence of the insects. Once more the sights and sounds of the landscape were being marshalled by a patch of still water.

When we approach a body of still water it welcomes us by playing with the light. The shining surface steals from the land

and sky, flips their features and gives them a polish. At the water's edge we peer in. The clarity of water can reveal its provenance. Pools tend to form above impervious rocks and if these rocks are acidic in nature then the water tends also to be acidic and low in nutrients. It will not support microscopic plants and animals and so remains beautifully clear. These are the good drinking waters we find on granite mountains the world over.

Water that lacks this clarity betrays clues about its journey. A yellow or brown colour can signal contact with a peat bog, as Patrick Whitefield explains. 'A river which rushes down the hills between woods and fields, Guinness-brown and topped off with a creamy foam, reveals its origins in a distant peat bog.'

As the top layer of mud in a puddle dries it shrinks, but the wet mud below it is not shrinking and so stops it from contracting: cracks form. These cracks are not random, they follow a pattern, one that will be recognisable in other local patches of mud. The process is almost identical to that which forms the cracks in oil paintings over time, known in the fine art world as 'craquelure'. Since the materials used in oil paintings and the conditions experienced by these paintings varies, art experts have learned to identify genuine paintings by Masters from their 'craquelure'. Italian paintings will differ from Dutch ones of the same era and two paintings from the same country but different eras will have a different signature of cracks. The drying mud of a puddle is an artwork, complete with its signature cracks. The cracks will be unique, but with a familiar form. It is reminiscent of the recognisable pattern that can be seen in the map of an old town's roads.

After the summer rain, an oak leaf bobs heavily. A couple of drops slide down along the leaf's vein until they merge at the tip. The enlarged droplet bounces once, then twice and then falls. The leaf springs upwards, freed of its burden, as the droplet falls towards the ground, a pulsing wet comet that lands in the puddle at the foot of the tree. The force of the impact sends a ripple through

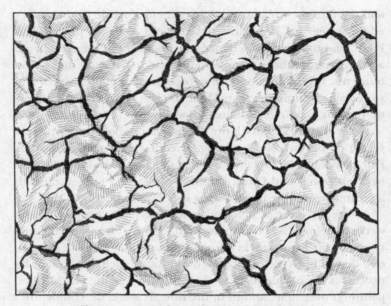

Signature cracks form as mud dries and shrinks

the puddle's surface and ejects a corona of water back up again, which arcs and forms tiny droplets at its edge. Extraordinary, tiny and transitory shapes form as the kinetic energy wrestles the surface tension of the water. The new droplets fall back into the puddle and then the motion dies down and all is still again, until the next drop falls. The same surface tension forms pearls of water on a spider's web in the oak above the puddle.

From patterns in mud and droplets, to the movement of animals around a pond and the desire of humans to live by a lake, water is an impressive sculptor for a passive element. John Ruskin, the emblematic Victorian social thinker and art critic, captured its ubiquitous wonder.

> Of all inorganic substances, acting in their own proper nature, without assistance or combination, water is the most wonderful. If we think of it as the source of all the

changefulness and beauty which we have seen in clouds; then as the instrument by which the earth we have contemplated was modelled into symmetry, and its crags chiselled into grace; then as, in the form of snow, it robes the mountains it has made with that transcendent light which we could not have conceived if we had not seen; then as it exists in the foam of the torrent, in the iris which spans it, in the morning mist which rises from it, in the deep crystalline pools which its hanging shore, in the broad lake and glancing river; finally, in that which is to all human minds the best emblem of unwearied unconquerable power, the wild, various, fantastic, tameless unity of the sea; what shall we compare to this mighty, this universal element, for glory and for beauty? or how shall we follow its eternal cheerfulness of feeling? It is like trying to paint a soul.

Embracing water's every mood and potential approaches the perfect and the near impossible challenge. Water constantly challenges our appreciation of the importance of scale in our journeys. If we allow ourselves to believe that the greatest view is to be found looking out across a sea, then we will surely miss the motion in the surface of a puddle. However, once we find fascination in a puddle by our feet, the danger is that we lose sight of the wind playing with the lake half a mile away. Or the raindrop that hangs from a leaf.

Not content to span the scales of distance, water partners with time to offer the places we know fresh disguises. Each day within each season will conspire to leave dust where we expected water on a February morning, or rivulets charging down a dry road on a summer afternoon.

The two sides of a path will dry at different speeds during the course of a single day; there is intrigue in this asymmetry and the footprints of sun and shadows that lie behind it.

Colour

Every spot of colour is a drop of wine to the spirit.

Richard Jefferies

*N*ear the point where the path turned north and then lurched downhill, a bright V shape forced me to re-examine a patch of ground that at first glance had appeared bare. I was rewarded with the purple flowers of the Viper's Bugloss. When I looked closer still, the purple disappeared and was replaced by two separate colours: the blue of the petals and red of the stamens.

● ● ● ● ●

There is an infinite variation in the appearance of the world thanks to mixtures of light, darkness, shade and tone, but it is light's ability to give us colours that elevates variety to something more exciting.

John Lubbock, a great admirer of nature's use of colour, wrestled with pragmatic considerations. If colour can be explained as a means for species to attract, repel or camouflage, why, he wondered, were there such brilliant hues in a mother-of-pearl shell, which is hidden during the animal's lifetime? Colour that has no obvious use or purpose hints at beauty for beauty's sake and this is a much more wondrous idea than colour as a tool for survival.

Colour suggests life where it has been scarce and this can be a cause for joy. The ecstasy of seeing purple, gold and silver flowers unfolding in a green plain after a period in a landscape of plain white snow and barren rocks, was the most beautiful spectacle that one Siberian traveller reported ever having witnessed. But there is always colour to be found, even in the often inhospitable canvasses of mountainous terrain. It may not appear instantly and in abundance, but with the passing of time and the changing light, colour will arrive and stay for a moment at least, as the nineteenth-century artist and essayist, Philip Gilbert Hamerton recounts.

I know nothing in the visible world that combines splendour and purity so perfectly as a great mountain entirely covered with frozen snow and reflected in the vast mirror of a lake. As the sun declines, its thousand shadows lengthen, pure as the cold green azure in the depth of a glacier's crevasse, and the illuminated snow takes first the tender colour of a white rose, and then the flush of a red one, and the sky turns to a pale malachite green, till the rare strange vision fades into ghastly gray, but leaves with you a permanent recollection of its too transient beauty.

White light consists of all the colours arriving together, that is to say light of many different wavelengths travelling as a group. When white light hits snow, the snow allows all the constituent colours to bounce back as reflected white light. This is true of nearly all the objects that reflect white light, from a chalk cliff to a daisy petal. All the other colours we see in nature need a different explanation.

Most plants are green not because plants like green light, but for the opposite reason. Light lands on a green leaf and the chlorophyll in that leaf absorbs the blue and red wavelengths because it needs them to complete the process of photosynthesis. It reflects the green wavelength as this is surplus to requirements – evolution has made green plants efficient in this way.

This mixture of reflection of some wavelengths and absorption of others is the process that gives us most the colours in the natural world, the colours we see are the wavelengths that are not absorbed by the object we are looking at.

Although he did not view it this way, when Ludwig Leichhardt stumbled upon green pegmatite rocks, he was looking at rocks that were absorbing the reds and most of the blue light and letting the green reflect back. When he later found lumps of violet sandstone, these rocks were holding on to most of the visible colours and reflecting back the violet colour that he saw. Black reflects no colours; it holds onto them all.

There is a relationship between the amount and type of light that an object absorbs and its temperature. A black rock will warm more than a white one, of course, but there is a lot more to it than that simple rule. Red light is the warmest light, it is closest to heat in terms of its wavelength. Violet light is the coolest light, it is at the opposite end of the spectrum. A red stone will warm up slowly as it is holding onto the cooler light and reflecting the warmer light. A violet stone will warm up much more quickly for the opposite reason.

The small stones that we trample daily become compelling even in the most mundane setting, when we look closely at their colours. The legendary fell walker, Alfred Wainwright, once stooped down to pick up some road chippings in the Pennines and revelled in the purples, turquoises, emeralds and pinks that he discovered in his hand. He found these small stones so entrancing that he put the 'beautiful pearls' in his pocket and kept them there for the rest of his holiday.

The other scientific principle that explains the colours we see is refraction of light, that is, light that has been bent. When white light enters a raindrop, the curved water droplet acts as a lens, which causes the path of the light to bend. Each wavelength and therefore colour has a different flexibility and so a single beam of white light separates into a full spectrum of colours as each one follows a slightly different path out of the raindrop lens. If there is enough light entering enough raindrops, we get to see the full effect as a rainbow. Blue light is deflected more than red light, it can be thought of as turning a sharper corner, which from the perspective of someone enjoying the sight of a rainbow means that its arc will appear at the inner part of the bow. Red light is bent less and appears near the outside of the bow.

Sometimes the light is bent by the raindrop but is also reflected twice inside the droplet, sending light out a second time, at a different angle. This causes a secondary rainbow, which appears outside the primary one. It will be higher, fainter, with a larger radius and reversed colours, with blues appearing on the outside and reds on the inside.

This reversal caught out the artist John Everett Millais in his painting 'The Blind Girl', which shows a blind girl feeling the warmth of the sun on her face and the grass in her hand as her sister enjoys the view she is denied. There are two rainbows in the picture, but unfortunately Millais repeated the order of the colours for the secondary rainbow. When his error was pointed out to him he repainted it to show the correct order.

A similar but different effect to a rainbow can be seen in the feathers of birds like the peacock. The colours appear brilliant and tangible one second and then they are gone. None of the vertebrate animals' bodies contain blue pigments, so the peacocks cannot be creating the beautiful blue colours through reflection alone. In fact the feathers contain thousands of microscopic ridges that scatter the white light that hits them. The effect varies depending on the angle of the feather, the angle of the light and the angle that they are viewed from, and since all three of these variables can change from one moment to the next we get the magical effects that created wonder for a Byzantine writer from the seventh century, as they do to this day.

How could anyone who sees the peacock not be amazed at the gold interwoven with sapphire, at the purple and emerald-green feathers, at the composition of the colours of many patterns, all mingled together but not confused with one another?

The colour blue is splashed all over great journeys and long distances and not solely in the imagination. Oceans really are blue and the landscape is imbued with blue as it stretches into the distance. Both of these effects are the result of blue light scattering more than red light. Beyond the most distant ocean horizon or blue mountain we can find deep red sunset colours or a 'convulsed orange inch of moon' as all the blue light has been scattered, leaving the other end of the spectrum to dominate.

The colours that seem rare or out of place create their own fascination. The green flash at the moment of the sun's limb dipping below the horizon has sailors and other sunset watchers debating and reminiscing until long after the cool has come in. The reds, oranges and yellows are not flexible enough to peep over the horizon once the sun has fallen below it. The blue light bends too much and is scattered before it reaches us, leaving a second or two of green light and a long memory.

The richness that colour lends to a landscape creates an appetite to understand it, and folklore filled the gap messily and voluptuously before science came along with its neat wavelengths and refraction.

Balder was the Norse God of Mirth and Merriment, which sounds like a pretty good role, but there was a drawback: he was not immortal like all the other gods. These other gods were understandably worried that they might lose their party man and so they petitioned Thor to grant their friend immortality. Thor agreed but only on condition that all the animals and plants on earth would promise not to injure Balder, and so his wife, Nanna, came down to earth to persuade all the animals and plants to agree. Loki, the God of Envy, disguised himself as a white crow and followed her, settling on a little blue flower and concealing it from Nanna as she did her rounds. The flower noticed Loki's game and cried out, 'forget-me-not, forget-me-not!' earning its name for posterity. Loki tried once more to thwart Nanna's efforts and flew up into an oak tree and this time sat in front of some mistletoe. Nanna managed to get the oak to promise not to harm Balder, but she did not spot the mistletoe. When Nanna returned she was convinced she had carried out her task perfectly and all the gods, including Balder himself, believed that he was now immortal.

One day the gods were playing the sort of game that only immortals could enjoy. They placed Balder against a holly bush and began to shoot at him with arrows. Loki, filled with his customary jealousy, tipped one of the arrows with a piece of mistletoe and then gave it to Balder's brother. The arrow pierced Balder's heart and he was killed. Some of Balder's blood spurted onto the holly, giving it the redness of its berries. The mistletoe felt terrible guilt for its role in Balder's death and has since borne fruit in the shape of tears. The crow, which had been white, was turned black in punishment.

The myth of Balder and the prisms of Newton are both supporting cast for the experience of light and colours, which remain a liveable joy even as we shift from one explanation to another. The reflections and refractions are woven between plants, animals, buildings and stories to give each place its own light. Our interpretation of this light will be a personal and subjective one. When somebody says, 'The light in Japan is often green,' there is more in that sentence than can be fully accounted for by science or myth.

Recent research is confirming one of the reasons that we should do our best to appreciate each colour, especially when it feels fresh or new in any way. Our brain is capable of creating colours if it anticipates them. A banana can appear yellow to us if we recognise its shape, even if it is not in fact yellow because it is situated in a different light. This has profound implications for explorers. We can only truly discover the colour of some-thing once, in an objective way; every subsequent time that we recognise the object, our brains 'paint' it with at least some of its remembered colour. The world becomes a richer more colourful place, and the object and subject are working together to create it.

The City

This City is what it is because our citizens are what they are.

Plato

The path joined a road and this was soon being led downhill towards Amberley by a perfectly trimmed hedge. The gradient steepened and almost immediately the sounds of traffic from a much busier road bounced up the asphalt to my ears. I am always delighted when I notice the way the shape of a hill determines the moment we are exposed to the sounds of the land below.

The sounds did not marry with the view. The top of a castle was visible in the direction I was heading, before it dipped and hid behind the trees. The sound of the road softened as the gradient shelved a little. The happy downhill flow of the road suddenly coagulated when the green edges became clotted with road signs. A red circle announced that the speed limit was now 40 miles per hour, then a red triangle warned of a crossroads and queuing up behind that another red circle reduced the speed limit to 30 miles per hour. There was no need for me to decelerate.

At the junction with the major road I waited two minutes for a pause in the roar. A line of cars was being eagerly shepherded from the rear by a collection of motorcyclists, who were keen to open their throttle. I crossed and continued into the outskirts of Amberley.

A bright and sparkling new police Land Rover was parked at the side of the road. The colours were all so different to the hills. The turquoises of some butterflies painted by children rested on the anaemic pink walls of a school *building. The sounds had become more urgent, I stepped off the pavement into the road, rattled as a car's engine started in a driveway metres from my feet. A helicopter banked overhead, signalling, in case there was any doubt, that I had crossed the Rubicon: fields had yielded to civilisation.*

But Amberley is hardly a sprawling conurbation, one local assured me that they bristle at anyone who calls it a town at all. It is a village and all the better for spotting those things that divide town from country. There was a 'No Parking' sign by the road. Caroline, who I met at work in her pottery, explained that newcomers from busier places 'wanted parking permits, double yellow lines, street lighting, a bar here, a this there . . .' She looked resolute, not threatened. 'They last about 18 months, maybe two years, these people, then they're gone. Amberley pops them out.' She returned to her work, before adding, 'The windows of the houses round here used to be open, we used to call to each other as we passed. They're all closed now.'

There were clues to frictions on the Parish noticeboard. Leaflets advertising bell-ringing, jumble sales and a village raffle sat uneasily alongside one that offered an 'Alternative Dispute Resolution' service. Above them all there was one that sought to clear up a mess and a mystery,

'There's no such thing as the dog poo fairy . . . Keep Britain Tidy.'

Each house had a character of its own, a great variety of stone had been used in their building and the less they conformed the more curious I became about the people behind them. I wondered whether this curiosity flowed one way. A feeling of being towered over by tree branches had been replaced by an awareness of satellite dishes and spiky aerials on roofs. Screens were being watched, but was I too? I waited to see if a curtain or blind would twitch, but one more pedestrian passing through was of little interest to these folk. Invisible inhabitants exuded a calm aloofness. Was I imagining the quiet confidence of a people who knew they they lived in a fascinating place?

I had asked Caroline the potter about those that Amberley did not 'pop out'. 'They are diverse.' She replied. 'They are interesting. They are caring.'

• • •

The city is the most enigmatic character that we will meet on our travels. One minute boisterous, the next taciturn. A formal, tidy, polite individual, until the mask slips and an unkempt and aggressively rude beast confronts us. The city draws us down its lanes with its morning hums and bakery scents, then flirts in wide open spaces before, rebelling against time and sky, it shouts at us and flashes neon warnings. If we fail to heed these warnings it tires of us and lays vomit at our feet down some tight alley.

The scarcely fathomable richness of feeling that the city offers makes deep relationships possible, but as with all relationships we must heed the stages. First impressions are often harsh, especially when a city is where a long journey is broken. Francis Bond Head serves up some of the unfair and narrow first thoughts that many towns prompt, when he arrived in San Luis in Argentina.

> I had hurt my right arm by my horse falling; however, I carried my cheese into my room, and then did not know where to put it. The floor was filthy – the bed was worse, and there was nothing else; so supporting it with my lame arm, I stood for some seconds moralising on the state of the capital of the Province of San Luis.

At first we pretend not to care for the place. It is a mere stepping stone, we rest and feed. We start to feel for a city when we watch one wake and sleep and grow – it is so much harder to spurn something once it has proved it is alive. And so we start to respond to the town's overtures. It invites us to come closer with its facades and signs, it winks at us with its wide windows and smiles crookedly with winding side-streets.

Early on in the relationship, cities will try hard to present only their best face. This visage is worth studying: what a city thinks of itself is as interesting as what it actually is. The face on view is found in the public buildings, the monuments and the statues. In the Viking heroes that look over our heads in Reykjavik we find braggadocio. In the Gefion fountain in Copenhagen, we find determination. According to Norse saga, the goddess, Gefion, was offered all the land she could plow in one night by the King. Rising to the challenge, she turned her four sons into oxen and ploughed a vast tract of land, which was lifted out of the earth and placed in the sea between Sweden and the Danish island of Fyn, forming the large Danish island of Zealand. The fountain hints at a wily, quiet determination to succeed, despite the city's isolation and watery context. In Edinburgh the lack of saints and heroes reminds us we are in a place with a reticent, Protestant past. Curious to know what lies beneath this public face, we look the city up and down, searching for clues. A dark sawtooth of high buildings breaks the dusk in silhouette: towers, a steeple and the top of a bridge bite at the sky. We hear stories of tunnels and catacombs that run silently alongside the rumbling arteries of the underground trains.

The Gefion Fountain, Copenhagen

Feeling through the clothes of the buildings to the body of a city, its curves please us. Geology, always persuasive, shapes the city in its hushed diplomatic ways. Streets are nudged one way and then another by hills and rivers. When geological diplomacy fails, tantrums ensue before pragmatism gets the upper hand. There are many low-lying buildings in cities that bow with the fear of earthquakes.

Growing comfortable in each other's company, we drop our defences, noticing for the first time the vulnerabilities and tenderness, the touching surprise of finding a green rice-field in the heart of a Japanese city. The things that used to annoy us no longer do, we learn to love the places that offer a dependable cacophony. But, inevitably, we also start to notice new things that grate. We discover the streets every city tries to hide from us and thinks we won't find, and the habits that are concealed under the thin burqa of nighttime.

Things grow stale; we want our space and we taste the claustrophobia that John Muir felt in Cuba.

The streets of Havana are crooked, labyrinthic, and exceedingly narrow. The sidewalks are only about a foot wide. A traveller experiences delightful relief when, heated and wearied by raids through the breadth of the dingy yellow town, dodging a way through crowds of men and mules and lumbering carts and carriages, he at length finds shelter in the spacious, dustless, cool, flowery squares; still more when emerging from all the din and darkness of these lanelike streets, he suddenly finds himself out in the middle of the harbor, inhaling full-drawn breaths of the sea breezes.

We grow old together, wrinkles appear in its face, but the city is still youthful in its heart. The green grimace of the war-hero statues no longer match the feminism and pacifism that beat through the city. We give each other space.

The space is more important than the city itself: just as a

poem cannot survive without the spaces between the words, so a city fails completely without the right spaces. It was Thoreau who felt most strongly that a city is also dependent on the wide open spaces outside itself. Thoreau believed that a town is saved not by its inhabitants, but by the swamps that surround it. He felt the cities trying to import this wildness 'at any price'. Thoreau would smile at the growing trend for gardens on rooftops.

The consequences if we become codependent, if the city becomes everything in our life and we are denied this wildness for too long are frightening. The Forest Schools initiative is an approach to outdoor learning that was imported from Denmark to the UK and other parts of the world. It seeks to teach and inspire children through outdoor play and learning. Children leave with greater confidence and self-esteem, but it is their first steps that send a shiver. One leader, Sian Jones, warns us, 'At first, some of them cry at the thought of going into the woods . . . some can't even walk on uneven ground; they've only ever been on pavements and carpets.'

A city must be built with order in mind, but should be explored with a penchant for anarchy. Rigid rules on how to get to know each city will only lead to a fair view of one layer and blindness to the others. It is good to follow the course of a river for a while, but then the pattern must be broken and a random series of lefts and rights through the streets that run away from the river is sure to unveil a delight or two. An air of purposefulness along the main arteries can be replaced with a tidal saunter that takes us in and out of the capillaries.

The role model for this urban mode of exploration is the flâneur. Derived from the French verb flâner – to stroll – the flâneur refuses to conform to a neat description. The French poet, Baudelaire, saw the flâneur as the person who walks the city in order to experience it, the 'solitary mortal endowed with an active imagination'. The flâneur, 'goes botanising on the asphalt.'

The senses must be kept working hard in a city, even through the fish markets that bear down on a warm summer lunchtime, for today's metropolises are faded versions of their own past. In the nineteenth century young girls would sell bouquets of violets to Londoners as a weapon against the smells that haunted the streets – garlic against the vampire of stench. Life and death give away their rich odours with effusive generosity, but steel, glass and stone hoard their cold smells. The town air that might manage a stale funk today is a mountain spring when set against the London smog that killed 4,000 in 1952.

The sounds of a city fluctuate by the second and the hour, but also with epochs. We hear different echoes in a Renaissance city than we do in a Baroque one. The stone of each place holds a different appeal. Ruskin found himself so drawn to touching Veronese marble that he likened the sensation to wanting to eat it.

The Scottish religious minister and writer, James Leith Macbeth Bain, was a strong advocate of barefoot walking and believed that the skin of bare feet was able to sample nature's pleasures in a deeply gratifying and therapeutic way, even in towns.

And if you wish to know even for once the fine intoxication of the radiant energy of the sun, you will soon get it by walking over the sun-baked pavements of the city.

The senses issue the battle cry for our imagination. If they detect something then we can interpret it in a positive or negative way and use our imagination to carry this train of thought forward into new places, but none of this is possible without the fresh prompt of alert senses. Where one explorer may have detected only the smell and sight of bland pollution, Charles Dickens could see a town of red brick stained black by smoke and ashes and in that he saw the 'painted face of a savage'.

When the art of the flâneur and the power of the senses are harnessed together a new level of experience becomes possible, one that marries a wonderful feeling of abandon and connection. This is the Paris Walter Benjamin found.

Not to find one's way in a city may well be uninteresting and banal. It requires ignorance – nothing more. But to lose oneself in a city – as one loses oneself in a forest – that calls for quite a different schooling. Then signboards and street names, passers-by, roofs, kiosks, or bars must speak to the wanderer like a crackling twig under his feet, like the startling call of a bittern in the distance, like the sudden stillness of a clearing with a lily standing erect at its centre. Paris taught me this art of straying.

In truth no amount of flâneuring or getting to know the city as a character can ever solve its greatest conundrum. The riddle that thrills and maddens every visitor and every resident is that of the crowd and the individual. The city is the crowd, but there could be no greater definition of a lack of awareness than to be oblivious to the fact that the crowd is made up of individuals. And yet, the faces that pass remain a mystery. As Hardy once wrote of London, all the individuals are conscious of themselves as individuals, but nobody is conscious of the collective group. Who are these people that form the mesh that binds the town? What role do they play in this great game of musical chairs? Is the man on the corner who sells us the newspaper merely a newspaper vendor, one small part of the fabric of that corner, or is he Ahmed with the wife who has terrible eczema and twin daughters who both want to be doctors? Has that corner changed if a different person sells the paper or is it just the individual that has changed? Each town is a living example of Plutarch's great paradox, the Ship of Theseus. If, over long periods and one by one, every person in a town leaves and is replaced by someone else, is it the same town? If not, then at what point did it become a new town?

Plato wrote in his Phaedrus dialogue, 'I'm a lover of learning, and trees and open country won't teach me anything, whereas

men in the town do.' Plato's words make perfect sense until we
realise, after a long, exhausting and intense relationship, that far
from learning more from living amongst strangers, we have started
to doubt everything. We feel a mute panic beginning to dilute
the blood and the relationship is brought to a swift end. We break
out of concrete and into the trees and open country that now
seem to be filled with simple truths and answers. And then the
lights of another city wink at us.

The Trees

> The treasures within the earth were long hidden, and
> trees and forests were thought of as her ultimate gift to
> mankind.
>
> Pliny the Elder, *Natural History*

*L*ooking west to the hills beyond Houghton there stood a lone tree
*in a steep field of wheat. It was too far away to be able to tell
exactly what species it was, but that did not take anything away
from this solitary giant's ability to hold court. How had it survived centuries of farming on either side of it? Perhaps it had not; I noticed now that
its branches were bare in the middle of summer, shaped like a crucifix
from this perspective. How long would it be before the farmer decided to
stop weaving his machines around this awkward monument and tear it
down, to straighten his lines?*

*I walked on a few steps, to improve my view. Until it succumbed, the
tree would draw quizzical eyes from all around but it would also draw
other spectators onto its branches. Birds of prey would be attracted and
songbirds repelled by the perfect perch it offers for surveying the land.*

*When I was half way down the hill I looked west towards the Arun
Valley and noticed an incongruous line of Leylandii that stirred suspicion.
The map revealed what lay behind the trees: a sewage works. Where it
suits us we uproot trees to provide land for our needs, and where we feel
ashamed of the ugliness we have created in their place we invite the trees
back to cover for us.*

By the edge of the path a lime tree shook off all that man had thrown at it. Its trunk had burst open a rusting iron cage that must have been placed around it in its youth for protection and was never removed. Fresh young branches shot upwards from its flat-topped pollarded trunk. The leaves were full and healthy, their vibrant green giving no hint of suffering in their shape or colour. I stared at the tree's bark for a few seconds, hoping to notice it slowly bending and engulfing the twisted iron around it.

• • •

The legend of Rome has the city founded by Romulus, but only after he and his baby twin Remus had escaped attempted murder. The servant charged with leaving Romulus and Remus to die of exposure instead placed them in a basket and set them adrift on the Tiber river. The river deity, Tiberinus, ushered the basket into the roots of a fig tree and in its shade the iconic suckling of the boys by a she-wolf takes place. There is a sense that civilisation springs from the sheltering and protection of the trees. They would cover most of the land on the planet save the high mountains if it were not for human intervention, so it is not surprising that we still have an intense and complex relationship with them.

Trees can colour each step of our journeys and nowhere is this colour more vivid than in the history of settlement in North America. English settlers planted the seek-no-further apple trees on hilltops in Massachusetts in the 1700s, using seeds they had brought all the way from Cornwall. Joshua trees reminded the Mormon settlers of prophets beckoning them on across the Mojave desert and Scandinavian settlers found a home from home in the pines that hugged the Great Lakes. But the trees were not always so welcome.

At the end of the eighteenth century, the Irish traveller and writer, Isaac Weld, found a young nation that had not yet fallen in love with trees. The ground could not be tilled until the trees were felled and so they stood for hunger rather than plenty.

Joshua trees, like those that beckoned the Mormon settlers across the Mojave

The Americans that Weld met found it astonishing that anyone could prefer the sight of trees to cultivation.

> To them the sight of a wheat field or a cabbage garden would convey pleasure far greater than that of the most romantic woodland views. They have an unconquerable aversion to trees; and whenever a settlement is made, they cut away all before them without mercy; not one is spared . . .

These are the two ends of the spectrum of the relationship, the elevation of the tree to almost mystical status at one end, its eradication as a hindrance to economic progress at the other.

A step in from one extreme is the use of the tree for economic gain. In Manaus in Brazil, there is an extraordinary opera house, designed and built in the neo-classical style popular in the 1880s and 1890s, which originally contained furniture from Paris, tiles from Alsace and marble from Italy. It was built using profits from the boom in rubber, drawn from the Hevea brasiliensis tree.

The podocarps of New Zealand span both ends of the spectrum simultaneously. They are vital to the religious traditions of the Maori but they are also vulnerable to economic practicalities. Recently the place of the tree in New Zealand society was tested when air traffic control at Rotorua airport demanded that a row of tall kahikateas be trimmed as they were getting too close to the aircrafts' approach to runway. The Maoris came up with a preferred solution: they suggested moving the airfield.

A different relationship is formed in towns, where the London plane tree has found a very successful niche for itself. Its roots are able to withstand compacting and it sheds its bark, which makes it able to withstand levels of pollution that would kill many other trees. Any tree that is prepared to tolerate conditions that deter most others tends to find its place to thrive and the London plane can now be found in cities all over the world.

Sometimes the relationship is more personal, we can relate to trees as individuals. The American naturalist, John Muir, felt the oaks spread their arms in support as he set off on his 'Thousand Mile Walk to the Gulf' and later in his journey he came across his first palmetto tree, standing lonely among the grasses. He did not find it especially beautiful, certainly less attractive than the Wisconsin oaks he knew, but still he connected with it in a profound way.

Whether rocking and rustling in the wind or poised thoughtful and calm in the sunshine, it has power of expression not excelled by any plant high or low that I have met in my whole walk thus far.

Muir does not elaborate on his feelings and this is not surprising. The depth of our relationship with a tree appears to be inversely proportional to our ability to articulate the reason for it. The most profound relationship with the trees can be found where no words are possible. The English naturalist, Gilbert White, wrote of the Raven-tree, a tall oak with an excrescence in its trunk. The local boys used to compete to climb the tree, but its swollen stem made it impossible for them to get as far as they wanted. A pair of ravens had taken to this tree and made a home there for many years, earning the tree its sobriquet.

One day the decision was taken to fell the Raven-tree as the land it stood in was being cleared. The trunk was sawn and then wedges were hammered in gradually. The female raven, which was nesting at the time, did not move. The wedges were driven in further until finally the tree came down, with the bird staying true to her nest until the very last second, when she made a bid for safety. She was too late, the twigs whipped around her and then smashed her to her death.

Proud and dominant individual trees come to mark the landscape as deeply as they mark us. All travellers come across a tree that stands as a local monument at some point in their journeys. Marco Polo describes a great tree that stood alone in a plain in Persia. Its isolation had earned it the name, The Solitary Tree, and, according to the locals, it marked the spot where the battle between Alexander and Darius was fought.

In Argentina, Darwin found a thorny leafless tree that he heard talked about as a famous local altar to a deity known as Walleechu. The tree was short and unremarkable except for one important attribute, the fact that it stood all alone. A gaucho explained to Darwin that he would lie in wait with his companions as the Indians arrived and made numerous offerings to the tree. The Indian ceremonies would include pouring spirits and mate into a hole, blowing smoke into the air and fastening threads to the tree. The more wealthy even sacrificed horses. The Indians would then leave gifts of cigars, bread, meat and pieces of cloth to Walleechu and head on their way. At this point the gauchos emerged from their cover and picked their way through the bones of the decayed horses to steal the offerings.

Trees that fail to mark great battles or achieve divine status still draw us to them if they stand proud and alone. In Venezuela Humboldt encountered a famous Saman tree. It was both vast and isolated, so vast and isolated in fact that it appeared from a distance as a hill or group of trees clumped together. The 'zamang de Guayare' had a trunk that measured three metres across and a dome-shaped crown with a circumference of two hundred metres. The tree was treasured by the locals and a local cultivator who had been caught sawing off one of its branches, was subsequently tried for this crime and found guilty. The tree still stands today, near the town of Maracay.

The power of trees to mark a spot has been used deliberately. Welsh cattle drovers walked huge distances in the course of their work and would be on the look out for a place to rest their head at the end of each long day. Farmers that were happy to offer hospitality would plant a group of Scots pines by the roadside as a welcoming sign. These clumps of pines can still be found by some Welsh roadsides.

Our relationship with forests is not the same as that with individual trees, but our connection to them is equally hard to articulate. We know when we have encountered a type of forest that is alien to us; it can be a daunting experience. The German traveller, Hermann Burmeister, felt acute discomfort in the Brazilian forests in the late nineteenth century. Burmeister attempted to describe his feelings and the causes of them and then exceeded his brief. He felt the vegetation was 'displaying a spirit of restless selfishness, eager emulation and craftiness.' He also thought that the European woods were more earnest and restful and that this 'formed one of the causes of the superior moral character of European nations.' Burmeister's bizarre sentiments may have been caused by the fact that he was intimidated by the sheer richness of tropical forests: they account for only two per cent of the world's land, but fifty per cent of its species.

Forests in all their wonderful varieties: montane, alpine, riverine, swamp and cloud to name a few, cover one third of the world's land. The urge to 'slash and burn, plant and earn' has not completed the purge, yet. The environment has been forgiving of our clearances so far, but there will come a point when the balance is lost. In the long term it is the trees that are more likely to survive than us, even if they have to struggle to recover after we are gone. In Norse mythology there is a giant ash tree called Yggdrasil, which supports the whole universe and holds it together. Its roots extend into the underworld as well as the home of the gods. After Ragnarok, the Norse Doomsday, Yggdrasil will survive to become the source of new life.

The regenerative power of the plants and their remarkable ability to bounce back from the excesses of man, which is magnified in the trees, can be felt in the words of the contemporary poet, Felix Dennis.

> I am marked to fell
> But warn them well
> That what they reap, they'll rue;
>
> When their bones are dust . . .
> Their axes rust . . .
> We shall cover the earth anew!

> Felix Dennis, from 'Sylva Anathema'

Woodlands can assault the senses with more force than isolated trees. The ascetic scent of a pine forest on a hot summer's day engulfs us and the autumnal palette of the different woodlands is one of life's great joys: scarlets, yellows and greens as the maples, birches and conifers reflect the shortening of the days in their own ways.

The long silvery green leaves of the Brigalow trees gave one Queensland forest a distinctive character that made it stand out in the mind of Leichhardt.

Forests can offer lots of riches within their dark perimeters but they do also occlude some sights. Leichhardt only spotted a comet that had been in the skies for a month once he emerged from a dense forest, in a place that became known as 'Comet River'. The forests' reputation for darkness is widespread and we need to remember that the forests will wrestle with the sky and sometimes keep it from us.

Woodlands have another reputation, one that is less deserved, and that is for monotony. It is true that plantations can be homogenous, but all natural (that is ancient) woodland is too rich for anything except diversion in all directions. In the UK there will be woodruff, wood anemones and wood spurge, herb paris and moschatel, wild service trees and small-leaved limes, not to mention the animals.

In densely populated areas, like the UK, ancient woodland is itself a clue to the land beneath: it is likely to be poor or inaccessible agricultural land; these forests have survived by clinging to land that no farmer wants.

Trees always whisper secrets about the land they grow in. The relationship between trees and soil has been understood for much longer than many people realise.

Palms grow in light sandy soil – usually one containing alkaline salts. They enjoy well-watered locations and take up water all the year round, although they also like dry places.

These observations, which would not look out of place in a modern garden centre, were written by Pliny the Elder, two thousand years ago.

Trees can give a clue to the environmental extremes that each area faces. Many conifers, for example, are expert at coping with extreme cold, their needles are good at retaining water in icy conditions. But the ability to survive and thrive in areas that are exposed to regular fires is rarer. Both eucalypts and cork trees can cope with fires and their presence, especially when combined with any telltale charring marks, is proof of forest-fire country. Conversely, a tree in a desert is a clue to the proximity of water.

The combination of soils, climates and geographical separation leads to species having preferences for broad regions. Oaks and willows are found almost exclusively in the northern hemisphere.

The eucalypts would only be found in Australia if it were not for their habit of travelling with people.

We can learn much about individual trees, beyond their species, by drawing closer to them. The age of dead trees has been estimated for centuries by counting the rings in the trunk, the art and science of dendrochronology, but the age of a living tree can be worked out in a similar way. Younger trees tend to be straighter, but it is possible to be much more precise. In the UK, standalone trees will have an age in years that is close to the circumference of their trunk in inches. In woodland their circumference in inches needs to be doubled. Trees will also grow thicker and sturdier in windy conditions.

The shape of trees reflects their location, in particular the angles and strength of sunlight and the competition from other trees. The firs, pines, spruces, rimus and kahikateas of the high latitudes are subjected to a lot of lateral light as the sun works its way around the horizon in a low bowl, consequently these trees grow tall and thin in a bid to harvest this light from the side. The cedars and umbrella pines of lower latitudes spread themselves out to catch more of the light from the sun that reaches high up in the sky above them. In dense tropical rainforests, where canopies block much of the light, trees are forced to grow tall and quickly in a bid to get any light at all. However, not all trees are heliomaniacs, there are many that are happiest with at least a little shade. Some of those are the source of our favourite hot drinks: the cocoa, tea and coffee trees.

As a general rule, trees that grow in forests tend to become tall and thin, whereas those growing in open spaces may, in the words of the arboreal author, Colin Tudge, 'spread themselves like a Persian cat on a feather bed, and take all manner of wondrous forms.'

Zooming into the marks on the tree itself we can often find a history, sometimes violent, of the trees' scuffles with the elements and animals. Tree wounds do not heal nearly as quickly as animals' wounds and they leave scars that are barely concealed. Older trees have a turbulent mix of broken branches, evidence of lightning strikes and occasions when man has wielded a blunt axe. The bark of many trees will show signs of other meddlers too: squirrels leave torn shreds hanging from branches, woodpeckers love to work their way into trees in search of grubs, although they prefer dead wood. If food is short then deer will tear off strips of bark with an upwards movement of their teeth and rabbits can kill a tree by ring-barking, gnawing the bark in a full circle close to the ground. Muddy claw marks at the base of a tree are signs a badger has come to clean its paws.

• • •

Pliny tells us that gold and ivory were once worshipped less than the trees. We are fortunate to live in an age where this idea, although not prevalent, is at least understood once more. The trees have been dedicated to the gods; the laurel is sacred to Apollo, the Italian holm oak to Jupiter, the olive to Minerva, the myrtle to Venus and the poplar to Hercules. The gods also bestow their divine mercy by turning people into trees. Philemon and Baucis were granted their wish to remain together throughout eternity and when they died were turned into a pair of intertwining trees. Buddhists venerate the Bodhi tree, which sheltered the Buddha as he meditated.

There is no compulsion for us to make offerings or prostrate ourselves before the trees. We can choose to be more or less aware of their existence, their connection to the land and the stories they are telling us about that land. If we do occasionally become aware of a forest or tree and a relationship develops, we are likely to find it challenging to explain. In Jean-Paul Sartre's philosophical novel, *Nausea*, Roquentin's moment of existential angst climaxes as he stares at the root of a chestnut tree. He can find no words to describe it. It is just there.

The Human Animal

A white man bathing by the side of a Tahitian, was like a
plant bleached by the gardener's art compared with a fine
dark green one growing vigorously in the open fields.

Charles Darwin, *The Voyage of the Beagle*

O *n one of the roads that lead down towards Houghton Bridge,
I found myself hungry for distraction, and food, and the two
came together in the sight of some wild damsons on a bush in
a neighbouring field. I made my way towards them, through a break in
the hedge.*

*Before I could try the fruit, my attention shifted to an unusual low-rise
building in the far corner of the field I now stood in. Open on one side
and neither old nor new, the red bricks and tiles were as neutral as it was
possible to be. There was movement within the building and then, when
my eyes had adjusted to the lower light, I saw a bearded middle-aged man
in a blue hat standing next to a tent. There was a sleeping bag drying
on a line next to the tent. Everything concealed within the relative
darkness.*

*The man and I looked at each other. This was not a spot that a camper
would typically choose and this made me a little uneasy. Whose property
were we both on? Not mine and not his either, I suspected. It was an
awkward moment: there was no greeting, no sounds at all. Then, the man
lifted an enamel camping mug full of tea, the mug continued up, higher
than his lips. A salutation!*

'Good Afternoon!' I called over. He nodded and I think I saw a smile.

Plucking one damson from the bush, I retreated to the road again, offering a half-hearted wave back to the man with the tea and giving him back his solitude. The damson was sour and I spat it out.

The path straightened. Then, in a tight lane that held a footpath more tightly still, I was passed by a young couple. Stepping to one side, I leant back against a wooden fence to make room. I tried hard not to wince as they squeezed through the small gap between my chest and a privet hedge, since that might have sent a strange signal. But it was difficult to keep my face from betraying me, as a stinging nettle was busy announcing itself by brushing at the back of my bare knee. I kept myself squeezed against the fence all the same, not just out of politeness, but because this couple seemed ill at ease with the close proximity of nature. Their faces betrayed a dislike of the foliage that leant out and brushed against them.

There was something peculiar about this couple. Not something furtive, I did not suspect them of hunting out some concealed patch of earth for the purpose of getting to know each other better. It was something else, almost the opposite of base suspicions, but for a minute I could not tell what had triggered this feeling.

Earlier in the walk I had been passed by several cyclists and held a gate open for two walkers who had also brushed close past me. The walkers and, as far as I could tell, the cyclists had smelled human. Neither pleasant, nor unpleasant, just human. Some sweat, perhaps, little more. The young couple who passed me on that narrow path smelled of something else. But what?

Sophistication. That was it. They left in their wake the faintest trace of the expensive pong of worldliness. They were wearing perfume and aftershave.

Continuing, I wondered for a second what the scented couple had thought of my face and smells. They might well have disregarded the former, but found it hard to ignore the latter: it was a hot day and I was in the third hour of my expedition by this point.

• • • •

In the late summer of 1803 Dorothy Wordsworth travelled to Scotland with her brother, William, and their friend, Samuel Taylor Coleridge. They bumped their way over tracks in an Irish jaunting carriage as they headed from their home in Keswick, up over Lanarkshire towards Loch Lomond in the south-west of Scotland. In South Lanarkshire Dorothy was struck by a sight that left a deep impression on her. Up to this moment she had not been overly impressed by the scenery, to her mind it lacked the beauty of some of the other valleys they had passed through.

> The forms of the mountains did not melt so exquisitely into each other, and there was a coldness, a want of simplicity in the surface of the earth; the heather was poor, not covering a whole hillside; not in luxuriant streams and beds inter-veined with rich verdure; but patchy and stunted, with here and there coarse grass and rushes.

Dorothy weighed up how the scene might have been made more pleasing, perhaps if the hillsides were interspersed with some trees and cottages it would lift the whole, she felt. It was whilst mulling these ideas that she noticed a large field opening up before her. In its centre a woman dressed in a grey cloak sat all alone. The melancholy figure did not move as they passed the desolate field. Dorothy could not understand this woman's reason for sitting in a field that was devoid of sheep or cattle. She concluded that the woman must have lived in the inhabited end of a partly ruined cottage nearby, but that did not solve the mystery of her sitting alone and motionless in an empty field.

> There was so much obscurity and uncertainty about her, and her figure agreed so well with the desolation of the place, that we were indebted to the chance of her being there for some of the most interesting feelings that we have ever had from natural objects connected with man in dreary solitariness.

In her account of this experience, Dorothy has beautifully illustrated two hugely important aspects of travel. The first is that a sense of connection can invoke a profound response in us and the second is that we find it easier to connect to a place when people are present. Even when the people we see are distant, motionless and silent, the effect can still be powerful. We can sympathise and empathise with the situation of another person in a way that is hard with animals and near impossible with plants. We transport ourselves to the centre of the field and wrap ourselves in that grey cloak. We borrow from our past and feel the melancholy that the lonely woman feels. We are catapulted into the field and into the world of cold solitude.

The moment we appreciate the impact that other people can have on our own emotions, and therefore our experience, is the same moment that we inevitably start to take a deeper interest in them during our travels and this further fuels their impact upon us. It is not long before the amorphous swamp of humanity that teems in ever greater numbers starts to break down into individuals with distinctly different and fascinating appearances and behaviours. We are most likely to notice this first among other travellers, when the tourist next to us ceases to be just the 'other fellow'. We learn to peel away the layers and this reveals more about the true animal beside us; all our senses join in this new game. We might notice beads of sweat on a stranger's forehead in a cool place and it gets us thinking: are they sweating because their heart or brain is working hard?

We smell different to each other and our body's smells waft more deeply than the scents we choose. Caucasians and blacks are hairier than Asians, sweat lingers amongst the body hair and feeds bacteria. Asian people have less body odour than non-Asian people – body odour was once so rare in Japan that it would disqualify an individual from military service.

It soon becomes clear that humans conceal themselves with differing methods and degrees of camouflage around the world. Richard Hurd, who was the Bishop of Worcester and an influential author, wrote a tract in 1763 entitled, 'Dialogues on the Uses of Foreign Travel; Considered as Part of an English Gentleman's Education.' In it he argues that we only truly get a picture of human nature when we have seen it in its many states of dress and undress. From the nakedness of North America and Africa, Hurd argued that the traveller must witness human nature 'cramped, contracted and buttoned up close in the strait tunic of Law and Custom, as in China and Japan. Or, spread out, and enlarged above her common size, in the loose and flowing robe of enthusiasm, among the Arabs and Saracens . . .'

We hide ourselves in scents, clothing, habits, fashions and customs, none of which must be allowed to deceive the explorer. These are not distinct areas, each one feeds into and influences the other. Habits have a bearing on our appearance and our smell. When Al-Masudi was in Cambodia he reported that the inhabitants were well-known for the freshness of their breath, due to their habit of using toothpicks.

Differences in any of these areas from our home or 'base' expectations have traditionally caused emotions that range wildly, but are often biased towards the disapproval or even disgust end of the spectrum. Even the enlightened Humboldt found the habit of one Aragonese missionary for delighting so much in eating beef very disagreeable. 'Thus does sensuality triumph when there is nothing to occupy the mind.'

A problem of perspective arises because we tend to judge other places from a position that is subconsciously and sometimes vocally assumed to be better. We tend to like the familiarity of the patterns of home and the people we find there. The infirmity of this position is best seen with the passage of time. Ludwig Leichhardt was quick to highlight the habits and customs of the Aboriginals that he saw as unsophisticated, but when one of his party, Mr Gilbert, died following an attack by the Aboriginals, Leichhardt's attempted solution to the problem was to cut open the veins on both of Gilbert's arms and his temporal artery in an attempt to bleed him back to life. Mr Gilbert remained dead. We are none of us perfect.

Those whose lives or livelihoods depend on an awareness of the state of mind of their fellow human beings, have always developed a greater understanding of their true nature than most. Leichhardt learned to read the differences between the 'smooth tongue of deceit' and the 'open expression of kind and friendly feelings' among the Aboriginals he met.

The French slave trader, John Barbot, wrote extensively of his experiences in West Africa in the latter half of the seventeenth century. Barbot learned how to tell when he was being offered counterfeit gold, not by studying the metal itself, but by studying the person offering it.

A cheat, who knows his gold is false and counterfeit, is very impatient, uneasy and in haste to be gone, under some colour or other, besides he commonly bids a higher price than usual for goods, and takes them in a hurry without too much examination; and if not found out, will paddle away to shore with the goods, as fast as his canoe will carry him. Nay, I have observed some of them to stand trembling and quaking, whilst their gold was upon trial; and such their behaviour is a sufficient indication to suspect some fraud.

Barbot's observations that dishonest people appear anxious and nervous are not extraordinary and from a cool distance would be realised by most, but in the heat of a transaction many may miss these signs.

There are thousands of these signals, many of them more subtle than the ones Barbot reports and they are being offered for our interest by everyone we encounter. Some of these signs are universal and benign and therefore reveal little, everyone in the world, regardless of ethnicity or cultural background, raises and lowers their eyebrows rapidly when greeting someone else, but we will typically fail to notice this and focus more closely on the culturally specific handshake.

If someone is resting their head on their hands they are

signalling tiredness, which would be registered subconsciously by most observers, but what if they bring their hand to their mouth whilst talking? And then a few seconds later cover their mouth with the same hand and a few seconds after that they lower both hands and keep them still? These signs are much more subtle and less instantly recognised by most. The action of bringing a hand to the mouth region is a sign that someone is experiencing tension, the hand covering the mouth is an attempt to conceal facial expressions and the still hands a sign that someone may be being deceitful. Covering the mouth and the restriction of hand movements are both attempts to cover the facial and hand signals that would otherwise betray deceit, but once recognised can ironically act as signals of deceit in their own right.

A clue that an individual is feeling exposed or threatened comes in what is known as the 'body-cross', when the arms are brought in front of the body. This instinctive defensive posture is commonly seen in the folded arms position, which is why this position is strongly advised against during important interviews, but it can be found in more fleeting moments too. Notice how public figures will often touch a cufflink, watch, bracelet or bag at a moment of raised scrutiny, such as crossing a threshold or stepping up to stage. If they lick their lips before speaking, this is likely a reaction to a dry mouth, which is a symptom of high levels of adrenaline. If on meeting these individuals we notice their head tip back then this may be a sign that they regard themselves as having a higher status than us. The backwards head-tilt by those who feel above the person they are speaking to is the likely origin for the expression 'looking down one's nose at someone.'

If all is fair in love and war, then it is acceptable for us to use every assistance we can to understand our targets in each case. A person with a pale white face is much more of a threat than someone with the stereotypically red face of anger. A white-faced person is in a high state of readiness, their blood has been redirected to the muscles in preparedness for action. The red face is a symptom of the stage after this, when the blood has flown back.

If we find someone attractive then our pupils will dilate. This response is not a reaction we can control and so it is a good window to the soul, and if not the soul, then at least our chances. There is an element of reflexivity in this too, because we tend to find large pupils more attractive. One thing can lead to another. This is why we are so sensitive to each others' gaze and also the reason why courtship includes a series of stages where we go from staring at the ground to being comfortable staring into each others' eyes.

If one thing has indeed led to another then it is worth knowing that it is possible to tell whether a man is a father by the way their eyes react on seeing a baby; childless men's pupils constrict, whereas the pupils of fathers dilate.

A fact that the West African gold dealers of John Barbot's acquaintance might have found interesting is that jade dealers in China have been known to wear dark glasses to conceal their eyes' involuntary response to any particularly valuable pieces that were passed beneath their nose.

Darwin noticed that the Fuegians in the far south of South America liked to watch the visitors' gesticulations very keenly and could imitate them perfectly.

> All savages appear to possess, to an uncommon degree, this power of mimicry. I was told, almost in the same words, of the same ludicrous habit among the Caffres: the Australians, likewise, have long been notorious for being able to imitate and describe the gait of any man, so that he may be recognised. How can this faculty be explained? Is it a consequence of the more practiced habits of perception and keener senses, common to all men in a savage state, as compared to those long civilised?

What Darwin does not seem to realise is that he is only mocking the habit of a foreign culture's own habit of mocking his own culture. Whilst mimicry does not impress Darwin, he does acknowledge that it is only a symptom of a heightened awareness of body language. The idea that the Aboriginals' 'more practiced habits of perception and keener senses' is synonymous with a savage state makes Darwin and the culture he springs from look regressive from our modern viewpoint.

Omai must have done well to disguise it, but when he visited London from Polynesia in 1774 he would surely have been almost overcome by the desire to laugh at some of the social conventions and costumes he witnessed in the capital of Georgian England. The temptation for one group to try to set themselves above another through appearance is universal, and just as universal is the response of the supposed underdog: to laugh.

This sheer ridiculousness provided the humour for a scene in the cult film of 1986, *Withnail and I*. We learn through the character, Danny, a mildly deranged and drug-addled individual that his associate, 'the coal man', has been arrested for drug-trafficking and recently appeared in court to defend himself. 'The coal man' elected to appear in court wearing a kaftan and a bell, which did not impress the judge. The judge informed him that this was not an occasion for fancy dress, to which the defendant, looking up at the judge in his wig and gown, replied, 'You think you look normal, your honour?'

The popularity of the sports and games that people choose as non-lethal replacements for the more traditional hunting and warfare may reveal clues to the nature of the competitors, their communities and philosophies. It is no surprise that rugby is widely watched and played in countries where warfare has formed an integral and nostalgic part of the national psyche. Rugby is very popular in its birthplace England and the contests between England and the neighbours it used to go to war with, Wales and Scotland, achieve the status of legendary battles amongst supporters.

One thousand years before rugby, Al-Masudi commented on the philosophical differences between backgammon and chess.

Each game of backgammon is shaped by the roll of the dice, there is a lot of luck involved and a bad player can beat a good one occasionally, but chess uses no dice and is a game of near pure skill. Al-Masudi made the point that chess is more popular with those who like to think that intelligence is what counts and is what will be rewarded in life, whereas backgammon is the choice of those who see chance as key.

Games may seem trivial, but conflict is often the best place to see character revealed. Games can offer an insight into the ways people like to pit themselves against each other, the importance they place on leisure itself and inevitably their vices too. Al-Masudi described how backgammon players in India would bet against each other using lengths of cloth or precious stones as the wager, but when they ran out they would bet parts of their body. Before games of this intensity, a copper pot would be filled with a special palliative red salve and placed on a brazier next to the contestants. If a player then lost a bet and had to pay with his finger, he could chop it off during play, cauterise it in the hot salve and then continue to play without the amputation causing too great an interruption. Al-Masudi no doubt recognised a gambling problem when he saw one, but this particular manifestation, through the choice of backgammon and then self-mutilation could not happen everywhere and certainly not in such a ritualised way, and is therefore a product of and insight into a culture.

Travel by its nature takes us from our familiar areas, which can be unsettling, but at least it also affords us the opportunity to observe this feeling in others. A very common alien is the townsperson who finds themselves in the country or vice versa. The German intellectual Walter Benjamin wrote for many when he described the jarring differences of the urban and rural landscapes, a battle that he saw being waged most ardently in the suburbs.

It is nowhere more bitter than between Marseilles and the Provençal landscape. It is the hand-to-hand fight of telegraph poles against Agaves, barbed wire against thorny palms, the miasmas of stinking corridors against the damp gloom under the plane trees in brooding squares, short-winded staircases against the mighty hills.

It is very common to encounter the countryperson who rails against the town, for some reason it is deemed a loftier position than the urbanite who lambasts nature's works, but both are borne of the same insecurity. They are both violent gasps for the air of familiarity that erupt when our heads are dunked too forcibly in the bucket of the alien landscape. And there is a sadistic pleasure on offer: it is fun to watch. The expensive watch catches the sun and an arm takes the hand to the mouth as the train carries the suited body too far from coffee-stained convenience. The farmhand scratches her head and then folds her arms as she is borne along the rails towards a great urban shed with no green around it.

Some of the loathing of towns stems from the discomfort that is experienced by many when forced to mix with crowds, but there are those that revel in this environment. The French poet Baudelaire found a sensual joy in mixing with crowds, a joy that multiplied with the growing numbers. Walt Disney included the theatrical impact of crowds on themselves in his vision for Disneyland. Shortly before his epic tourist attraction opened, Walt Disney was driving around the site with his guests, but even as they marvelled at it he was quick to point out that the biggest attraction had not yet arrived. 'Fill this place with people,' he explained, 'and you'll really have a show.'

At the other end of the spectrum from Disney are those who harbour a devotional love of nature and they often find themselves driven to anger by man's place in it. John Muir felt this rage.

Well I have precious little sympathy for the selfish propriety of civilised man, and if a war of races should occur between wild beasts and Lord Man, I would be tempted to sympathise with the bears.

The people do not even need to be present to send a chill down some spines. Inside the Neolithic tomb of Maeshowe in the Scottish Orkney Islands there is a slimy green coating on some of the stones. When visitors breathe in the tomb, the moisture from their breath condenses and allows algae to grow on the stone. The tomb is stained by past gatherings and this smear of recent humanity is more repellent to some than thoughts of ancient corpses.

For many, the space between vacuum and compression, is the garden. The garden is nature that is neither raw nor roasted to destruction. It reassures us that the human hand is not far away, but still allows a certain solitude and proximity to nature. Francis Bacon, the philosopher and pioneer of scientific method, considered that a garden was the 'greatest refreshment to the spirits of man, without which buildings and palaces are but gross handy-works.' For the lovers of gardens they form the tonic that dilutes the harsher liquids of both man and nature.

Whatever our individual stance on the human's role within the broader natural world, there is no denying the fascination this creature offers. We learn about the human being by watching its habits within an environment, but we also get an opportunity to reflect on ourselves. The more we study others and the deeper we go, the more we are forced to reflect. Leonardo da Vinci believed that the structures and shapes of the exterior natural world would also be found within man, and he was right. The branches of rivers and trees mirror the veiny branches in our bodies. Studying the human animal is a way of holding up a giant convex mirror: we learn much about ourselves.

Worldly Goods

> Among the mulattos whose huts surround the salt lake
> we found a shoemaker of Castilian descent. He received
> us with that gravity and self-sufficiency characteristic in
> those countries where the people feel they possess some
> special talent. He was stretching the string of a bow, and
> sharpening arrows to shoot birds. His trade of
> shoemaking could not be very lucrative in a country
> where the majority go barefoot.
>
> Alexander von Humboldt

*A*pproaching the village of Houghton Bridge, the noise levels rose *once more. Sounds of steam and hammering emerged from the Amberley Working Museum on my left, drowned temporarily by the occasional passing car. After I passed Amberley train station, the village centre announced itself with a riverside café on one side of the road and a pub called the Bridge Inn on the other. The train station, museum, pub and café were drawing the tourists in, entertaining them, feeding them, watering them and then sending them on their way.*

This corner of Sussex has not always been a tourist destination. High above the museum, towering chalk cliffs hinted at a past that was confirmed in the name of one of the first buildings that I passed, 'Quarry House'. As in so many places, one source of income had withered and another had been found. In each case the line of work had come to give the place much of its character.

• • •

The human being indulges in many activities that the rest of the animal kingdom forego and none of these habits is more prevalent, peculiar or revealing than its penchant for economic activity.

In Venezuela, Humboldt was frustrated by a local guide who could not be dissuaded from resting frequently, even by the bait of money. Humboldt did not think that this man or the local population as a whole were lazy, he testifies to watching them paddling a canoe against the current for fifteen hours when necessary; they were just uninterested in marching to Humboldt's tune solely for financial reward. Neither was this a problem purely of indifference to the value of money. Later Humboldt found his desire for the Venezuelans to be more motivated by money turned on its head, and he lamented their obsession with mining gold.

This rage for searching for mines amazed us in a climate where the earth needs only to be slightly raked in order to produce rich harvests.

It would appear that Humboldt had encountered an element of pride in the Venezuelans he met. They were not immune to riches and could see the value in attaining wealth, but it lost a lot of its sheen if the price was to submit oneself to the demands and whims of a stranger. Much to his frustration, Humboldt found that in Venezuela there was a noticeable geographic distribution of this shift in attitudes.

Money means less the further from the coast you go, and there was no way to shake the imperturbable apathy of the people when even money meant nothing!

Humboldt never tackles the inherent contradictions in his conclusions. Why is the pursuit of gold wrong if economic gain is desirable? But equally, why is the unwillingness to work wrong, when the population is able to survive without working for the white man?

The people of Venezuela demonstrated how alien Western economic mores were by taking off into the forests for periods of self-sufficient nomadism and emerging only when they felt like returning to a settled life. Subsisting from nature was arduous and thus they proved they were capable of living without being industrious in the European sense and without being lazy either. This was clearly confusing to a man such as Humboldt, who could not see a way to fit these observations neatly into the world order as he saw it.

The lust for riches in the ground, especially gold, condenses and epitomises any people's susceptibility to greed. Humboldt was not the first explorer to be revolted by a craze for gold. Almost three hundred years before Humboldt's travels, Sir Thomas More had cleverly sown a contrarian idea about gold into his fictional hero's travels on the island of Utopia. On Utopia, gold is disdained and is used for the manufacture of prisoners' chains and chamber pots. One and a half thousand years before More, Pliny had lambasted the greed of gold miners and jewellery wearers.

If only gold could be completely banished from life, reviled and abused as it is by all the worthiest people, a discovery whose only purpose was the destruction of human life!

Both Humboldt and Pliny seem saddened by the physical attack that mining forced on the land itself and this lament was not restricted to gold. Pliny noted with regret that the marvel of the crossing of the Alps by Hannibal had been replaced by a hunt for a thousand types of marble. The history of exploration has a seam of stories running through it tainted with the lust for mineral wealth.

When Meriwether Lewis read the letter from the US President, Thomas Jefferson, that detailed his instructions for his expedition he must have spotted that the objects 'worthy of notice' as far as the President was concerned included, 'the mineral productions of every kind; but more particularly metals, limestone, pit coal &

saltpetre;' in short, a shopping list for any mining opportunities that would bolster the economics of industry and war. The contemporary explorer is less likely to be tasked with finding minerals, but more likely to encounter evidence of their extraction.

In 1994 an academic study estimated that each year in the USA, 0.8 billion metric tonnes of sediment was being moved for construction, 3.8 billion tonnes for mining and 3 billion tonnes for roads. Globally about 30 billion tonnes of earth was moved by industry in 1994. By comparison, each year rivers move an estimated 14 billion tonnes of sediment to the world's oceans and the wind moves 1 billion tonnes. Man's etchings in the surface have become a major force in shaping that land. The Bingham Canyon Mine in Utah has produced more copper than any other mine in the world. It is 2.75 miles wide, deeper than two Empire State buildings on top of each other and can be seen from space.

A quarry or open cast mine will stir the emotions of any traveller that stumbles across one, but this is because these relatively small landforms jar with the landscape that we have already come to know. They evoke scenes of violence, but the total change they have wrought is minuscule in comparison with one that we are now accustomed to. Before the first minerals were hauled from the ground there was a human economic activity that shaped the land far more broadly and dramatically than mining ever will: agriculture. We only need glance out of an aircraft window as it passes over land where agriculture is practised to see its power. Flying across Spain or North Africa we notice how a little water forms an invitation for the ground to be assaulted by the green and yellow quilts of agriculture.

The first farmers arrived in the UK some six and a half thousand years ago and began the process of keeping animals from each other and from their crops. Early agriculture has a ruthlessness to it: the land was completely reshaped to suit human beings' ends. It often started with the clearance of woodland. Forests that once covered vast areas of Europe have so often found themselves on the wrong side of a utilitarian tussle. If the woods could not be more profitably used for agriculture, they were frequently felled for construction and shipbuilding. The smell of trees engaging in a battle with economics emanated from the eighteenth-century forests of Lithuania, where they were drawn into the manufacture of potash, a useful ingredient for bleaching textiles or making glass and soap. It was a smelly business. 'The smell of rotting eggs overlaid with the cloying scent of boiling birch tar and pine pitch.'

The trees that have proved their worth have been offered protection in the form of plantations and each country's climate and soils will host their own varieties, from the spruces that are grown for paper in Sweden to the Cork Oaks of Portugal and Andalusia that are harvested for the use in the wine industry. Each tree's value will grow into the character of the people who live in an area and flavour their towns. The Cork Oaks provide a perfect habitat for black pigs and the streets of Andalusian towns are consequently filled with the scents of some of the finest hams in the world, wafting from shop doorways. The Cork Oaks, and the pigs, are being threatened by the rise of the plastic wine cork. Economics is change.

There are vocal proponents and opponents of all economic change and its consequences, those who lament the death of a lichen with each wash of acid rain and those who argue that conservation is a rich person's dilemma. Many find themselves somewhere in the middle, willing to accept a certain amount of change before railing against development that undermines the character of a place. The debate rages partly because the work that is done in any area comes to define it. The northeast of England was synonymous with coal mining for many communities and now it is not, or, more sadly, it is defined by the *lack* of coal mining. The geology shaped the economics, which in turn shaped the identity of a people and therefore the character of a place.

On the far southern tip of Chile, in the Wollaston Islands, Darwin encountered a poverty that it would be hard to exceed. The local Fuegian people hunted with their dogs to catch otters and buried any excess of washed-up whale-meat in the sand for future consumption. But it was not always sufficient to get them through the vicious winters and they regularly suffered famine. One of their solutions to this problem was to kill and eat the old women of the community. When pressed to justify eating the women before eating the dogs, they offered an answer that was as practical as it was desperate. 'Doggies catch otters, old women no'.

Travel is notorious for its ability to make us confront uncomfortable extremes of wealth and poverty, neither of which are new phenomena. Ibn Battuta was aghast at the consumerism he witnessed seven hundred years ago in Tabris, in modern day Iran.

I passed through the jewellers' bazaar, and my eyes were dazzled by the varieties of precious stones that I saw; they were displayed in the hands of beautiful slave boys, wearing rich robes and their waists girt with sashes of silk, who stood in front of the merchants exhibiting the jewels to the wives of the Turks, while the women were buying them in large quantities and trying to outdo one another. What I saw of all this was a scandal – may God preserve us from such!

God has clearly not preserved us from such, as this scene is reminiscent of some of the boutiques in the departure lounges of airports today, but wealth itself is usually a camouflage. A people's wealth, or the lack of it, is not the same as their philosophy. When contemporary travel writer Colin Thubron is seeking to understand a place he tries to remain alert to anything that betrays people's values, rather than be too focused on their material state. Thubron resists the temptation to associate wealth with either values or outlook.

When Seneca travelled north from the comfort of Rome and saw the harsh life of the German tribes, he was surprised that their austerity was not matched by melancholy. Despite the 'perpetual winters', he did not find gloom in the hearts of the people to match the gloom in the sky.

Are they unhappy? No, there is no unhappiness in that which has become natural through habit; what has become necessity soon becomes pleasure.

Whenever we are in new territory, we tend to place a high value on goods that are novel. We often mistake novelty for scarcity early on in our journeys, until we learn better. From the plastic models of the Statue of Liberty, through the local food specialities to camel rides, vendors will prey on our weakness for new objects and experiences. Mark Twain used the example of the joy of hearing yodelling in the Alps to perfectly demonstrate the way the exchange rate for novelty ebbs with time.

> After about fifteen minutes we came across another shepherd boy who was yodeling, and gave him half a franc to keep it up. He also yodeled us out of sight. After that, we found a yodeler every ten minutes. We gave the first one eight cents, the second one six cents, the third one four, the fourth one a penny, contributed nothing to Nos. 5, 6, and 7, and during the remainder of the day hired the rest of the yodelers, at a franc apiece, not to yodel anymore. There is somewhat too much of this yodeling in the Alps.

As travellers our economic interactions are often in the form of currency swapped for access or knowledge and we depend upon those we meet to help us understand each place. There is a risk of learning little if we assume that the gatekeeper in each place is the key to its soul – even good guides will only show what has been seen many times before and describe it in a way that has been well-worn. But the real problem is more that those we assume will be guardians of vast repositories of local knowledge so often disappoint. Ibn Battuta recounted a story that illustrates this point.

The Sultan in Damascus once visited one of his orchards and

asked the superintendent of the garden to fetch some pomegranates for him to try. The superintendent in turn asked the orchard keeper, Abu Ya'qub Yasaf, to fetch some pomegranates, which he dutifully did. The superintendent tasted the pomegranates and, finding them sour, sent the keeper back to fetch some more. Abu Ya'qub Yasaf returned with some more pomegranates, but the superintendent found that these were also sour and asked Abu Ya'qub, 'Have you been looking after this orchard for six months and cannot tell the sweet from sour?' Abu Ya'qub replied, 'It was for keeping that you hired me, not for eating.' This proved Abu Ya'qub's honesty and he was rewarded for it, but sadly the modern equivalent of the keepers – the ticket vendors and cashiers – often appear motivated as much by a zeal to achieve new levels of ignorance, as by honesty.

To find the people who really know a place we do well to look beyond those who man the gates and handle the normal flow of money. William Gilpin, pioneer chronicler of the picturesque, learned much from the underbelly of places like the New Forest, where he befriended black-economists like poachers and woodland squatters. These colourful characters, who hid behind the façade of the main economy, made a living by flirting with and regularly breaking the laws of trespass; they knew the place more intimately than its owners.

The image we project will shape the reactions of those we meet, not least when business must be done. John Dundas Cochrane, a determined pedestrian traveller, found that an image that would oil the wheels of one transaction could grit up the next. In Russia he carried a letter of introduction from the Tsar, a powerful imperial endorsement that helped prise open many heavy doors and secured him a great deal of hospitality. However, when he reached the Arctic coastal region, where the indigenous Tchuktchi lived, they read his letter and then interpreted its meaning very differently. If Cochrane was travelling with the Tsar's blessing, then surely he could spare the cash to pay his way? Surely such a nobleman could offer a gift of a vast quantity of tobacco without any trouble? Cochrane could not and his journey came to a cold halt.

Travel can bring us into contact not just with differing levels of wealth and attitudes to wealth but whole new perspectives on property itself. Theft was once an alien concept in the Pacific islands, as was discovered in the eighteenth century. The explorers arrived with the Western belief that theft was understood universally as wrong, but they had landed on islands where notions of private property and therefore theft were as foreign as swords and gunpowder.

Differences of opinion remain, much closer to home. The UK and the Continent have different philosophies of state and individual economics and this filters through each place. A 2010 survey found that only six per cent of the French strongly support the concept of the free market, and this can be felt in the country; it has a bearing on almost every institution that goes beyond offering a cup of good coffee. It may even explain why it is hard to get things done at lunchtime and why a strangely relaxed feeling pervades large parts of the country.

Marco Polo came across one convention in eastern India that is of interest in relation to the ever-growing complexity and challenges of the finances of the modern world. If a debtor repeatedly failed to repay a creditor, Marco Polo learned, then the creditor could try to draw a circle on the ground around the debtor. If successful, the debtor was not allowed to move outside the circle until he had arranged to come good on his debts. The penalty for failing to repay in these circumstances? Death.

Whatever economic differences we encounter, it is always helpful to remember that there is no simple correlation between the wealth and the wisdom of a population. In fact the opposite is often true. Studies have found that there is an inverse relationship between income and knowledge about the natural environment. This has been found to be true from the UK to Indonesia: the poorer people are, the better they are at identifying the names and uses of local plants and animals. In the words of the writer, Jules Pretty, 'the poorest know, and the richest have forgotten.'

Behind the items for sale there is usually a philosophy that differs slightly from our own, although it is often hidden by a price tag. A king in ancient India felt sorry for his people, who had to walk each day upon the rough earth of his kingdom. He was a benevolent man and wanted to change things for the better so he proposed a solution: the whole territory should be carpeted with soft animal skins to protect the tender feet of those who walked upon it. One of his wise counsels dared to suggest an alternative approach. Could not the same end be achieved more simply and economically by cutting small pieces of skin and binding them under each person's feet? And so the sandal was born.

This Hindu parable has very little to say about feet and much to say about our attitude to the world. It is easier for us to adapt ourselves mentally and physically to the world we find than to change the world itself. Changing our own views and behaviour to suit the place we are in is not always the right thing to do, but it is sometimes worth considering; particularly if every economic world we encounter leaves us wanting less of something or more of something else.

Food and Drink

Hunger is insolent, and will be fed.

Homer

I n the heart of Houghton Bridge village, I was greeted by a board with the words, 'Cream Teas', chalked on it. These two words bypassed the part of my brain that analyses the land around me and plunged deeper into my software. I could smell the scones baking, taste the jam, feel the bread crumbling, held together only with the unctuous cream cement. The rest of the landscape around me disappeared. I wrestled to gain some control over my thoughts and fought to suppress a primal urge to gorge.

It took a few seconds. The scones and jam and cream had been clumsily levered away from my appetite, but the words, 'Cream Teas', continued to hang in my mind. They would not shape me, but they were now shaping the land around me. The words painted the village as more English than England.

• • •

Whatever plans we make, our stomachs will at some point disagree with them and urge a slight tweaking of the timetable. On some occasions this is because our guts have something to say and are not feeling very patient about the matter. Early on in his travels, Marco Polo enjoyed a wine made from dates and spices, but warned others that when not used to it, the drink did have the effect of loosening the bowels. Its effects would have been welcome compared to those of some green and brackish water that lay ahead of him, one drop of which apparently makes you 'void your bowels ten times over.'

More commonly our stomachs rebel less emphatically, instead nagging at us to fill them. The satisfaction of eating when hungry brings joys that can be shared and provide an opportunity to connect with others. The Bantu feel that sharing food forms a contract between two people, who are then joined in a 'clanship of porridge'.

The travel writer, Eric Newby, resigned from his job in a London advertising agency, annoyed that he was deemed 'too unimportant to be sacked', and began a life of adventure. Soon afterwards he found himself on board a four-masted sailing barque that was setting out on a 30,000-mile round voyage, carrying grain between Ireland and Australia. The ship's captain was Finnish and so were many of the crew; Finnish customs prevailed. Weeks of hunger at sea were broken on Christmas Eve of 1938, when the captain unveiled a banquet below decks that included traditional Finnish rice-porridge, potato pastry, sardines, salmon, corned beef and apricots. Silence bar the sounds of munching filled the ship as the men gorged happily. One of them then turned to Newby and, with a face contorted around a piece of ginger pudding and a beard flecked with rice, said, 'To spik nothing and eat, is bettair.' Newby knew what he meant and thought to himself, 'We all love one another now.'

Our arrival in a new place coincides with hunger more frequently than not. First impressions are filtered through the gauze of the signals our stomachs are sending to our brains. The minute details are shrouded behind a veil of low blood sugar, and mighty minarets lie invisible behind the small stall of the street-food vendor. Caught up in our own hunger, it becomes easy to forget that those who we meet may be experiencing the same or worse. Sir Richard Burton felt quite strongly that religious fasting had a detrimental impact on the ambience of certain places.

Like the Italian, the Anglo-Catholic, and the Greek fasts, the chief effect of 'the blessed month' upon True Believers is to darken their tempers into positive gloom. Their voices, never of the softest, acquire, especially after noon, a terribly harsh and creaking tone. The men curse one another and beat the women. The women slap and abuse the children, and these in their turn cruelly entreat, and use bad language to, the dogs and cats. You can scarcely spend ten minutes in any populous part of the city without hearing some violent dispute.

More urgent still than hunger becomes the desiccated call from our cells for water, but our sufferings are unlikely to approach those who have gone before us. In the Gobi desert, the Swedish explorer Sven Hedin wrote what he feared would be the last lines in his diary before attempting to drink the spirits in his Primus stove. Thesiger learned how the desert Arabs would deal with a serious thirst by killing a camel and drinking the contents of its stomach or by ramming a stick down a camel's throat until it vomited and then drinking that.

Even if our sufferings are pale, it takes a passion to notice the small things through even a modest thirst or hunger. Our bodies will argue convincingly that it is the energy in the honey that is most interesting, not the fact that its distinct and wonderful flavour speaks of the marjoram that grows nearby. The Greeks and Romans could tell which waters the fish they ate had come from, but this stemmed from a refined fascination in fish as a food, which would have been unlikely had they not got enough to eat.

When our stomachs are full our interest in food, even in a cultural sense, diminishes; books with narratives about food are hard to pick up when our stomachs bulge. There is a window for us to connect with the food of a place, those moments when we are neither starving nor gorged. It is at these moments that the subtle connections can really be enjoyed. The superb olives that arrive before a meal in Melbourne whisper stories of the waves of emigration during the Greek civil war between 1946 and 1949, but the stories can only be heard by those who have allowed a few of the olives to line their stomachs first.

Cultures with sophisticated food like to wear it as a badge, they see their own sophistication reflected back at them in the complexity and refinement of their dishes. There is also a gradient within each country, typically one between the major cities and the minor ones and a steep one between town and country. In the rural wilds of countries that have always had a tradition for simple food the fare that we encounter is likely to be homogenous to the point of exasperation if we stay for a long period. Desert travellers in North Africa tend to eat the same meals each day, breads cooked in sand and monotonous dishes of meat or chickpeas bombed into submission by the harissa spoon.

Francis Bond Head had been warned that in the Argentinian Pampas he would find a simple diet dominated by beef and water, but still he could not hide his disappointment at the repetitiveness of the cuisine.

> I went to the door of the Maestro de Posta (Postmaster), and told him that I had ridden all day without eating; that I was very hungry, and begged to know what we could have. 'Lo que quiere, Señor, tenemos todo.' (Whatever you want, we have everything).
>
> I knew too well what 'todo' meant and he accordingly explained to me that he had 'carne de vaca and gallinas' (beef and fowls). I ordered a fowl, and then went to my room.

Near the aptly named Port Famine in Tierra del Fuego, Darwin found the inhabitants of this harsh land eating a hard, pitted, yellow fungus (Cyttaria darwinii) that they collected off the bark of the beech trees. In Venezuela Humboldt found that the ant and cassava-flour mix preferred by his Indian hosts tasted like rancid butter mixed with breadcrumbs, but the missionary he was with, Father Zea, was clearly more accustomed to the taste, describing it as 'an excellent ant paté.' Driven by necessity, the inventiveness of man knows few bounds in the search for edible food-stuffs. But starvation is a crude motivation and some of the more interesting foods are those that are eaten purely for pleasure, not out of desperation. James Holman came to know each place through his fingers, ears, nose and tongue. St Petersburg delighted him with fresh caviar, reindeer's tongues, snipe as rich as butter, a new fruit called moroshka and pea pudding.

There are foods that are consumed for a pleasure that tran-scends the taste buds and the heavy satisfaction of a full gut. The poisonous fugu fish is savoured by connoisseurs in Japan, but only after an expert chef has removed the organs containing the toxin, tetrodoxin. If the poison is accidentally ingested it causes muscle paralysis: the diner remains conscious, but their respiratory muscles fail them until they asphyxiate. The proximity of death adds a spice to the dish that cannot be found in a jar.

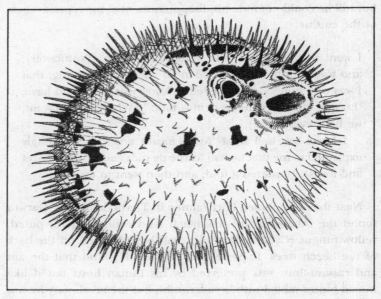

The fugu fish

There are many drinks that do more than quench a thirst. Leichhardt delighted in the ability of a simple cup of tea to banish feelings of fatigue, without doing any harm, but there are more potent brews in most lands.

In 1907 Manuel Cordova-Rios was fifteen years old and had barely left school to begin a career in the rubber trade. One day he found himself all alone in a rubber camp near the Jurua river, off the Brazilian Amazon. He was waiting for his companions to return from a day's excursion to tap some new latex-producing trees, but they did not show up. Hearing a sound he turned around and found himself surrounded by naked Indians armed with bows and arrows and lances.

The Indians took Manuel's knife from him and bound his hands before kidnapping him. The Indians had no intention of harming the boy, quite the opposite: he had been selected to be groomed to succeed as their next chief, when the current ailing chief died. Manuel spent seven years with the Indians, being schooled in their traditions and learning their ways. It is a little-known story, told well in F. Bruce Lamb's book, *Wizard of the Upper Amazon.*

After six months living with the Huni Kui tribe, Manuel Cordova-Rios had grown used to being naked and living off jungle game and wild fruit. Then one day, quite suddenly, his diet was altered by the older women who looked after him. He was given roasted breast of white partridge to eat, supplemented with roasted yucca and mashed bananas or sweet potatoes. Next he was urged to drink a series of herbal preparations that tasted odd, although he was assured they would do him no harm. One of these concoctions caused violent vomiting, the next was a laxative, another caused his pulse to soar and gave him a fever and left him drenched in sweat. After this ordeal he was given a bath and massage and the total effect was to make him feel exhilarated.

This series of bizarre rituals lasted ten days and was overseen by the chief of the tribe himself. Manuel was then led through the jungle to a clearing with a small creek running through it.

One of the Indians mimicked several different bird calls and the birds responded. The group then began to make preparations.

A fire was lit and guards were posted. A branch of dried leaves was placed on the fire and the chief began to make a strange chanting sound. Each of the participants was wafted with the smoke from the leaves with the help of a fan made of brightly-coloured feathers. Manuel felt the mood and the chanting sounds change slightly, as a clay vessel was fetched and placed next to the fire and then, from this pot, a dark green liquid was decanted into six cups, one of which was then handed to each of the men sitting by the fire. Manuel received his last and was encouraged to drink it.

The chanting continued, but Manuel could now hear a high pulsating whine in his ears, followed by a shock, which passed through his nervous system. He felt intensely nauseous, but this sensation passed and was replaced by feelings of incredible eroticism. His senses began to become confused and his vision swarmed with flashes of many different colours. Jungle animals danced before him, until he succumbed to tiredness and fell asleep.

Manuel was woken by sunlight shining in his face. The Indians conducted a kind of debrief of their experiences and then the party made their way back to the village. Manuel later learned from an old man called Nixi Xuma Waki, the Maker of the Vine Extract, how the ingredients for this hallucinogenic potion were collected and then brewed.

Seven years after his kidnap, Manuel Cordova-Rios broke away from the life of a chief that had been laid out for him. He made his own way back out of the jungle to rejoin his old world.

More common than the hallucinogenic drinks of the South American jungles are the alcoholic beverages that are enjoyed, abused and banned in differing measures across large swathes of the world. The role of alcohol in the socialising of each culture has a dramatic impact on the shape of that socialising. Most cultures enjoy coming together for a drink, but in Islamic countries there is a very different look and feel to the tea- and coffee-drinking that lines the streets and squares to that of the glasses of wine and beer of other nations. Alcohol is a more powerful drug than caffeine, its effects less predictable and the scenes we encounter in countries that have a penchant for alcohol will be as unpredictable as the strength of that liking.

Hopefully none will match those encountered by Marco Polo in Russia, where he tasted the local mead and learned of the extraordinarily zealous all-day drinking festivals called 'stravitza'. He explained that, in these festivals, teams are formed of up to fifty people and each team elects a captain. Each team then gathers and drinks as much as they can during the course of the day. This, from Polo's account, would appear to be the limit of the sophistication of the rules.

So focused were these Russian drinkers during the stravitza that the women would not leave the drinking tables to relieve themselves, preferring to ask a handmaid to mop them with a large sponge as they continued drinking. So addicted were they to the desire for more that they pawned their own children in return for credit with the mead merchants.

On one occasion, a husband and wife were returning home from a stravitza bout when the woman decided she needed to relieve herself and squatted by the side of the road. Unfortunately, this was during the Russian winter and it was freezing. The woman's hairs became frozen to the ground and left her as stuck fast as a ship that had run aground on a sinking tide. Her husband saw the seriousness of the situation and devised a solution: he knelt down as close as he could and began to blow the warm air of his breath onto the icy pubic anchors that held his wife down. Unfortunately the effects of the mead had clouded his judgment a little and he failed to see the one flaw in his plan. The husband's beard became frozen to his wife's hair and the two of them had to be rescued by passers-by who helped break the ice. No doubt with straight faces.

Contrasting Lines

The same impression repeated again and again may
prove fatiguing. Sublime upon sublime scarcely presents
a contrast, and we need a little rest from everything,
even the beautiful.

Victor Hugo

*here were cars waiting to cross Houghton Bridge. It was too
narrow for traffic to flow in both directions simultaneously. The
drivers waited for the oncoming stream of half a dozen cars to
pass, without the need for traffic lights or other paraphernalia.*

*Somebody must have shown a little too much patience, their eyes perhaps
drawn in search of the river they were about to cross. A car horn sounded.
The hoot was truncated, as though the driver was aware that it would
not be well received. They were hidden behind reflections in the glass, but
I pictured them resting their fingers on the button, like a trigger, and then
lifting their fingers swiftly off as soon as the deed was done.*

*The noise jarred us all, I think, but I may have felt it more than those
wrapped in their cars. The aggressive, industrial sound railed against the
calm, open hills. The sounds of traffic and the feel of the hills hated each
other. I knew that the horn would linger. I would love to have let the experience fade to nothing or at least put it to the back of my mind, but we cannot
control our memory so easily. Things that jar stay close to the surface.*

• • •

Francis Bond Head was alert as he travelled through a notoriously tough part of central Argentina. The locals dissuaded him from travelling alone and instead he set off one morning with the postal courier's postilion and three heavily armed guards.

The party stopped at one postal hut and the courier, a man of about fifty-five with 'a face like a withered apple', struck up a conversation with 'a rough mongrel-looking fellow'. The courier kept his pistol in his hand as he spoke, and told the rough-looking man that he had managed to get his only son, a boy of nineteen, a position as a postal courier but that his son had set out on his first job unarmed. The whole party, including horses and a dog, had been found dead, with their throats cut. His son must have died like a lamb, he added.

The haggard man listened to the story as he sat on a stone by the hut, while his young daughter combed his wooly hair and then began to plait it.

'En dos?'

The little girl asked her father if he would like his hair in two tails.

'Si!' he grunted in reply.

The contrast between the image of a daughter tenderly plaiting hair and her implacable father makes this image from Bond Head's travels evocative, but it is the fact of the teenage courier's vicious murder being recounted in front of the innocent young girl that is probably what made the scene stick in his mind. Contrast, like conflict, triggers a response in us. We react, we feel something.

Exploration is fuelled by the search for contrast. The travel writer, Colin Thubron, has spoken of how he has been invited to write about home but he finds it very difficult; travel writers seek the unfamiliar. The contrast does not need to be negative to resonate: think of Captain James Cook standing on the deck of his ship in full formal naval attire and gazing out to shore as he becomes one of the first Westerners to witness the bare locals of Hawaii riding planks of wood in the waves, surfing.

The power and importance of the effect of contrast in each

journey makes it worth contemplating. The contrasts arrive in all dimensions, including time. When the French naturalist and archaeologist, Henri Mouhot, studied the incredible city and temple ruins in Angkor in Cambodia, he was struck first by the scale of the gigantic works there, but then more profoundly by the mirror they held up to the current state of the country. He thought one of the temples would rival Solomon's and described its creation as the genius-like work of an ancient Michelangelo, but it jarred with his perceptions of the state of contemporary Cambodia.

It is grander than anything left to us by Greece or Rome, and presents a sad contrast to the state of barbarism in which the nation is now plunged.

A change in terrain is the most common contrast we encounter and, as we have seen, it will always bring with it a change in vegetation and animals. If the terrain becomes hostile then the land becomes barren, but as Darwin discovered on Santiago in the Cape Verdes, an absence of life can offer a pleasing contrast to anyone who is accustomed to a consistent abundance of it.

The island would generally be considered as very uninteresting; but to anyone accustomed only to an English landscape, the novel aspect of an utterly sterile land possesses a grandeur which more vegetation might spoil.

On a much smaller scale the contrast between smells reaches deep into our memory and allows a place to reside there forever. Who can forget the place where, as a child, we doused ourselves in autumnal leaves? The licensed messiness and abandon fuse with the rich wet funk of decomposition and set themselves apart from the orderliness of the rest of our lives. The scent of a specific location and nostalgia are regularly found holding hands.

Colours can burst out from a background and steal our

attention. The cherry blossom is adored in many countries because so many trees' flowers are green and do not stand out. The cherry and almond blossoms shrug off the Procrustean shyness of the neighbouring trees and win our admiration for their boldness.

The ability of contrast to command our attention in this way has been harnessed by artists. Caravaggio and Rembrandt use depth of shadow in their paintings to draw our focus to the subject, which our eyes then find 'embedded like a precious object on a dark velvet background.' 'Chiaroscuro' is the artistic technique of using the contrast between light and dark for effect, particularly for giving a two-dimensional representation a bold three-dimensional feel.

Contrast is standing out and standing out is rebellion. The aware traveller will find in nature many organisms that are both rebellious and lacking any malevolence, a combination of traits that a traveller, who is already going against the grain of a largely unobservant and sedentary home country, will find it easy to relate to.

There are few greater contrasts than the line that is drawn between sea and land and this must be one of the reasons for the coastline's allure. But any place that promises differences with such assuredness is also, occasionally, going to raise expectations so high that let down is inevitable.

In 1811 David Thompson's explorations along the Columbia river in North America culminated at their goal: the Pacific Ocean. Thompson was understandably delighted. Thompson's men on the other hand, were seriously underwhelmed. They had seen the great lakes of Canada and it wasn't clear what this ocean offered them, as a visual spectacle, that a large lake did not. Thompson wrote that his men had expected to find something beyond the power of their senses. Thompson tried to light their enthusiasm by explaining that they were looking out at a body of water that stretched for five thousand miles and that the next land mass was the Empire of Japan. It was in vain; the men remained nonplussed.

Often it is the less grand boundary line, the one that does not promise so much, that can offer the most uplifting experiences, unladen as it is with unfair hope or expectation. The humble hedge will offer much if the curiosity is there. It was more than enough for John Lubbock.

> I love the open Down most, but without hedges England would not be England. Hedges are everywhere full of beauty and interest, and nowhere more so than at the foot of the Downs, when they are in great part composed of wild Guelder Roses and rich dark Yews, decked with festoons of Traveller's Joy, the wild Bryonies, and garlands of Wild Roses covered with thousands of white or delicate pink flowers, each with a centre of gold.

Hedges are indeed fascinating micro-worlds. Wherever a forest meets open land the transition is very rich in life, hence the work that has been done in recent decades to encourage farmers not to farm right up to the edge of woodlands. Hedges can be thought of as forest edges on a smaller scale. Hedges are teeming with life, but they are also clues to the history of the land itself. In his book about hedges, Dr Max Hooper put forward an interesting hypothesis. Although it was widely known that older hedges are more diverse, Hooper had investigated this trend empirically and then devised a formula that summed up his finding. Hooper's Hypothesis, as it became known, states that if you count the number of different tree species in thirty yards of hedge, this will give you an estimate of the age of the hedge in centuries.

There are other clues to the nature of the land in the ingredients of field boundaries. The efficient use of land in farming has led to a clearance of the rocks that would normally lie strewn across the land. The large rocks have been hauled aside and a lot of the smaller ones were used for building the earliest walls that marked territory. There are very few stone walls in chalk country, but there are a great many beautiful dry-stone walls in upland granite country.

Contrast is implicit in the notion of natural boundaries between territories. The north-south border between Argentina and Chile is drawn by the summits and watershed of the Andes mountains. Rivers divide nations, states, counties, properties and families. On a smaller scale any feature that dominates the landscape is likely to be invoked if it lies anywhere near disputed territory. Humboldt admired a formidable dragon tree in Orotava in Tenerife and learned that it served as the local boundary marker.

Borders and boundaries are inextricably linked to the politics of private property. The moment something clearly belongs to one person it is equally clearly denied to another and therein lies a large portion of human friction throughout history. Great wars have been waged and smaller ones too. The protest movement that led to the formation of the National Parks in the UK was sparked by a mass trespass of Kinder Scout, the highest point in the Peak District, in 1932.

Some boundary lines are temporary, but no less influential for it. Many cities used to close their gates at sunset and open them at sunrise. All these arbitrary lines will have a bearing on our journeys, physically and mentally. Rebecca Solnit has linked the closing of the city gates of Geneva in the face of a teenage Jean-Jacques Rousseau to a change of course for the rest of his life. Returning from an afternoon's walking to find he had been locked out of his home city, Rousseau 'decided to abandon his birthplace, his apprenticeship, and eventually his religion; he turned from the gates and walked out of Switzerland.'

The Western traveller has become deeply inculcated with the creed that there are certain places that you are allowed to go and certain places that you are not, there being a lot more of the latter than the former. Contrasts and boundaries illuminate differences and these suggest that alternative thoughts and actions are possible. Jean-Pierre Gontran de Montaigne, Vicomte de Poncins, was the son of French nobility and born in 1900 on his family's nine-hundred-year-old estate in southeastern France. He is better known now as the man he became, Gontran de Poncins, an adventurer and travel writer. Gontran travelled around the world, but it was his observations of the Arctic that touched him most deeply.

Here he found a place and people that impressed him as being utopian. While others saw the world of the Inuit as harsh and unpleasant, Gontran de Poncins was impressed by the freedom from boundaries and property. This offered surprising benefits to the Inuit people. There were no invasions and nobody stole their land or possessions. Theft within the communities was just as unlikely; selfishness was impossible as survival depended on cooperation. In a land that was undesirable to most people, Gontran de Poncins found the ideals that escaped the most liberal of societies further south. The Arctic Inuit had achieved a harmony that contrasted starkly with the world he had left behind.

The River

The face of the water, in time, became a wonderful
book—a book that was a dead language to the
uneducated passenger, but which told its mind to me
without reserve, delivering its most cherished secrets as
clearly as if it uttered them with a voice. And it was not
a book to be read once and thrown aside, for it had a
new story to tell every day.

Mark Twain, *Life on the Mississippi*

I had first glimpsed the Arun from the highest ground, the South Downs
ridge. The river, oblivious to its own notoriety for speed, meandered
calmly through the almost perfectly flat flood plain as far as I could
see. Each section of the water borrowed light from a different part of the
sky and the land appeared to be tied with a ribbon of silver, white and
blue.

Having descended and met the water once more in its valley, I paused
before the bridge over the river, in the small village of Houghton Bridge.
The bridge funnelled keen traffic over its narrow back. Lorries edged past
cars, a handful of cyclists and pedestrians hesitated at either end, picking
their moment to head across. A wooden sign on an old building politely
announced that the tollhouse was built in 1813 and listed the tolls for
crossing the bridge. Coaches, chariots, landaus and 'berlins drawn by six
horses' were chargeable at two shillings each.

A car approached the bridge as I made my way across and I slipped
into one of the recesses in the stone walls. There was no room for

pavements and these thoughtfully-placed refuges were necessary for the preservation of walkers. Jutting out over the water, these stone hollows reminded me of pulpits, the perfect place to preach to waterborne travellers. Below, there was a young family preparing a kayak at the water's edge, but I had no sermon for them. Instead I stared at the stone pillars below me and then at the hypnotic ripples and eddies that danced away from the grey stone.

Shapes formed in the water from above and below. The surface was still like a mirror in the places where the bridge blocked the breeze and cast a wind shadow. Elsewhere the tidal current formed bows among the ripples.

• • •

There is a mighty pink granite monument to John Hanning Speke in London's Hyde Park and it would not be there had he not correctly identified Lake Victoria as the source of the Nile. It was the solution to a puzzle that had vexed great men for nearly two thousand years. Julius Caesar offered to abandon his wars in return for a glimpse of the source of the Nile.

The historical obsession with finding the sources of rivers can be seen as an attempt to understand the source of life. The contemporary equivalent might be the search for the beginning of time in events such as the Big Bang. The early universe is the cradle that the modern mind now sees as its spring; rivers are no longer grand enough but for a long time they were, before our gaze moved outwards.

Rivers nurtured life by forming the accessible artery in an aqueous circulatory system that was vital to many of the great ancient civilisations. The Tigris, Euphrates, Yellow River, Indus, Nile, Tiber . . . without these rivers the whole course of human history would have been very different. Some of the most powerful stories come to us from the banks of rivers: the flight in Exodus, for example, can be seen as a migration from the Nile to the Jordan.

Rivers sustained civilisations, but they also periodically devastated them. The Akkadian empire was destroyed in the third millennium BC by the drying of the Tigris and Euphrates. It is unsurprising that rulers were obsessed by and desperate to control the flow of water. The ancient Egyptian King Necho tried to force a canal to the Red Sea. He gave up, but only after the loss of 120,000 workers' lives. It was inevitable that the cycles of rivers should become intertwined with the cycle of life.

Water evaporates from oceans, rivers and lakes, it transpires from the leaves of trees, it condenses as clouds and then falls again as rain and snow. The rain runs downhill or it seeps underground to emerge elsewhere in a spring. When a trickle joins another trickle it forms a brook, the brook joins a stream and soon a river is running. Mountains dispatch rivers out from summits and ridges, like messengers from a royal court.

The water that runs and then gathers in the Lake District can be seen from above to be radiating from both the summit of Scafell Pike and the line of high ground that heads east-southeast from that summit. In high country, rivers and lakes radiate from points, like blood vessels in the iris of a tired eye.

The Rocky Mountains separate the flow of water with a broader cleavage, the rivers that flow down their western flanks provide drinking water for Utah, Arizona and Los Angeles, on the other side they feed the mighty Mississippi. Mountains shape rivers and rivers shape life. Marco Polo paid tribute to the nurturing effects of one river on a hillside by declaring that the pasturage it provided would allow a lean beast to grow fat there in ten days.

The cycle is endless, no sooner has a river come into being than it begins to evaporate. The water is never constant and if the river dries then death is ushered up from the dusty riverbed. Osiris was the god that gifted the Nile its annual flood, the water that broke out of the banks and gave the valley and its civilisation sustenance, but he was also the ruler of the dead.

Water is maternal, she gives life, but she turns into a ruthless

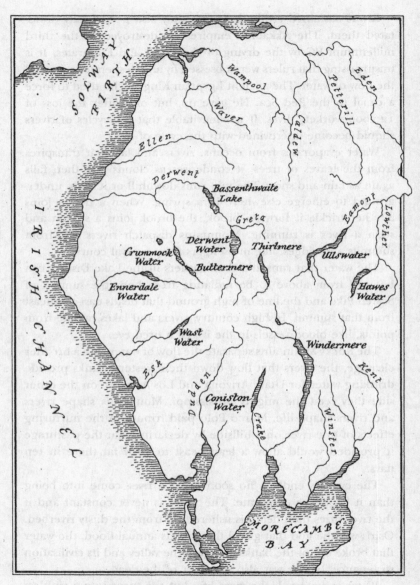

The rivers and lakes of the Lake District

tyrant of a parent to any child who forgets her power. The Egyptians watched this parent lovingly, but nervously. A Nile depth-gauge was also a gauge of mood: twelve cubits meant famine, thirteen spelled hunger, fourteen equalled cheerfulness, fifteen was security, and finally sixteen cubits brought happiness and delight, or perhaps parental approval.

The power of rivers over people lies in their whimsical depth, but also in their capricious speed. In the July of 1873 Nikolai Przhevalsky, the Russian soldier, geographer and explorer, was investigating an area at the edge of the Gobi desert when he noticed that the mountains were enveloped in mist, which he saw as a certain forecast of rain. Soon after, the rain began and Przhevalsky was forced to dig trenches around his tent to keep the water from filling the inside. It rained hard for an hour and the soil could not absorb all the water, it began to run down the mountain in 'every cleft and gorge', cascading from cliffs and joining the water that had already begun to flow in the ravine where they were camped. Soon the water had formed a torrent that gave an audible roar.

> Dull echoes high up in the mountains warned us of its approach, and in a few minutes the deep bed of our ravine was inundated with a turbid, coffee-coloured stream, carrying with it rocks and heaps of smaller fragments, while it dashed with such violence against the sides that the very ground trembled as though with the shock of an earthquake . . . the rain continued with undiminished violence, and the torrent kept ever swelling. The deep bed of our ravine was soon choked with stones, mud, and fallen timber, which forced the water out of its channel on to higher ground. Barely twenty feet from our tent rushed the torrent, destroying everything in its course.

The power of a river lies in a simple but terrifying relationship. As the speed of the water doubles, the size of the particles it can carry goes up by a factor of sixty-four. Since a river flows faster as you move away from its banks towards the centre, a single step from a manageable shallow edge can take a person into water that is only fractionally deeper and faster, but more than powerful enough to steal them away and drown them, long before they have had time to appreciate the ruthless physics. During a rainstorm in the Tehachapi Mountains in California, a swollen river carried a train half a mile downstream and buried it.

None of this diminishes the beauty of rivers, perhaps it even enhances our respect and therefore our love of them. Nan Shepherd was sensitive to this paradox in her beloved Cairngorms.

For the most appalling quality of water is its strength. I love its flash and gleam, its music, its pliancy and grace, its slap against my body; but I fear its strength. I fear it as my ancestors must have feared the natural forces that they worshipped.

Somewhere beyond love and fear there is a relationship between people and rivers that is both more mercurial and more fundamental than either. Rivers have been credited with everything from the practical ability to wash clothing to their psychological value in cleansing the mind. The river's role in life and death means spiritual and religious associations must follow.

In ancient times a river's running waters were proof that witchcraft and sorcery were not present. The Jordan was the sacred river of both Christianity and Judaism. The Roman Emperor Justinian prohibited paganism across the Empire and yet could not overturn the practice of making offerings to the watery god Osiris at Philae. Some waters run deep and rivers flow into hearts and minds in a way that counter-insurgencies struggle to. Even those poor souls that feel nothing when spending time near a river are likely to experience a pang on leaving it.

The early Egyptian explorers followed the Nile south and then back again, and one of the most extensive accounts we have of these expeditions is carved into the rock tomb of an explorer named Harkhuf. It is one of the most surreal accounts of early exploration in existence and warrants a minor digression. According to the account in his own tomb, Harkhuf made several upriver expeditions and each time returned with tales of the Nubians who lived to the south and some of their wares, including incense, ebony, panther skins and ivory. Harkhuf was clearly sensitive, as so many explorers are, to a feeling that his achievements were not being given their due credit and so he brought back something from his final expedition along the Nile that created the stir that he sought: a dancing dwarf. A letter from the king to Harkhuf, which is transcribed in full on the inside of his tomb, shows the monarch's keen curiosity.

Come north to the court [at Memphis near Cairo] immediately and bring with you this dwarf that you have brought alive, healthy, and in good state from the land of spirits, for the god's dances, to rejoice the heart of the king, lord of Upper and Lower Egypt, Nofr-ka-Ra, living forever.

The instinct to follow rivers is still with us and can be testified to by the number of paths, roads and railway lines that hug them. These arteries are often forced to congregate by the valleys that like to squeeze the traveller, but there is more to the pull than mere practicality. The acclaimed naturalist and traveller, W.H. Hudson, who was born in rural Argentina in 1841 and ended his days in Worthing, felt that the most fascinating pastime of all was to follow a river from its source all the way to the coast.

A river will twist and turn as it etches into the land, unlike the straight, bulldozed glacial valleys. Each meander forms an impediment to its inclination to head downhill and the river tries hard to negotiate with this barrier. It erodes the banks it hits, picking up sediment and then dropping it in stiller waters downstream. The sinuous shape of the river is in flux.

On 3 August 1804 Captain William Clark, one half of the better known Lewis and Clark team, was chasing some turkeys when he came across a place where the Missouri river was working hard to change its own course. The banks were falling in as the river's current dashed the sides and Clark noticed the river building up deposits of the soils it had robbed from a bank downstream. He concluded that the river would break through the weakest spot in two years' time.

Where the river nears the sea it adopts a new shape, name and persona. Here the river becomes an estuary, a mix of fresh and saline water, and it broadens to form a triangle or delta (the word 'delta' here comes from the shape of the fourth letter of the Greek alphabet, a triangle). The estuary is still the river, but it has come under the might of the sea's salt water.

It is not a fair fight between freshwater and seawater. After heavy rains the river will push at the sea, but the latter enlists the support of the moon and besides, is in virtually limitless supply. If all the world's seawater was spread over the surface of the Earth evenly it would be over two kilometres deep; if the freshwater of the world was spread in the same way it would reach a depth of forty-five centimetres. The imbalance is clearest at the coast itself, where the tides are able to dictate the water's movement and the salt has such a powerful effect on all life it touches.

There are not many organisms that are happy to tolerate conditions that fluctuate between wet and dry, fresh and saline so as the land around the river changes under pressure from its salty tides, the life on its banks changes, too. Many terrestrial plants and animals give up as freshwater yields to salt, but specialists emerge to replace them: bladderwrack and bright orange lichens, worms that love the mud and birds that love the worms. The common shore-crab has evolved to cope and manages to survive in the upper reaches of an estuary, where the water is almost fresh, by adjusting the salt levels in its own blood. Thousands of bar-tailed godwits enjoy estuarine mud in Britain in winter, before returning to the Arctic in summer.

Rivers tinge the air with their odours and an estuary is a pair of sweaty gym shorts to the clean laundry of a freshwater stream. The medieval Arabic scholar, Ibn Juzayy, believed that the air in Basra was unhealthy, because the town was subject to a river where at high tide the salt water from the Arabian Gulf overpowered the sweet water (freshwater). This in turn made the inhabitants of Basra unhealthy and gave them yellow skin. He quotes a poet who had observed the same thing.

> A citron here amongst us shows
> The image of the lachrymose.
> So God hath clothed in sickly hue
> The Slaves of love – the Basrans too!

The medieval traveller, Ibn Battuta, who covered even more ground than his contemporary, Marco Polo, found a river playing a more positive role in Baghdad. For him the Tigris is the only thing of beauty in the city, acting like a mirror between its eastern and western quarters, or 'a necklace between two breasts'. The ability of a river to act as a mirror is as true in the wild as the town, but there is something sublime about seeing the upside down crenellations of a city skyline from a riverbank in twilight.

The pressure on space in a town and a river's adamant and volatile habits have forced us to try and mend, bend and straighten its ways. Bridges, canals, dams and locks persuade rivers to accommodate our ambitions. The river that gave birth to civilisations and then great metropolises can become a nuisance to later generations, who pen and cover it. It is fitting that the industrial revolution that spawned the wealth that oozes through cities now was itself born at Ironbridge on the river Severn. And it is ironic that one of the most vibrant temples to modern retail and commerce, Oxford Street in London, runs over a river that nobody can see, hear, smell, touch or taste. The more determinedly we cover over nature, the harder we need to scratch to reveal it again.

In the Second World War a German bomb fell on Oxford Street and allowed the Tyburn river to breathe again. Then it was covered over once more and ever since.

Water runs through the struggle between conservation and economic progress. Hydroelectric plans threatened the Cree people's hunting and fishing way of life in Quebec in the 1970s, and the Three Gorges Dam spanning the Yangtze river in China has caused consternation more recently. Flowing water forms the line between life and death, but also between one type of life and another.

The ancient Chinese philosopher Lao Tzu wrote that water does not strive, it flows and it flows in places that men reject and is therefore like the Tao. The flow of water is something that has fascinated many great minds, it is a natural form that effortlessly bridges the worlds of science, maths, art and literature. One of history's great polymaths, Leonardo da Vinci, was fascinated by the flow of water and his sketchbooks are filled with pictures of water in motion. These were not idle sketches, Leonardo was gripped by a desire to know more.

Jean Leray was a French mathematician, best known for his work in the field of topology undertaken in an Austrian prisoner of war camp in the Second World War. When the war ended Leray returned to France and took up a post at the University of Paris as a mathematics professor. In Paris Leray liked to pause on the Pont Neuf and gaze down into the swirls and eddies of the Seine below. The hypnotic dances that mesmerise were the ones that most intrigued Leray and he set about fathoming these patterns. Leray went on to become one of the great pioneers in understanding the way fluids behave.

There is a complex and daunting world of maths that models fluid behaviour awaiting those who are brave enough to venture there, but there is also one simple and beautiful relationship between flow and patterns in the water that was discovered near the end of the nineteenth century.

Water will flow past a pillar in smooth straight lines until it reaches a certain speed and then turbulent eddies suddenly form. The speed at which this happens is defined by something called the Reynolds number, which is calculated by multiplying the speed of the water with the diameter of the bridge's pillar and then dividing by the viscosity of the water. The beautiful and strange thing about this calculation is that all the units cancel each other out, the result is a dimensionless number, i.e. a number with no units attached to it at all.

When the Reynolds number exceeds 40, eddies form, but below that number the water will run smoothly. The speed of most rivers is such that the Reynolds number will regularly exceed one million, but in tidal rivers the water stops flowing twice each day before changing direction of flow and starting again. For a brief second at each high and low tide the water will move slowly enough past the pillars not to form eddies.

The tendency of fluids to become turbulent as described by the Reynolds number shapes everything from clouds in our sky to patterns in Jupiter and even the way bubbles rise in a champagne glass. This is clearly one of nature's numbers.

There is another apparently universal relationship between fluids and surfaces that shapes our environment and a distant alien environment, too. Whenever water runs down over a gently sloping grainy surface it will form into braided rivers, channels that loop in and out and converge, forming islands. There is a famous braided river in the South Island of New Zealand called the Waimakariri. There were also braided rivers on Mars.

The British photographic artist Susan Derges was as entranced by the flow of water as Leonardo da Vinci and Jean Leray, although her methods of enquiry were very different. Derges went to great lengths to capture a moment in the turbulence she saw. Realising that all photographs of water from the surface had so far failed to do justice to the wonder of its forms, she placed photographic paper between glass plates and then submerged this below the surface of the River Taw in Devon, at night. Next she lit up the water from above with a brief flash of light, allowing

The braided Waimakariri River in New Zealand

the photographic paper to capture the image of the underwater eddies.

While mathematicians can see the beauty in numbers, Derges' work is very much concerned with our more personal relationship with these flows. She underlined this by printing her images in a vertical format, reflecting a human scale. Derges wants us to get away from the idea of a view through an aperture or even an eye. The vertical format invites a more direct, immersive experience with the water. For Derges the turbulent flow of a river parallels the workings of our imagination.

Having spent time in Japan, Derges is familiar with the Taoist philosophy of appreciating the universal from the specific. The swirls in a river add Oriental philosophy to the mix of maths, literature, art and physics.

The complexity we find in the flow of rivers threatens to become too much, it might drown our minds, but there is an unlikely philosopher who can sum things up and save us from that fate.

Sometimes, if you stand on the bottom rail of a bridge and lean over to watch the river slipping slowly away beneath you, you will suddenly know everything there is to be known.

The name of this philosopher is Winnie the Pooh.

Lines in the Earth

Sehnsucht – the passion for what is ever beyond – is
livingly expressed in that white riband of possible travel
that severs the uneven country.

Robert Louis Stevenson

*In the distance a golden crop had lines running through it. The lines
were neither random nor anarchic, they criss-crossed and merged, ran
parallel in places and then diverged. I suspected the deer of having
had some fun.*

*The paths made by the animals in the field made me think back to the
quality of the tracks I had walked on so far. The best sensation had been
an unexpected patch of perfectly flat mud on the path that led away from
the River Arun. There, some long-gone farm machinery had compressed the
wet chalky mud, leaving it now dried as a perfectly flat table, with a glass-
like smoothness. It would have been possible to play snooker on its surface.
Only in a few places had this mysterious machine, capable of ironing mud,
left a few scratches in the surface. These parallel lines were like the striations of a glacier in rock.*

• • •

Roads, and even tracks and paths, evoke mixed feelings amongst
explorers. Ibn Battuta recoiled from the staleness of roads and
tried to avoid retracing any one he had travelled over before. By
way of contrast, the writer of science fiction and political novels,

H.G. Wells, assured us that there would be many footpaths in Utopia. And there were few sights that pleased Wordsworth more than a public road. The American author, Jim Harrison, thought that any trail that was not an animal trail was 'an insult to the perceptions' and Thoreau declared that roads were for horses and men of business, neither creature beloved by him. For the minimalist artist, Carl Andre, roads are pieces of sculpture.

Paths and roads offer us a way ahead but they also have a whiff of routine, of journeys that have been 'done' until the ground has become stained. Are these lines in the earth a lure for new adventure or the scars of indifferent feet and wheels? Tracks divide the land and they divide our thoughts. Some journeys are a search for something more than the chance to stop moving again and this is where roads are struck dumb. As the philosopher Alan Watts put it, 'To the mind which pursues every road to its end, every road leads nowhere.'

Our feelings about paths and roads are not static, they are influenced by our enjoyment of the feel of long grass brushing against our legs or cresting a hill in a convertible as the sea comes into view, minds full of of Steve McQueen in San Francisco. If we are merely the passive pedestrian being squeezed at the verge and choked and hoot-hooted at, our feelings are twisted in a contrary direction. We will feel differently about the same road at the start and end of a long day, and the bone weariness of a trudge along life's road provides a powerful metaphor for the poet, Christina Rossetti.

> Does the road wind up-hill all the way?
> Yes, to the very end.
> Will the day's journey take the whole long day?
> From morn to night, my friend.

Once there were no paths, and then the animals made them, and then the animal that wears shoes made its own. Animal tracks in wild places can delight and then frustrate, they draw you along, urging you to follow a confident line through the undergrowth and then they evaporate, as abruptly as they appeared. Animals are as interested in efficiency as humans, their lines have a logic and some of our first paths were formed by human feet stomping a firmer declaration on top of the animals' suggestions. But many others are not, for paths are always an invitation to follow a certain route and simultaneously a reflection of the intent of those who went before us. Animal and human intentions diverge and human ones are the more mysterious.

When a path is born its hold on life is tenuous and can be snuffed out by a handful of subsequent travellers choosing an alternative. The few who bring nascent paths into the world and fear for their wellbeing protect them by marking the route with cairns, stones in small heaps that remind all who follow that a path has been born and exists for them. Cairns can be made from any materials to hand and offer clues to the land the path is passing through. In Badakhshan, Marco Polo found tracks marked with piles of the horns and bones of the sheep that had fallen prey to the wolves that stalked all around.

If a path can be seen as an invitation to proceed, then for a few the absence of a path is an invitation to forge one. In a general sense this is the trade of the explorer of course, but on a more local level the process is full of intrigue. If you had walked into the Forest of Fontainebleau in the middle of the nineteenth century you might have encountered a small man, dressed in wood-coloured clothes, with an over-sized hat, spectacles and cheeks that were autumnal red with veins. This was Monsieur Claude-François Denecourt, a legend in the history of the Forest of Fontainebleau, whose name and ideas have reached well beyond that vast woodland.

Denecourt spent years pioneering paths in the forest, making a wilderness accessible and opening the eyes of many to what lay within. Keen not to arouse the ire of the authorities, he crept into the woods at night with a pot of paint concealed under his coat and a lamp at the ready. He then spent long hours painting blue arrows on rocks and trees to show the way for those who chose to follow. And this they did. Denecourt had marked the first trails for walkers and his legacy can be found in the many coloured and coded arrows and bright painted footprints that mark trails all over the world today.

For thousands of years, exploration for most people was accessible primarily through pilgrimage, the following of a specific route to a particular destination. Henry David Thoreau would have us believe the word 'saunter' derives from those who passed themselves off as pilgrims on their way to 'Sainte-Terre', but who in actual fact were 'idle people who roved about the country'. Thus, to have a purpose, to follow a true path, was respectable (and there was nothing more laudable than the route to a holy destination) but to amble off a path could be seen as degenerative behaviour. Many pooh-pooh Thoreau – the etymology of the word 'saunter' is not so clear – but holy places have certainly led pilgrims on long journeys and their feet have forged clear paths. One of the most famous in Europe in medieval times was the Way of St James, the pilgrimage route to the cathedral in Santiago de Compostela in Galicia, Spain. The path had been followed by the Romans and it is still a popular walking and pilgrimage route to this day.

In Venezuela, Humboldt witnessed an interesting moment in the adolescence of a path. He set off to climb La Silla peak and his guides told him that the track they were leading him along was a favourite of smugglers. It was also frequented by the militia who had been formed to chase off these traffickers. These mutual antagonists were being joined by a new category that Humboldt was himself spearheading, perhaps unknowingly: the leisure walker and their professional guides. A path that had been born as a route for contraband had now blossomed into a fuller and more rounded life.

Whether springing from holy yearnings or wicked trade, a path is a condensation of the wisdom and motivation of those who have gone before. If the purpose is efficiency then the path will be economical, direct where possible and utilitarian. But where the purpose is leisure, the line in the earth will be happy to take in small meanders for the sake of a view. Today the most popular routes in hillwalking country are not determined by their pragmatism but by the experience they offer the walker. Sometimes it is possible to spot where the practical path is being threatened by the enriching one: perhaps a fork offers one branch leading directly to the next village and one that takes a short detour with a view of a river.

Paths cannot distill a wisdom that was never there. They are not all-knowing, they do sometimes err. Tourists who visited Niagara Falls in the nineteenth century were underwhelmed by what they saw. The landscape designer Frederick Law Olmsted was hired to improve things. He altered the route and sequence that visitors followed and created a better experience for the visitor.

The relationship between the directness of a route and its history has a modern illustration in the roads we encounter in hill country. Older tracks are often straighter as those who travelled on foot or horse were quite content to be taken over the tops of hills, not least because this was where the paths became drier. Since the advent of the wheel and road-surfacing, impeding gradients could instead be circumnavigated with a sinuous road that hugged the hill. Clues are often to be found on a map, where the old road is marked running along the edge of field boundaries, but the newer roads cut through the fields themselves – any road that cuts through a field must be younger than the field.

The experience that a path or road offers will be shaped by more than the land it moves through; its surface will also influence our journey. Darwin enjoyed a 'gentle chirping noise' as his horse placed each hoof down on some fine siliceous sand in Brazil, but all too often we are only sensitive to the unpleasant intrusions from the track beneath us. The historian, Edward Gibbon, claimed to have been nearly killed as he travelled 'between Sheffield Place and East Grinsted, by hard, frozen, long, and cross ruts, that would disgrace the approach to an Indian wigwam.' The blind traveller, James Holman, tuned as ever to his other senses, liked to remain 'joyfully awake to the path itself' and was sensitive to the way a track would change with the passing seasons, as the soft snowmelt of March was firmed by a warming April.

The reputations of the worst roads reach out to us through the tales of those who have gone before. This is a tradition that has evolved into the droning traffic reports on the radio and surging tide of data on the Internet, but there was a time when the information was slightly less reliable and much richer. Over to the Chinese explorer Hsuan Tsang for the latest reports on the roads and weather in seventh century central Asia.

The roads are steep and dangerous, the cold wind is extremely biting, and frequently fierce dragons impede and molest travellers with their inflictions. Those who travel this road should not wear red garments nor carry loud-sounding calabashes. The least forgetfulness of these precautions entails certain misfortune. A violent wind suddenly rises with storms of flying sand and gravel; those who encounter them, sinking through exhaustion, are almost sure to die.

With each boot, carriage and car that passes, a track eats more deeply into the land around it. Roads sink lower than the land they pass through and can be found looking up at villages on either side of them. On the way to Alton, Gilbert White found roads that had worn their way down through eighteen feet of rock, exposing tangled roots and frozen streams that apparently frightened the ladies who passed that way. Modern roads have a vicious way of accelerating this process as rock is blasted out of the way, although this does at least allow a chance to inspect the rock strata on either side of a road.

The life at the roadside will reflect the artery throbbing through the land. Few plants can survive in the centre of paths and only a minority are happy to endure the constant trudging along the edges, but a few hardy types persevere. In the UK we might find pineapple weeds and greater plantains braving the verges.

It is not all take, though, the pedestrian will also bring some life to a path. Patrick Whitefield reports that in Wales the best blackberries are found along the edges of old drovers' roads. The drovers had the choice of blackberries throughout the day and could afford to be very selective. They picked and ate only the best berries, whose seeds passed through to the other end of the drover and were deposited by the roadside, coming to life as the next generation of fruit.

We carry seeds across continents, too. The botanist and explorer to whom Darwin first told his theory of evolution, Sir Joseph Dalton Hooker, found the shepherd's purse weed growing alongside the path he was following in India. These weeds are common in Britain but are not native to India. He concluded that they must have been exported unwittingly.

The salt that we scatter on the roads each winter deters ice and many species of plant, but it welcomes in coastal plants like the Danish scurvygrass that lines motorways with small white flowers in spring. There are young apple trees to be found alongside the same motorways and train tracks too, the descendants of the cores that flew out of windows at great speed.

Choosing mechanised transport will seal off many opportunities for connecting with the land we pass through, but it will also bring some new perspectives. A hermetically sealed and air-conditioned car might not be quite the thrilling ride that a Tuareg nomad experiences aloft a camel, but the car will pass through much more scenery than a camel and so is not a total loss to those who remain aware. It's a shame, but we become inured to new modes of transport so very quickly. Barely one hundred years ago many a traveller would have been happy to give a year's wages for the opportunity to climb on board a flying machine and yet now we immerse ourselves in inflight magazines and plug our eyes and ears with piped entertainment. We do anything, in fact, to avoid the extraordinary view out of the window. The train journey has become sullied by associations with commuting and the need to get to meetings in towns. The romance has been leached out, but it would do us a lot of good to remind ourselves how foreign these iron road-dragons are.

The Sioux Native American, Plenty Kill, lived from 1868 to 1939 and became known as Luther Standing Bear. He remembered a Sioux scout reporting that 'a big snake was crawling across the prairie'. This snake was the Union Pacific Railroad. In 1879 Standing Bear was playing with some friends near some government buildings when he noticed two other Sioux boys who were dressed as the white man dressed. Standing Bear was persuaded to join the boys and go east with a government agent, who was armed with sticks of candy, to be taught 'the ways of the white man'. He found himself aboard a train for the first time. The older boys teased the smaller boys that the white people were taking them to the place where the sun rises and would kill them by tipping them over the edge of a world they all believed was flat.

Standing Bear looked at the full moon ahead of them as they headed east. It did appear to be growing larger and he worried that they were getting too close to it. Very tired, he dozed off for a while before being woken by the older boys who said they had made a discovery. They told the younger boys to look out of the window.

We did so, and the moon was now behind us! Apparently we had passed the place where the moon rose! This was quite a mystery. The big boys were now singing brave songs again, while I was wide awake and watchful, waiting to see what was going to happen. But nothing happened.

We afterward learned that at Harrisburg, Pennsylvania, the train turned due west to Carlisle, which placed the moon in our rear. And to think we had expected to be killed because we had passed the moon.

Train journeys can remind us that the parts of a mundane journey that seem to offer nothing but frustration can provide windows if we look for them. John Muir became one of America's most revered naturalists not because of the extraordinary things he saw, but because of his extraordinary desire to see things. Once, when delayed for five hours between trains in Chicago he managed to spend the time botanising in some vacant lots nearby.

Rails, roads and paths might raise some grievances if they could speak to us. The words 'taken for granted' and 'under-appreciated' would doubtless surface at any meeting. A road finds it hard to win. If a road proves popular it becomes a victim of its own success and is chastised for its popularity, in the UK we need think only of the M25. But if it is unpopular then it is an unnecessary blight on the landscape.

If we could wish the paths, roads and railway lines away, we would doubtless feel a rush, a giddy abandon at the opportunities to wander the virgin land without the ushering and coagulating of the lines in the earth. This dizzy freedom might become intoxicating very quickly so that we forgave our old friends, the roads. All who have struck off the path know how quickly a liberating stroll can turn to a desperate sense of being lost. They will also know the joy that follows fear on finding a tempting way to guide them back.

Time

> Nobody sees a flower, really, it is so small, we haven't time . . .
>
> Georgia O'Keeffe

There was a moment when, sitting, looking through the rusty leaves of some dock, my eyes were drawn to a pattern in the grass on the opposite hill. I began to wonder. How long I would need on that grassy spot before I became fully aware of my surroundings? The problem then occurred to me that everything would have changed before I managed to come close to achieving that level of awareness. The light on the hill opposite had altered even as these thoughts formed. The sheep below had no intention of staying still for my convenience, either. Is this daunting feeling what landscape painters experience?

Even if I did spend long enough in that one spot to really know it in that moment, how long would it take to know it throughout the year? I remembered walking these same slopes, the ones now dry under the sun, in Wellington boots. The deep snow had still managed to drop down inside the rubber and melt into my socks.

I pulled a small lump of chalk from under a buttock. It rolled in my palm for a second. The chalk was formed 90 million years ago, from creatures that had lived and died before that. I let it fall onto the path, before that line of enquiry took me back to atoms and then the Big Bang.

• • •

A change in light is one way of marking time, as Jesus demonstrated in the way he prayed. Jesus needed to pray at the correct times according to the scriptures. Morning prayer was signalled by the cock crowing at dawn, the middle of the day was determined by the sun reaching its highest point in the sky and evening prayers came when he could make out three stars. When it was too cloudy to make out stars, Jesus was still able to use the shifting light to read time: he waited until he could no longer tell the difference between a blue thread and a black one. Time brings change. Even the mountains that seem to stand for permanence when measured against our brief stay on the planet, are in a state of flux, rising and being worn away.

Change brings us many things, but it also snatches them back; we cannot hold on to a moment, we are powerless to stop it falling away. The desire to fight this can be seen in the banks of faux-clicking digital cameras marshalled by contemporary holidaymakers, tiny tools for trying to beat back the slow rolling boulder of time. A photo of a sunset cannot stop the shifting scents and ebbing heat from rolling past the lens.

Later we must wrestle with the fact that our minds, bodies and perspectives change with each passing moment, which brings the realisation that even if two sunsets could appear identical, which they cannot, they could never feel identical. For now, it will be a fair challenge to appreciate the beats of the drums that our environment dances to.

Experiencing the passing of time is not difficult but explaining its meaning is. St Augustine of Hippo summed up the challenge well when he wrote. 'What then is time? If no one asks me, I know: if I wish to explain it to one that asketh, I know not.'

Parcels of time are far easier to define than time in the abstract, as they are all rooted in the sky. On 24 March 1800 Alexander von Humboldt and his entourage left the Venezuelan town of Calabozo. That afternoon they stumbled across the body of a twelve- or thirteen-year-old girl, stretched out and lying on her back in the savannah, completely naked. She was still alive, but exhausted and dehydrated. Her eyes, nose and mouth were filled with sand.

Humboldt attempted to revive her with some of the water and wine that their mule was carrying. Regaining consciousness, the girl was initially terrified to find herself so vulnerable and surrounded by so many strangers. When she had calmed down she looked to the sky and explained from the shift in the sun's position that she must have fainted and lain unconscious for several hours.

The poor girl had been suffering from a long illness and had recently been sacked by the hacienda owner that she worked for. Humboldt offered her a lift on a mule, but she refused, accepting only a refill of water in her jar, before disappearing into the distance on foot. Humboldt noted that she was not only inured to suffering, but that she lived for the moment, with no thought to the future.

The unfortunate girl had managed to communicate her experience of time with Humboldt because of their shared experience and understanding of the sun's passage across the sky. She, unlike Humboldt, was probably not conscious of the fact that this was being caused by the Earth's daily rotation, but this did not matter. The passage of time for humans, animals and plants is defined by the sky as it appears, not the science behind it: a day stretches from sunrise to sunset regardless of what astronomers discover about the cause of these phenomena. However philosophically shattering the heliocentric revolution of Copernicus was, it did not change the way people experienced the passing of a day.

Each sunrise and sunset is slightly different from the previous one. Everywhere in the world the position of sunrise and sunset travels north from December to June and then south again from June to December. The days grow longer in the northern hemisphere as the sun travels north and it rises higher in the sky each day. These are the physical changes in the sun's behaviour that we can note with the passing of the seasons. The annual cycle marked by the change in sunrise and sunset positions, the height of the sun, length of days and seasons all find their cause in the Earth's orbit around the sun.

The summer solstice, around 21 June, is when the North Pole is tilted as much as it ever is towards the sun and the winter solstice, around 22 December, is the turn of the South Pole. The four points that punctuate our daily and annual existence are sunrise, sunset and the two solstices. These are the moments that corral the majority of events that we know as cyclical. Plants and animals, including humans, are all marshalled in some way by these four points in time. From the sighs of workers as they hit their alarms to the groans of timber as a great oak begins another spring's heave up and out: the solar drum beats.

Pliny the Elder noticed that thyme flowered around the summer solstice, that the sheep came to graze on it, on the stony plains of Gallia Narbonsensis and that the thyme flowers also drew the bees. Here is a moment in the cycle when land, plants and animals come together, all dancing to Earth's orbit around the sun, but each probably oblivious to this great clock.

The clock can be read beyond the sun: the stars also rise and set at different times of the year. Pliny noticed that bees went into hibernation when the Pleiades set and woke up when these seven stars rose again. The annual habits of the stars had been appreciated since the earliest times by all whose work depended on understanding the plants' relationship with the annual cycle. This same constellation of Pleiades finds its way into *Works and Days*, the great poem of the ancient Greek writer Hesiod.

When the Pleiades, daughters of Atlas, are rising, begin your harvest, and your ploughing when they are going to set. Forty nights and days they are hidden and appear again as the year moves round, when first you sharpen your sickle.

Works and Days is a cautionary poem, which gave contemporaries guidance into the nature of peasant work, but for us it is a rich source of insight into the methods and habits of the era: it captures time. Immediately after explaining the seasonal rhythms as measured by the stars, Hesiod warns that those that failed to heed this advice to work hard and in step with the seasons would starve.

Between the daily and annual posts driven into the ground by the sun there are monthly patterns that are more loosely shepherded by the moon. Unlike the stars, the moon appears to move across the sky more slowly than the sun. If the sun and moon are in line one day, then the sun will have overtaken the moon the following day. After a couple of days the moon will have slipped back sufficiently to emerge from the glare of the sun and be just visible for the most observant to the east of it, as a very thin crescent. Five more days after this it will be lagging behind the sun by half the visible sky and appear as a waxing half of a disc. Seven days later it will have fallen so far behind that it is now opposite the sun as they both wheel across the sky, which is why it reflects all the sun's light and appears as a full moon. Two weeks later the sun has caught up with the tardy moon, it is new moon once more and the cycle starts afresh.

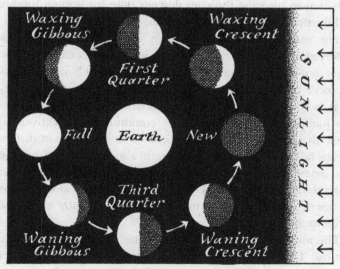

The phases of the moon

There are not as many cycles on Earth that are driven by this monthly circuit (it takes 29 and a half days from new moon to new moon) and the tides are the best known of these. There are a few lunar cycles in the animal kingdom and unsurprisingly they are mostly related to the sea, like the palolo worms of the South Pacific, whose breeding cycle is dictated by both sun and moon. This worm lives in crevices in coral reefs and reproduces by dividing. Reproduction is triggered by the moon's phases in October and November.

Lunar influences on natural cycles are discovered regularly by scientists, but for each discovery of a natural phenomenon there is probably an artificial one too. The regular appearance of the new moon is too neat a marker and breaks the long annual cycle up too well for it to have been ignored by humans. It features particularly strongly in the Islamic calendar.

The moon has long been held by distinct cultures across the world to have a connection with menstruation and the womb. Ishi, the last survivor of the Yahi people, explained to anthropologists that in his tribe the convalescent time for women following childbirth was dictated by the moon.

The moon acts as a particularly convenient calendar when different cultures need to communicate with each other about time, but lack a common language for it. When the French explorer Jacques Cartier was exploring the St Lawrence river in what is now Quebec in the first half of the sixteenth century he was hampered by his inability to communicate effectively with the native population. With no common units of time or distance, he was failing to learn anything useful about the river from those who knew it best. A breakthrough was made when the locals managed to explain to him that he could navigate along the river for three moons: Cartier understood this instantly as meaning three months.

The ability to gauge time is only one small part of its appreciation. Time is a key to understanding the richness in many of the fluctuations that engulf us. Colin Pittendrigh, a pioneer in researching biological clocks, hinted at the philosophical hurdles that appear when we fully appreciate time's role in nature.

A rose is not necessarily and unqualifiedly a rose; that is to say, it is a very different biochemical system at noon and at midnight.

Each species of flower follows an individual circadian rhythm, but their respective dependability led the Swedish botanist, Carl Linnaeus, to propose a flower clock in 1751. Linnaeus proposed that the varying opening times of each flower could be used to tell the time: Goat's Beard would mark 3.00a.m., Rough Hawkbit 4.00a.m., Dandelion 5.00a.m. through to Sand Spurrey at 9.00 to 10.00a.m. The flowers' closing times were also staggered and marked the end of the day. These were the times that Linnaeus proposed for Uppsala, where he taught. At different latitudes the times of opening and closing would need to be amended, but latitude has this effect on all clocks and dials that take their cue from the sun.

The end of the day is also signalled in non-visual ways by flowers that fill the air at dusk with their scents, like jasmine and Evening Primrose.

The seasonal cycle of plants is familiar to most, but the way plants responded to the seasons was a mystery until scientists in America solved the problem in the 1920s. The most obvious clue to seasonal change, the rising and falling of temperature, is too volatile for plants to depend on it for their major seasonal efforts, like the production of leaves or flowers – shock frosts and heat-waves would throw a plant out of sync in a life-threatening way. For temperate plants at least, the length of day is a much more dependable way of gauging season and this regulation of stages through the use of light is known as photoperiodism. A plant's secondary stages, such as the blossoming of its flowers, can then be triggered more safely by changes in temperature.

It turned out that plants do not actually keep track of the length of day, but the length of night. This knowledge is now used by commercial plant growers to trick the plants into believing it is a different season. A light bulb switched on at night in a greenhouse for only a couple of minutes is enough to fool a crop of strawberries into believing that they have just experienced two very short nights instead of one long one – winter has been turned into summer in seconds.

Photoperiodism in plants is not limited to their world, but spills into the lives of all animals, not least those that drive tractors. Wheat flowers as the days get longer, barley as the days get shorter; the colour of land and the rhythms followed by the farmer are being shaped by the length of the night.

The animal kingdom's sensitivity to the annual cycle was documented as long ago as 13,000 BC by the Cro-Magnon people in southwest France. Paleolithic paintings in the Font de Gaume cave in the Dordogne show bison, mammoth and reindeer migrating across this region. In a much colder part of the northern hemisphere the seasons are marked precisely by the sound of hooves on the ground: reindeer in Lapland make an annual migration, and amazingly they seem to depart on the same day each year, the 29th of July.

David Thompson, the English explorer of Canada, found himself squeezed by the seasonal habits of two animals of very different size. As summer passed and the temperature dropped, Thompson felt some relief as the number of insects that had plagued him and his fellow team members also fell. 'The myriads of tormenting flies allow no respite, and we see the cold months advance with something like pleasure, for we can now enjoy a book, or a walk.' But in early winter the cold had not fully set in and this prevented one large creature from hunting for its favourite meal, forcing it to scavenge and hunt closer to Thompson and his colleagues. 'Our enemy the polar bear was prowling about, the sea not being sufficiently frozen to allow him to catch seals.'

The animals punctuate the daily cycle as they follow its cues.

The king-of-the-morning cockerel was replaced for Ludwig Leichhardt in Australia by something more colourful still.

> I usually rise when I hear the merry laugh of the laughing-jackass (Dacelo gigantea), which, from its regularity, has not been unaptly named the settlers' clock.

It is not just the actions of plants and animals that mark time, more subtle shifts can be picked up in colours and shades. We enjoy the purple that emerges from a beech forest seen from a hill as winter sets in or the shifts in tone that moulting of animal fur will reveal as warmth returns. Nan Shepherd noticed that hares change colour from brown to white to offer better camouflage for the winter season's snows, but that sometimes their clock is not set perfectly and the change comes too early, 'Breaking suddenly into a hollow, I have counted twenty white hares at a time streaking up a brown hillside like rising smoke'.

There are some creatures that refuse to be governed by either the daily or the annual markers. Among the noisy cicada family of insects are two that keep intriguing inner-clocks. One emerges from beneath the surface of the ground every thirteen years and the other every seventeen years. They feed underground on the roots of trees and detect each passing season by being sensitive to the blossoming habits of the tree. (In experiments where a tree was manipulated to blossom twice in one year the cicadas emerged a year early.) But nobody yet knows how they count up to thirteen or seventeen. The numbers thirteen and seventeen are themselves interesting as they are both prime numbers, which means that any predator would struggle to predict their emergence by any smaller factor of years. An animal that expected to find these cicadas every three or four years would miss them very regularly, perhaps taking fifty years to get it right.

While we will always be happy to wallow in the delusion that the animals are shepherded by us, this is not a one-way game. Marco Polo observed that the Tartars moved with the seasons to improve the grazing for their livestock, but also to avoid the horseflies of the summer. This is something that might bring a smile to the faces of the thousands who voluntarily head into the Scottish Highlands during the summer each year and take on peak midge season.

We may move to accommodate time, but our battle to manage time itself has turned on us. We can trace the measurement of time, from 4,000-year-old sundials through the mechanical clocks that started appearing seven hundred years ago, to the atomic clocks that will lose less than one second in 10 billion years. Never has a creature trapped this mercurial substance more tightly, and never has it gripped a people more savagely. Many would like to turn these accurate clocks back a bit and there is an African proverb that captures this idea. 'The white man has the clock, but the African has the time.'

We appear to be more conscious than other species that our time is finite, we can never 'remount the river of our years', and to compound this consciousness we have created systems that measure time exactly. We also separate ourselves from the animal kingdom by creating endless occupations that devour every second of our lives. Time's greatest irony might be that ancient peoples found the time to stop and stare at the great celestial clocks in the sky, while we are too busy for that, barely glancing at very accurate digital clocks as we rush around. One poem by the Roman writer Plautus would suggest that even the ancients were not immune, and that the problem has been creeping up on us for many years.

> The gods confound the man who first found out
> How to distinguish hours! Confound him, too,
> Who in this place set up a sun-dial,
> To cut and hack my days so wretchedly
> Into small portions. When I was a boy
> My belly was my sun-dial; one more sure,
> Truer, and more exact than any of them.

> This dial told me when 'twas proper time
> To go to dinner, when I had aught to eat.
> But now-a-days, why, even when I have,
> I can't fall-to, unless the sun give leave.
> The town's so full of these confounded dials,
> The greatest part of its inhabitants,
> Shrunk up with hunger, creep along the streets.

Perhaps 'busyness' is the preferred response because deeper contemplation of time is too terrifying. It is hard not to feel insignificant when we measure our short sojourn on the planet against that of the Giant Sequioas, some of which were casting shade a thousand years before Rome had a Republic. But even these mighty arboreal monuments wilt against the story of geological change as it is served up in its epochs, eras, aeons and super-aeons, parcels of time so weighty that our minds struggle not to be crushed by the mere attempt to conceptualise them.

The oldest rocks on Earth are four billion years old and are located in parts of Canada, Western Australia and Greenland. The oldest rocks in the UK are found in the northwest of Scotland and date back as far as 2.9 billion years ago. In the eighteenth century, James Hutton looked out at the layers on layers of rock that were visible in the Scottish mountains and used this awesome message of time to galvanise himself into becoming one of the founding fathers of geology as we now know it. With the knowledge we now have of geology we can pick up a smooth grey pebble on the shore, and by gazing at the thin white lines that run across it, allow ourselves to be taken back over two hundred million years to the deposits forming in the Paleozoic era.

However we look at time during our waking hours, it is likely to frighten us, and when we rest our heads at the end of a day, at the time dictated by the earth's rotation relative to the sun, and consider how the day went, we realise that we are about to slip into temporary unconsciousness and so give one third of our short time away to sleep, that 'brother of death'. If this thought keeps us awake, then we can at least decide to give the sheets a rest from our restlessness by stepping outside in the hope that some fresh air will bring on drowsiness. Breathing in the cool night air, we gaze up and catch sight of the milky smudge in the Andromeda constellation that is the Andromeda Galaxy. This galaxy is 2.5 million light years away, so the light we see is actually the galaxy as it was 2.5 million years ago. From pebbles under our feet to the scintillating night canopy so very far above our heads, time taunts us. We cannot escape it, so we must somehow learn to love it.

If looking at time in a linear way is too much to bear then perhaps American Indian philosophy may offer a solution: everything of importance that occurs is part of a cycle and time is no exception. Hehaka Sapa of the Oglala Sioux, also known as Black Elk, pointed out the attractive foundation of this idea: the wind whirls, the sun and moon move in circles, birds make circular nests and the life of man is circular, from childhood to childhood. Some American Indian languages lack words for past or future, since everything exists in the cyclical present.

Whether or not we choose to subscribe fully to a philosophy of time as cyclical, it has one cyclical aspect that colours every journey. Time's march is always accompanied by both decay and regeneration. Around 10,000 BC the majority of the population of northwestern Europe lived in an area of plains known as Doggerland. This was the land that joined Britain to northern Europe before the sea levels rose after the last Ice Age. This whole area is now underwater. But as one civilisation is destroyed or displaced, another emerges. Cities grow and wither or grow and grow again. Rome was once mighty and today is again seen as one of the great cities of the world, but when the founder of the *Spectator* magazine, Joseph Addison, visited at the start of the eighteenth century he was aghast at the desolation he found in the city and surrounding countryside.

The power of this decay and regeneration can be seen by looking among the bays, coves and creeks of a place visited in

September 1609 by the English explorer Henry Hudson. Hudson admired the mighty oaks of the area, its poplars and hickories too. There was plentiful fruit ready to drop from the plum trees at that time of year and when full bellies made them feel sluggish, Hudson and his companions could enjoy resting on the grass between the trees and by the side of cool freshwater brooks. This idyll of natural abundance is now The Bronx, Brooklyn and Queens areas of New York City.

The trees of New York may have felt the axe, but trees remain powerful symbols of regeneration, of nature's ability to wrestle time. Laurens van der Post certainly felt this as he came across Mapani trees on a plain, 'They are a brave sight. I know of no tree which partakes so deeply of the nature of Africa, and is so identified with its indomitable spirit of renewal.'

The English travel writer, Charlotte Anne Eaton, visited the battlefield of Waterloo only a month after the battle and found a predictable scene of carnage: heaps of burning bodies, pistol holsters filled with blood and a hand, reduced almost to skeleton, stretching out of the earth as if rising from a grave. She also found trees torn to pieces during the battle and some with more than thirty scars from cannonballs, but it was these same trees that offered her some hope for the future.

> The broken branches were strewed around; the green beech leaves fallen before their time, and stripped by the storm of war, not by the storm of nature, were scattered over the surface of the ground, emblematical of the fate of the thousands who had fallen on the same spot in the summer of their days. The return of spring will dress the wood of Hougoumont once more in vernal beauty, and succeeding years will see it flourish.

The natural world's resilience and reinvention does more than signal hope, it provides endless precursors of the future. With an ear close to the ground, the sounds of wet grasses and mosses springing up from underfoot are so clearly the bubbles popping at the top of a fizzy drink that it is a wonder Coca-Cola was not invented before the wheel. When the next billion-dollar invention comes along we will find it already etched in some rural landscape, blueprints whispering to us across a plain, 'I told you so.'

Close to our minds and hearts are our own deaths, and our sex lives. One cuts our time short, the other allows us the feeling of cheating it. Organisms that manage the life cycle seamlessly, like some lichens and corals, appear to live forever. We are a long way from such tidy attempts to project ourselves into the future. The lichens colonise a rock and feel a few thousand years pass as we die in plagues, wars and car crashes, but somehow live again through sexual reproduction that lurches from fun to functional and back, through predilections and inefficiencies. A journey might make us confront the pornography and sexual mores of another culture, which can leave a bitter taste or we may smile as we find another pool of genes that are also keen to cheat time, however inefficiently.

Change is the only thing that time offers us with certainty and so embracing it would seem a simultaneously philosophical and pragmatic way to enjoy the things we observe on our journeys to their fullest. This may be easier for some cultures than others, though. The religious and philosophical traditions of the West have seeped into our subconscious and given us a dislike, if not fear, of change that the East does not fully share. Christianity is a religion that blossomed in cities – the original meaning of the word 'pagan' was 'country-dweller' – and cities foster a spirit of battling to impose permanence, whereas rural-living becomes an accommodation with inevitable change, the cycles of the seasons and of life and death. Buddhism is characterised by an embrace of change.

In March 1835 a young Charles Darwin was studying rocks in the mountains of Chile. He visualised the landscape around him in strata, layers of time. Later that day, when Darwin and his travelling companions encountered several herds of cattle being shepherded down the mountain, they realised that the locals were telling them indirectly that winter was approaching. They decided it would be prudent to descend with them to the lower slopes and Darwin cut his geologising short. In the valleys there was not much in the way of vegetation, birds or insects, but Darwin was able to enjoy the end of season alpine flowers.

Darwin's account of his experiences in his book, *The Voyage of the Beagle*, remains an accessible and vibrant read. They have survived the man. Time won the battle with the human being, as it always does, but it has so far failed to snuff out his works. The creative arts are one more way we try to cheat death, beat time and satisfy an ache for immortality, and creativity is a recurrent response to the natural world. For the many who never met the man, Gauguin's colour-saturated images of the Pacific live on more vividly in their minds than their creator.

One of the perennial opportunities presented by travel is that we can at least attempt to use our time in a more controlled fashion than during the normal course of our lives. Therefore, indirectly, we ought to have more control over our feelings about it. We can choose to stop in one place and stare at rocks, leaves or clouds for hours on end, or we can set ourselves the challenge of fitting as much as possible into a time frame, perhaps even racing across a continent. Those who choose the latter may view the former as a waste of time and vice versa. Each person must find their own accommodation with time. There are no clear morals available from its study. But there are some practices that seem to help.

If the fear of time in our travels is too much to bear, it is probably a good idea to think less and do more. If we wish to heighten the fear we can do less and think more. If a fear of the future is the specific problem, a haunting sense that this journey of ours amounts to little more than the dust that is blown across these rocks from other aeons, then it may be a good idea to write, paint and have sex, and to do all three as well as possible.

Language

Language is the dress of thought.

Samuel Johnson

The country I was walking through was rich with 'hams' and 'stokes', traditional English words for settlements. I had begun my walk near the village of North Stoke, across the river was South Stoke and beyond them behind a hill lay Burpham, its name meaning either 'place by the water' or 'defended settlement'.

I passed the purple flowers of the nettle-like black hoarhound and far from making me want to stoop to inspect the plant, it made me look up and to the south. Its castle made the town of Arundel easy to spot from all of the high ground. One theory is that its name derives from the abundance of hoarhound in its valley, making it a 'hoarhound-dell'. I then looked higher, but could not find the bird I was hoping to spot. There is a swallow on the Arundel crest, and the French for swallow is 'hirondelle', which is the other likely source for the name.

• • •

The missionaries at the Capuchin convent in the Caripe mountains of Venezuela held religious classes for the indigenous Indians of the area. When Humboldt was bored one day he tagged along to one of the classes and witnessed a scene that is strangely familiar to all travellers.

The Indians' language was very different to Spanish and

consequently a lot of the Spanish words sounded alike to them. The missionary teacher lost his temper as he tried desperately to explain that the words 'invierno' and 'infierno' were not the same: 'winter', the priest puffed, was definitely not the same as 'hell'. The missionary's efforts were in vain, he totally failed to explain the difference in sounds or meanings and since winter meant the rainy season to the Indians, they could not be parted from their belief that hell was an extraordinarily rainy place.

Language can be a means and a barrier to understanding each other as well as a key to unlocking hidden significance. The lessons that Humboldt witnessed were called 'doctrina' by the Spanish missionaries. It is a word that carries a heavy meaning, without translation, across the language divide to English. Words can unlock the nature, culture, history and geography of a place.

The Amazon, that most South American of rivers, was named by the Spanish explorer, Francisco de Orellana, in 1541. After encountering tribes of female warriors, he chose to name the river after the female warriors of ancient Greek mythology. The river's name betrays the cultural influences and Eurocentric views of one of its explorers.

There is a river in Turkey called the Buyuk Menderes. Its name contains within it a clue to the geography and history of the area. The 'Menderes' part of the name comes from its classical Greek name of 'Maiandros'. The river flows into a broad, flat-bottomed valley at Saraykoy, where it does what all rivers do in flat valleys, it twists and turns. It meanders. Over time its name was borrowed to mean this characteristic of twisting and turning.

Rivers are a good example of a feature that so marks and defines a landscape that it cannot be separated from it. The importance of the features to a landscape can be felt in the retention of local words for them. When all other words in a local language or dialect have surrendered to a dominant new tongue, these words frequently survive. So we find the streams adopting new names as we move around the UK. There are brooks in Cumbria and Lancashire and burns in Scotland. The becks and gills in the north of England owe their allegiance to Old Norse (and place names ending –by or –thorp have likely played host to Scandinavian guests in the past).

Popular expressions can also contain clues to the land. Patrick Whitefield makes the claim that the expression 'chalk and cheese' stems from the difference between the two starkly different landscapes of the West Country, one well-draining and the home of sheep and the other a heavier clay, ideal for grazing and dairy farming.

We can find clues in much smaller forms too. The common 'daisy' flower is a corruption of the 'Day's Eye', the name it earned for its habit of opening at the start of each day and closing at its end. Once we know the etymology it deepens our relationship with this humble plant.

Names can alter perceptions. Who can see anything but beauty in a shooting star? They lose a little of this beauty when described with the expression, 'the piss of the stars'. This is what the Indians that Humboldt encountered near the Orinoco called them. Dew was no less romantically described as the 'spit of the stars'.

Sometimes there is as much fascination in the gaps we find in languages as in the words themselves. Why did the Romans have no word for the colour grey? Why did the Japanese take so long to invent a word for the colour blue?

When our knowledge of languages fails us, our relationships with local people will also change. Humboldt was warned before leaving a mission in Uruana that he would become a mute, rendered dumb by the absence of European languages or translators amongst the inhabitants in the area he was heading into. Humboldt was forced to communicate through sign language. Instead of hampering his efforts to relate to the indigenous population, this development had an unexpected benefit.

Humboldt had grown tired of the apathy of the Indians who had served him as interpreters and the daily struggle he faced to understand what was being said through their half-hearted responses, but it was only when he was forced to do without interpreters altogether that he discovered the real problem. He had assumed that the difficulties in communication all lay in language barriers, but there was a simpler, more human explanation. The interpreters had tired of being used as a means to an end and once Humboldt was forced to go without an interlocutor, once he was compelled to communicate with the Indians directly, they delighted in the interest being paid to them as people. They opened up and became enthusiastic and, despite the need for sign language, communication actually improved.

Leichhardt assumed a direct relationship between the natural geography of the land he travelled through and the languages spoken within it. On 5 December 1845 and nearing the end of his journey, he wrote, 'The natives seemed to speak a less melodious language, which might be ascribed to the mountainous character of their country.' Although it is hard to credit this observation with any definite truth, it becomes harder still to refute it entirely when we let some of the words he collected there roll on our tongues: Kobboyakka, Nobungop, Kanbinycx, Manguradja, Apirk, Yaganyin, Kolar, Kadgupa, Gnanga Gnanga . . . Do we not feel closer to the land he describes through these sounds? Do they not somehow contain the land itself?

Styles of speaking and expressions come to assume meanings within countries, towns and smaller communities, and they develop between two people. When one of Leichhardt's party, Charley, returned from a foray to search out a safe descent through some rocks, Leichhardt asked him how he had got on. Charley replied that he had found a descent but that it was 'very far off'. Leichhardt entered his thoughts on hearing this, to his diary. 'This "very far off" of Charley was full of meaning which I well understood.' Leichhardt had learned to read the significance of Charley's speech beyond the words themselves, he had become familiar with Charley's personal use of them. Each person uses styles of speech including slang, exaggeration and irony, in differing measures. We come to understand these over time as surely as we become more comfortable with new accents.

Languages are alive and, like pets, their health reflects the care of those who keep them. Words and expressions are born, they change, grow old and die. Like people, words come to assume the character of the places they inhabit. As Rebecca Solnit has pointed out, the word 'street' no longer means just a road with houses on either side, it has assumed the 'rough magic' of those who live there, it has become a word that evokes the common, the erotic and the dangerous. It is a word with edge.

Like animals, languages move and spread their reach. Leichhardt noticed that the use of English words grew as he got closer to his destination of Port Essington. British influence was spreading beyond the Port through the English language, it reached beyond the politics or the law of the land with a life of its own. This is a process that has accelerated with globalisation. The areas of the world where the words 'Coca-Cola' mean nothing shrink each year.

There are limited resources for languages to feed off and if a dominant language comes into an area and outcompetes a native language, then the older language may starve and wither. It is maddening and saddening for those who feel protective of their native tongues to see them suffer in this way, and although it is not a new process it is hard not to sympathise with the underdog in each of these cultural struggles. There is a bully lurking in languages that displace others and we can smell its unpleasant attitudes in the words of Samuel Johnson.

The conversation of the Scots grows every day less unpleasing to the English; their peculiarities wear fast away; their dialect is likely to become in half a century provincial and rustic, even to themselves. The great, the learned, the ambitious, and the vain, all cultivate the English phrase, and the English pronunciation, and in splendid companies Scotch is not much heard, except now and then from an old lady.

The suffering of a language so often mirrors the melancholy of a people. Bundled with the sadness, there is undeniably a morbid fascination in watching something that reflects life wither. It is like watching a very slow car crash.

Humboldt was told of a parrot that lived in the Maypures region of the upper Orinoco. It was famous as the last surviving speaker of a local Indian language. Nobody could understand what the parrot was saying, but they recognised it as having a vocabulary that it had learned from the very recently extinct Atures tribe.

In 1835 the priests on the Californian mainland travelled over to San Nicolas island and transported off the Indians who had settled there. As their boat was departing, a mother noticed that her baby had been left behind in the confusion and the captain of the boat was implored to return. He deemed it too risky to go back and continued on his course towards the mainland. The mother leapt overboard in desperation and swam for the island to rescue her baby. All on board assumed that the poor woman had perished in the waves.

Eighteen years later, sealers spotted a lone woman on the island and a boat was dispatched to rescue her. Everyone who had been carried off the island had since died. Her baby had also died. She was the last surviving member of her tribe and there was nobody left who could speak her language. She died a few months after being taken to the mainland, possibly the loneliest woman in the world. Before she died, four of her words were noted down and used posthumously to identify her as being from the Shoshonean tribe, a different tribe altogether from the one that the missionaries had long believed. The final four words of her language told the world something of the identity of the people who had passed away with them.

Companions

They don't do that in Haywards Heath!

Colin Thubron

I had not once felt lonely on the walk. Everyone feels lonely after a certain amount of time, it is the time that varies, not our vulnerability to the feeling. In my case it is usually at the longer end of the spectrum. I have spent weeks without seeing another person and not felt lonely, but I have also felt that familiar chill of loneliness during a short walk in central London. Loneliness likes to pick its own moment, it is its own timekeeper.

● ● ●

When Amundsen's polar ship, the *Maud*, became frozen fast in the winter ice for the whole season he was forced like so many polar explorers before him into a surreal life of close companionship and limited exploration. When it was time to head south so that the ship could be repaired in Seattle, Amundsen decided that he needed more crew, as the journey would require him to pass through ice under sail. He invited some of the Eskimos that he had befriended at the settlement to join the boat. They replied, 'Anywhere you go, we will go with you; anything you ask us to do, we will do – except if you asked us to commit suicide, we would ask you to repeat your question.'

The Eskimos duly joined the crew and sailed with Amundsen for a year.

The bonds that we form on our travels have an extraordinarily powerful influence on the whole experience, but they remain slippery and unpredictable.

When we decide to embark with another person we know we are introducing an element of chance into the journey, a variable beyond our control. It is a risk most are happy to take, for solitary travel holds its own portents and they are dreaded by many.

Our companions are a roll of the dice, we can load the odds a little by choosing carefully, but we cannot make the dice land the way we want. We feel the six dots land up when a sympathetic bond allows a moment to be shared, one that marks a journey for better or worse. These are the moments that are recalled and referred to for many years over coffees and laughs. The solitary dot lands upwards when we argue over the smallest things, when a whole morning is dominated by discussion of some minor grievance.

Perfect companions learn to read each other, they come to know the moments when light banter is needed, when serious discussions are called for and equally importantly, when silence is welcome. Nan Shepherd enjoyed company during her walks in the Cairngorms, but she also loved silence; she needed to be careful to select the right companions. She abhorred people who made conversation for the sake of it and especially entertaining, witty and incessant types who would not allow the hills themselves to speak. When she found the right person she felt their company enhanced the silence of the mountains, their identity merged with the mountains.

It is the need for this sensitivity to each other during our travels that makes the state of companionship fluctuate and range across the full spectrum. One of the most difficult decisions during a journey is to part ways with a close companion. We know that our fates will be different. We also know that we will be deprived of the qualities that drew us towards them in the first place. There are countless platonic relationships that have flourished and then foundered under way. Wordsworth and Coleridge got on famously during their walks together in England and then famously did not get on during their journey with Dorothy to Scotland; their relationship decayed permanently.

Hopefully the romantic couples who have embarked together and returned separately are exceeded in number by the friendships that have blossomed into romance during longer journeys. Romantic exasperation has itself been the trigger for many journeys. Austen's Elizabeth in *Pride and Prejudice* jumps at the chance to get away to the Lake District, speaking for so many women at so many moments with the words, 'Adieu to disappointment and spleen. What are men to rocks and mountains?'

For all the romantic liaisons that are consummated, our journeys are fizzing with moments that might lead anywhere but never quite do. Who has not felt their pulse quicken on a meeting of eyes that goes before a parting of ways and a silent question to ourselves? Flirtation is the match lingering over a puddle of petrol in any staid location. The writer, Italo Calvino, sees us busy in this department when sheltering from the rain or pausing beneath an awning. These are not innocent comings together of strangers for Mr Calvino, but a hive of seductions, copulations and even orgies; even when no words are spoken, even when our bodies do not touch.

If journeys fail to offer sufficient romance or the hope of that romance, they can lose their magic. Francis Bond Head was revelling in a view across a snowy landscape when he called to one of his companions, 'What thing can be more beautiful?' After a rueful smile, his friend replied, 'Them things, sir, that do wear caps and aprons.'

We travel with our families and the blood bond that cannot be voluntarily broken holds us together, often to the point where we can no longer stand the sight of each other. Marco Polo heard a story in India that may be of interest to families travelling together, particularly those undertaking long flights or car journeys.

Once there was a king who had five hundred concubines and every time he saw a woman he found attractive he brought her into his circle of 'wives'. But this was not enough for the lustful king and one day he decided that he fancied his brother's wife and took her from his brother and ravished her. The brother who had lost his wife was tempted to kill the brother who had taken her, but was stopped by their mother who had had enough of the quarelling. The mother quelled the arguing with the line, 'If you fight with each other, I will cut off these breasts which gave you both suck.'

Some of the most endearing and intriguing friendships on our travels are the fleeting ones, encounters driven entirely by circumstance, where neither party has volunteered to spend time with the other. There are times when we are brought together by chance, but then we rue that chance does not keep us together for longer. The urgency with which we catch the last train is the measure of our company at dinner.

The ability of strangers to be kind and generous, when they are almost guaranteed not to receive anything in return is one of the most uplifting aspects of travel. It can feel like evidence of one of humanity's redeeming qualities. Darwin rounded off his wonderful account in *The Voyage of the Beagle* by saying that we will all probably travel with distrust, but we will also inevitably encounter many kind-hearted people, strangers who help us regardless of the fact that both parties know that they will probably never hear from each other ever again.

It is our love of this widespread kindness and generosity that makes us angry when it is abused. Charles Dickens was incensed by tramps who pretended to have been gentlemen, who talked of their glorious pasts and their plans of giving future lectures, in the hope of eliciting this generosity from strangers. For Dickens, this is the traveller who would take a farthing from the poor and get between the mother's breast and her infant if only it would help them.

The people we meet shape our initial feelings about the people we meet after them, however illogical this is. Pity the kindhearted locals who extend a hand of friendship to a visiting foreigner, one who has unfortunately been robbed by others the day before.

Sometimes, what we crave is solitude, not companionship. John Muir was invited by a Kentuckian to stay the night at his farmhouse. During the course of a convivial evening, Muir's host asked if he wouldn't stay on until the following spring, a full six months away. Muir was not tempted. For many explorers the point is not ongoing conviviality but the train of experiences that solitude brings. Muir was in the same mould as Thoreau, who enjoyed solitary travel to the point of bristling, 'I never found the companion that was so companionable as solitude.'

More recently Colin Thubron has spoken of a preference for solitary travel because of the problems that travelling with others brings, in particular the impact it has on our perspective. A single companion, Thubron found, could create 'a bubble of Englishness' and risk a personal reaction to a scene being replaced by another's finger-pointing, accompanied by the words, 'They don't do that in Haywards Heath!'

For many, the issue is not so much dictated by the desire or otherwise of companionship, but the pull of nature itself, which draws so many to solitary spots. Once there, the urge to drink more deeply of the experience can be powerful, primal and spiritual. A walk in the country can spiral in our minds, a breath of fresh air becomes a longing for reclusiveness and for retreat. William Gilpin tasted this pull at Tintern Abbey, where the woods, river and ruin came together in a heady mix.

Every thing around bears an air so calm and tranquil, so sequestered from the commerce of life, that it is easy to conceive, a man of warm imagination, in monkish times, might have been allured by such a scene to become an inhabitant of it.

Marco Polo was one of the first to document a symptom of extreme loneliness that has been written about by explorers through the ages since. Those who endure or enjoy long periods of isolation (it doesn't seem to matter which emotion dominates) sometimes come to sense another person close by. Marco Polo wrote that those who fell asleep whilst riding and awoke to find themselves all alone and separated from their fellow riders would hear spirits talking as if they were their companions. Mountaineers and singlehanded sailors have often experienced the presence of an extra person, particularly during difficult times. During the final exhausting bid to cross the mountains of South Georgia, Shackleton wrote of feeling that there were four of them travelling together, not three.

Many travellers enjoy the richest and most vivid sense of liberation on embarking alone, but it is not a panacea. To set off is a romantic dream for many, but the first steps for a few are pulled less by dreams than they are driven by demons. The French writer, Isabelle Eberhardt, was one such tortured soul.

The illegitimate daughter of an aristocratic Russian émigré, Eberhardt was born in Geneva and went on to become a sensualist, a heavy drug-user, a cross-dresser, a convert to Islam and Saharan explorer. Eberhardt suffered a series of personal tragedies in her life and wrote from Cagliari in 1900, 'I am alone, sitting facing the grey expanse of the shifting sea . . . I am alone . . . alone as I'll always be throughout this seductive and deceptive universe . . . ' Less than five years later she was killed by a flash flood in Algeria, at the age of twenty-seven.

There is a world of difference between solitude and loneliness. The nineteenth-century writer Charles Kingsley never felt loneliness on his solitary excursions, he considered that he had companions in every bee, flower and pebble. This is a sentiment that the anthropologist, Richard Nelson, found echoed among the Koyukon Indians of north central Alaska. The Koyukon people felt that the natural world, however wild, was aware of their presence and was watching over them: the forests are alive, they have feelings and must be respected in return for their care.

Wilfred Thesiger craved privacy in the desert, something the Bedu he travelled with never did, but however much he found himself the solitary white man, he never felt lonely. Instead,

Thesiger knew the feeling of loneliness in crowds and in towns. The loneliness that towns throw at us washes us in anxiety. Look at all these people with their busy lives, their manic sense of definite purpose, their secret knowledge, their silent bonds . . . why do they exclude me so?

In describing his reasons for setting off on his journey alone, Ibn Battuta wrote of being 'swayed by an overmastering impulse within me and a desire long-cherished in my bosom'. There are many motives for embarking on solitary travel – the explorer and advocate of tribal people's rights, Robin Hanbury-Tenison, has jokily claimed that all explorers have overbearing mothers – but there may be an interesting study to be done into the relationship between the desire for solitary travel and an individual's comfort among large groups and crowds. There is an awkwardness among many pioneers. Those who are comfortable in the group probably see no reason to march hundreds of miles out of it. If the motto of the townsperson is, 'If you can't beat them, join them', then the motto of the solitary traveller is, 'If you can't fathom them, abandon them.'

Despite the differences in background, culture and religion between Wilfred Thesiger and his Bedu friends, he formed bonds with them that were stronger than those of blood ties between the Bedu themselves. Thesiger realised that for the Bedu, being companions on the road meant they had become so close that they would be expected to fight in each other's defence, even against their own brothers if necessary.

One of the sensations that tells us with a dull constant ache that it is time to bring one chapter of travels to a close is the absence of old friends. Andrew Archibald Paton, a British diplomat and author in the nineteenth century, wrote from his post in Belgrade, Serbia.

> I have been four years in the East, and I feel that I have had quite enough of it for the present. Notwithstanding the azure skies, bubbling fountains, Mosaic pavements, and fragrant narghiles, I begin to feel symptoms of ennui, and a thirst

for European life, sharp air, and a good appetite, a blazing fire, well-lightened rooms, female society, good music, and the piquant vaudevilles of my ancient friends.

He missed a lot of things, but above all, he missed his mates. Are the bonds of our new companions stronger than the longing for our old ones? This thought so often triggers a desire to head home.

Customs and Habits

Nothing so needs reforming as other people's habits.

Mark Twain

I retraced my steps down the slope and looked back at the branches of an ash tree. They had left an imprint on my mind and I was curious to learn more about their shape.

I stared up at the twists in the wood for a moment, trying to read their relationship with the sun and the wind, before continuing uphill again. Then it struck me that although I had walked this same stretch of path just moments ago, the experience was not the same. My feet had churned the Melilot on the path and it was throwing up its scent in a way that it had not on a first passing. I pulled my notebook and pen from my pocket and was about to scribble, when I resisted the urge. This was a moment to enjoy. The writer's habit of trying to note everything is one that it is good to resist at times. It was one of those times.

There may have been a moment during my walk when I picked my nose. I did not note it and I do not recall.

• • •

We do something a certain way once and then twice and then before we know it we have developed a habit. These habits go, to paraphrase the Talmud, from the lightness of a spider's web to the strength of a cable. Despite their growing hold, our own habits remain opaque to us and this is because we have probably borrowed them from others. Customs and habits are territorial.

Once we move from our familiar territory into a new one, the weird, wonderful and terrifying habits and customs of others stand out as a luminous pink against a grey background. Locals only see a homogenous sea of behaviour; this is one way we can tell that we have truly settled in a new place: the habits fail to stand out.

The way we greet each other morphs from a handshake to a kiss to four kisses as we cross cultural borders. Our dress and the amount of skin we show each other fluctuates in each place at a pace that the local population is comfortable with, but which visitors notice instantly. The map of the acceptability of topless-ness among women is not static, it is tidal. Native cultures failed to see the problem with breasts being on display until Christian missionaries arrived in America, Africa and the Pacific and wagged their fingers. This tide ebbs and flows, Christian countries with Mediterranean beaches are now ablaze with bare skin. It fluctu-ates within each territory too, the fashion for toplessness in the South of France comes and goes. It is vulgar one year and a symbol of the 'new feminism' the next.

So ingrained is the general sense that nudity is wrong and at least some clothes are needed that we have made even the animal kingdom aware. Al-Masudi met a famous war elephant called Manfarqalas in Mansura, in what is now Pakistan. This elephant had many credits to his name, not least the occasion when he helped an unfortunate woman in the street. During a procession of eighty war elephants, a startled woman had panicked on coming face to face with this great elephant. The poor woman fell backwards and her dress lifted up revealing her private parts. Manfarqalas appreciated the delicacy of the situation and called the procession of other elephants to a halt by turning sideways in the road. He then used his trunk to signal to the terrified woman that she should get up and finally pulled the woman's dress down for her with his trunk.

When the blind traveller, James Holman, returned home from

his travels he had been away long enough for the clothing fashions to have shifted in his homeland. In London Holman could hear that the men's taste for silks had been replaced by quieter wools and linens. Women on the other hand had grown noisier, with a trend now favouring layers of petticoats, lace and skirts of ever-greater dimensions. Holman found the new styles made it easier to tell that a woman was approaching, from the louder rustling sounds, but he found it harder to politely make enough room on the pavement for their large noisy skirts.

After our differing appearances, we are most likely to notice any habits or rituals associated with the consumption of food or drink. Marco Polo would not have been the first to notice the habit, in countries that use no utensils for eating, for there to be a preference for using one hand for eating, while the other is reserved for attending to the other end of the food's visit to the body.

It is customary in many countries for a formal meal to be preceded by a few words. Grace is said in Christian countries and so it cannot have been a surprise to the explorer, linguist and author Sir Richard Burton to encounter local variants on this tradition, but the frequency and enthusiasm of some for such rituals prior to any and every drink clearly began to irk him.

Look, for instance, at that Indian Moslem drinking a glass of water . . . In the first place he clutches his tumbler as though it were the throat of a foe; secondly he ejaculates, 'In the name of Allah the Compassionate, the Merciful!' before wetting his lips; thirdly, he imbibes the contents, swallowing them, not sipping them as he ought to do . . .

Although there is obviously no single right way to eat or drink something, it appears that we are guaranteed to find offensive anything that differs from our own well-honed but no less peculiar habits. Is this not one of the great joys of going to restaurants in places we don't know?

Toiletry and sanitation habits are not far behind eating and drinking when it comes to arousing curiosity and frequent revulsion. According to his autobiographical account, Olaudah Equiano was born in what is now Nigeria in 1745 and kidnapped, tied up in a sack and forced into slavery at the age of eleven. On arriving in Falmouth in England as a twelve-year-old, Equiano was exposed to a bizarre new world. He could not understand why the deck was covered in salt, until he touched and then tasted his first snow. Equiano was also confronted with a number of customs that were as new to him as the whiteness of the faces that surrounded him. He was shocked that nobody seemed to make any sacrifices or offerings and equally appalled that nobody appeared to wash their hands before eating. (Equiano was transported to Barbados and then into the employ of a naval captain in Virginia. In 1766 and barely into his twenties, Equiano bought his own freedom and then travelled back and settled in England, where he became a passionate and effective member of the abolitionist movement.)

Working habits will always come under scrutiny from travellers. Countries that take siestas are regarded with some small suspicion by visitors from northern countries, who, rather enviously, find such habits indulgent. Our working habits precede us too, then they take on a life of their own and stomp about the world as phantom stereotypes. Humboldt found that everyone he met in South America expected him to know a lot about mining. He soon discovered that the South Americans believed the vast majority of French to be doctors and Germans to be in the mining business.

Any clue that illuminates the bedroom habits of the people of a new area is sure to encourage interest – even if we pretend otherwise. It was not always clear how Marco Polo gleaned so much detail about the sexual practices of those he visited, but it must have been one of his major preoccupations as he rarely fails to keep us informed about the cohabitation and carnal antics of each place.

If the husband of a woman who lived in Pem (in modern

Turkistan) left her to go on a journey of twenty days or more, then the second he was out the door, she was expected to take another husband. A male stranger who visited a house in Kamul (north of the Gobi desert) where the inhabitants, 'take great delight in the pleasures of the body', would be left by his host in the house with the host's wife to lie with her in her own bed for two or three days, where 'they lead a gay life together'. In the city of Kanchau in the province of Tangut (northwestern China) it was acceptable for a man to make love to a woman, providing she had made the first overtures, otherwise it was lecherous and sinful. It was also allowed for the men to marry their cousins and their father's widows, but not if that widow was their own mother. Marco Polo assures us that 'they live like beasts'. Tartar men might take as many wives as they could afford, for each time they married they must pay a dowry to the bride's mother, but after marriage the women were afforded a higher status than the man. The women of Cathay had no hair on their body at all and the men were 'much addicted to sexual indulgence'.

Polo tells us that near the Tibet–China border the men would not consider taking a virgin bride and insisted that their wife should have had knowledge of many men. Whenever men from a foreign land were passing through this region and set up camp, the matrons brought their daughters and begged the travellers to sleep with them. This continued for as long as the men stayed in their camp, but they were not allowed to leave with the young women. When it was time for them to depart, the visiting men give the girl or girls they had slept with a trinket. Each girl could then present this token to her future husband as proof that she had had a lover. The girls with the greatest number of these tokens were the most highly prized brides, as they had clearly been favoured by the gods. Marco Polo recommends the region as an excellent place to visit for men between the ages of sixteen and twenty-four.

A curiosity about sexuality combined with conventional inhibition leads to a lot of interest in its manifestations. We consciously and subconsciously read a lot into each others' clothes, body language and public displays of affection. All three are often on display in a country's dancing traditions. Sexual liberation is mirrored in the form of dance: countries with liberal sexual habits will have relaxed approaches to and views about dancing, but those with conservative sexual habits will tend to have at least a formal approach to dancing, if it is not repressed altogether. Visible courtship rituals, including dining, walking, swimming and dancing, give us an insight into the sexual activities that are hidden. This is why we each have a threshold for what we deem acceptable levels of public displays of affection. One person's holding hands is another's intimate kissing.

We can stop ourselves from committing transgressions that upset the people we live among, but we cannot avoid moving through areas rich with the tales and gossip of others' transgressions. A village without a rich flow of such rumour is a village without people and even there the walls would be imbued with the many-coloured tales of sexual adventures of earlier times.

We cannot escape them, even when we leave the city for the country. When Humboldt fled the marsh-air miasma of the Colombian city of Cartagena to indulge in some botanising in wilder parts, he could not avoid the sexual tapestry of the land. His guides pointed to an *Acacia cornigera* bush that was well-known to all the locals. A wife who clearly had no respect for the tradition that in the wake of infidelities it is the cheated party that seeks revenge, not the perpetrator, had become incensed by the jealousy of her husband – a jealousy that he was well entitled to. One night the wife, with help from her lover, tied her husband up with rope and then threw him into this thorny bush. The harder he struggled, the more his skin was torn by the thorns. He was rescued by passers-by, but not before he had become covered in blood and severely stung by ants.

There are enough similarities between the sexual customs of different cultures for us to read and understand those in foreign countries most of the time; we are all the same animal after all.

However, there is always the potential for a misunderstanding. On his way back to his camp near Mount Lang in Central Queensland, Ludwig Leichhardt and his companions encountered a group of young Aboriginal men. There was some tension, but it eased when Leichhardt offered to make them a gift on his arrival at camp. The men appeared to relax, even offering suggestions on how Leichhardt could avoid the water on his way. When Leichhardt arrived back at his camp he discovered that some Aboriginal men had beaten him to it.

When Leichhardt asked what had happened, his colleagues explained that they had done their best to keep things on a friendly footing, seeing as how they were outnumbered, and they had kept the conversation flowing as best they could. The Aboriginals seemed extremely curious. One of the things that they were keenest to ascertain was whether the bullocks that were accompanying Leichhardt's team were being brought along for the white man's sexual pleasure.

Religion

> In the worshipful attitude toward Nature there is a
> highly religious feeling that I should like to see even in
> these days of science and economics and war.
>
> D.T. Suzuki

A s I approached the church of St Mary the Virgin in the village
of North Stoke, the building began to tell stories of time and
place. On the southern wall I found a Mass Dial, a partial
circle of scratched lines that would have been used for telling the time with
shadows. A few feet from the Dial, on an eastern wall, I found a benchmark
– three lines forming an arrow up towards a short horizontal line. Again
the lines had been scratched into the stone, this time by the Ordnance
Survey to mark the point where height above sea level had been accurately
measured.

There were clues to the construction of the church too, in the anomalous
stones that had been used to fill the putlog holes left by the removal of the
wooden internal scaffolding. Near the western end of the building there
appeared to be a mason's mark on one of the stones. Masons were paid
by the number of stones they worked, and these marks were a way of keeping
tabs.

The unsung builders of the church were the millions of fossilised shells
that formed the quarried stone. This stone was ferried all the way from
the Isle of Wight for the church of this small settlement, underlining the
labour, cost and therefore the importance of the building to those who lived
here.

The village of North Stoke is small, just a modest set of brick and flint buildings. I counted fewer than a dozen homes. There are no shops or cafés, no village hall, no pub. I found a post box and matching traditional red telephone box, with some missing panes. Other than that there was only the impressive church of St Mary the Virgin. The villagers' predecessors may have gone without food or drink at times, but never without their God. The church is described as redundant now, it is preserved as it was, but not used for services. I went in.

St Mary the Virgin's Church in North Stoke

When Marco Polo arrived at each new town or region he made a point of noting the religion of its inhabitants before launching into more detailed analysis of the place and the people. Religion has historically been a more important and fundamental descriptor of who a people *are* than what they *do*, which has been of subsequent and inferior interest.

In Venezuela, Humboldt did an excellent job of summarising

the ubiquity of religious beliefs, the underpinning similarities, and the lunacy of some religious differences. In Caripe, in eastern Venezuela, he learned that once each year the locals headed into a cave, harvested thousands of nocturnal birds and then boiled them down for their fat. The cave was a mystical place for Humboldt's hosts and it was in the midst of this unusual economic ceremony that he learned of the Indians' religious beliefs. The Indians believed that places that were not reached by the light of the sun or moon were to be feared and that at the threshold of the cave the *guacharos*, the bird harvesters, entered the realm of the dead. Each time the bird farmers ventured into the dark grotto, they were on their way to meeting not just with the squawks of thousands of terrified birds, but more chilling still, their own ancestors. Magicians were called upon, spells were cast and the supreme evil spirit Invorokiamo was called up. Humboldt recognised in these traditions the local flavour of more universal beliefs.

All over the earth similarities may be found in the early fictions of people, especially those concerning the two principles ruling the world: the abode of souls after death, the happiness of the virtuous and the punishment of the guilty. The most different and barbarous languages present a certain number of similar images because they have the same source in the nature of our intelligence and our sensations.

Humboldt is enlightened in his consideration of the views he encounters and identifies the primal triggers for the superstitions and religious beliefs that unite us, but he cannot help talking down from his Western pulpit with the words, 'early fictions', simultaneously patronising and trivialising these beliefs.

The folly of a follower of one belief system belittling another was in full evidence for Humboldt by the time he reached the Rio Negro in Venezuela. The rivalries between Spain and Portugal had manifested themselves along the banks of this river and led to friction between the Indians who had come under the influence of the two nations, not least in their religious affectations. Two groups of Indians who were separated only by the water and could see each other on its banks, learned to hate each other. When Humboldt tried to ascertain where this loathing stemmed from he discovered that chief among their reasons was the fact that the missionaries on each bank wore different coloured robes. This is hardly less ridiculous than the enmity felt between the two camps of egg-crackers, the Big-Endians and Little-Endians, in Swift's Lilliput.

In Venezuela Humboldt had found the great undercurrent, the wild human hope that there is more to the jungles of life than the mundane, that out there somewhere is a world of spirits that can lift us as we try to raise ourselves to it. He had also found the equally universal truth that as soon as these aspirations are materialised in any way the consequences are rivalries and tension.

Marco Polo saw enough of the relations between religious groups to form some strong opinions and he noticed a similar trend. There is a fractal quality to the enmity between religious groups: it does not matter how closely we zoom in, we still find bitter lines of division. Marco Polo thought he witnessed some very broad lines, stating, 'It is a fact that all the Saracens in the world are agreed in wishing ill to all the Christians in the world.' But looking more closely, he noted lines within each broader pattern. In Baghdad all Christians liked to observe the same anniversary of a miracle of a mountain that was made to crumble by a humble shoemaker, but the different sects did not see eye-to-eye on how this should be done and 'since Armenians, Nestorians, and Jacobites differ in certain points of doctrine, they repudiate and abhor one another.'

The lines that divide the doctrines are a specialist concern, but the tangible borders they leave in the dirt are worth uncovering. When Ibn Battuta visited Antalya in Turkey he found a segregated city: the Christian merchants lived in an area called al-Mina, which was a harbour encircled by a wall, but the Greek Christians lived in a different walled-off area. The Jews had their own space, as did the mamluks – a military caste – and the Muslims too. These habits pass down through the generations as the religious influences wax and wane and give the modern town its hidden flavours, even as more and more secular tourists flood in.

In the eighteenth century, Mohammed Ben Abdullah, the Sultan of Morocco, encouraged the Moroccan Jews to settle in the coastal town of Essaouira and trade with Europe from there. A thriving Jewish quarter was formed and one corner of a Muslim town in a Muslim country became home to many synagogues. Essaouira was a rare beacon of Muslims and Jews living harmoniously. Although the ageing synagogues remain, there are few Jews still living in Essaouira today – the Jewish Quarter has changed most of its inhabitants and become the Old Jewish Quarter – but it remains a distinct part of the town, which feels very different to the rest. These lines and patches of historical and contemporary difference can be found in most towns and cities.

Religions stamp their marks on individual buildings too, not just with the construction of mosques or synagogues, but in more subtle and emblematic ways. We find cockerels perched aloft churches, for example, typically as part of a weather vane. This followed a ninth-century papal edict that the cockerel – a symbol of St Peter since he denied Christ three times before the crowing of the cock – should be raised above every church. But these symbols step down from the roofs and out into the streets and into the art of each area. Religions will spread and adopt – where they cannot build an identity from scratch they will dress up what they find in new clothes. Many of the aqueous Christian sites of the world, like the holy wells in Ireland, were holy pagan ones before being given Christian robes. It is only the most outrageously proud ancient monuments that escape any attempt at 'baptising the customs': no bishop was going to be able to find clothes big enough to restyle Stonehenge as Christian.

Religious buildings will reach out and shape the nature that surrounds them, too. Japanese Buddhists are drawn to Buddhist temples by the planting of alluring cherry blossoms and the spirit of renewal is engendered in Christian churchyards with the help of yew trees. But the flow is much stronger the other way. The attempts of religious people to shape nature are feeble compared to the power of nature to inspire divine feelings.

In Hebrew the word 'ruach' means both wind and spirit and it appears in the first sentence of the Hebrew Bible.

> When God began to create heaven and earth – the earth being unformed and void, with darkness over the surface of the deep and a wind [ruach] from God sweeping over the water . . .

In the Hebrew Bible the wind brings about the birth of the world and for the bushmen of the Kalahari it ushers us off the planet after our short sojourn. 'When we die, the wind blows away our footprints and that is the end of us.' In between it offers so many people that feeling of coming closer to a god of some kind and if not a god than an ascetic purity that has a soul of its own. This must have been the feeling of John Tyndall, the Victorian scientist and mountaineer, when he declared, 'There is assuredly morality in the oxygen of the mountains.' It is this purity in nature that has led many into the deserts of the Middle East or the forests of Europe in search of penitence and away from the temptations of the hectic world. It has also led many to contrast the ugly religious contrivances of man with the beauty that nature offers, and nobody summed up this feeling more emphatically than Carl Jung.

> It seemed to me that the high mountains, the rivers, lakes, trees, flowers, and animals far better exemplified the essence of God than [did] men with their ridiculous clothes, their meanness, vanity, mendacity, and abhorrent egotism . . .

It may be the destiny of humankind for there never to be any consensus in this area, and fortunately it is not the task of the explorer to weigh religious issues, only to try to be aware of their influences on each place. However, there is a likelihood that the Natural Explorer will be drawn into strong feelings, nonetheless. It is not possible to have it both ways, to desire a greater level of awareness and simultaneously remain oblivious to the emotions that can come with it. In the words of the Zen scholar, D.T. Suzuki, 'the appreciation of the beautiful is at bottom religious.'

Interest in the divine is heightened near death and the funeral rituals of each place can reveal much about a community's view of life, death and religion. In the Goat's Hole Cave in south Wales, remains were found of a burial that dates back to about 27,000 years ago. There is evidence that the cave was a focal point for centuries and that people travelled long distances to visit it. Fascination with the journey after death becomes intermingled with fascination with natural features in the landscape and helps underline those that locals deem most important. The Ganges gives and takes life on many levels, the water sustains crops and people but it also sustains potentially lethal levels of faecal bacteria. Despite the excrement, the river has a reputation for its purifying powers and the water does indeed contain unusually high levels of oxygen and bacteriophages, which kill many bacteria. A vast watercourse so full of life and death would inevitably become a focus of reverence and the river is famous for its human burials.

If life is hard and the belief in a better afterlife is strong enough then it can lead to some extreme behaviour amongst the living. In the tenth century the Arabic traveller, Ibn Fadlan, travelled to visit the Bulgars of Middle Volga. He witnessed a traditional Viking ship burial of a Viking chief and wrote one of the few accounts in existence. In it he describes how the pages and girls of the chief were invited to accompany him into the afterlife and on this occasion one girl – it was usually a girl – did indeed accept. The young volunteer was led through a religious ceremony, which culminated in her being drugged, ritually and repeatedly raped, held down with a rope noose placed around her neck and then stabbed to death. The male Vikings stood outside the sacrificial tent, some of the same ones who had just raped the girl, and banged their shields to mask the sounds of terror, lest the girls that were also outside would become wary of volunteering in the future. The young woman was then sent on her way on the ship with her chief.

It does not take long to realise that our own religious convictions, or lack of them, colour our perceptions of a place as dramatically as those of the people who live there shape it. They determine our actions too, although we may not know it until a dilemma of the magnitude that confronted John Hanning Speke presents itself.

Speke was the British Army officer and explorer who discovered the source of the Nile. Near the heart of the African continent, he reached the city of the violent King Mutesa of the Baganda and here he received a curious welcome that tested his morality. Thirty naked virgins, the daughters of a vanquished foe, were paraded before him, greased and ready for his pleasure. Those that he selected would be spared and become his concubines, those that he declined would be executed. Speke, a bachelor, wrestled with this viper's nest of morality, before awkwardly selecting one girl, passing her over to his servant and turning his back on the other twenty-nine. As historian Simon Schama puts it, 'Everybody is offended except the Explorer, who has surely done the Christian thing.' Modern morality being as it is, young single male explorers of the world confronted with such a dilemma today may find it in their hearts, however much it tries their conscience, to spare more of the greased virgin girls.

A change in religious outlook can move mountains, or their place in our minds at least. Before Buddhism arrived in Japan in the sixth century, mountains were deemed too holy to set foot on. Shrines were built at the foot of a mountain, but nobody saw fit to climb them. With the advent of Buddhism this relationship changed and the Japanese began to climb mountains, going on to become a nation of keen mountaineers. Certain Japanese religious sects emphasised the spiritual value in communing with mountains, foremost among these Shugendo, which, like many Asian religions, brought together many influences including Buddhism, Taoism and Shinto. The aim of Shugendo was to offer enlightenment through raised awareness of the relationship between humans and nature, with the mountain as its central focus. The ascent of mountains came to be viewed as a physical metaphor for the spiritual ascendancy towards enlightenment.

John Muir came from a deeply religious family, his father believed that anything that led away from Bible studies was frivolous and punishable and he did indeed thrash his son many times. Muir's father may therefore have smiled from the grave at the extreme irony, when his son went on to become a hugely influential naturalist and writer and managed to use religion to defend this vocation against doubters. When questioned on his travels across America by one stranger about the value, or virility, of botanising – 'Picking up blossoms doesn't seem to be a man's work at all in any kind of times' – John Muir's hours of Bible study were loaded into the breech of his response and he blasted politely back with examples from both the Old and New Testaments. He reminded his inquisitor that the wisest man of all, Solomon, had studied plants and that Jesus told his disciples to consider the lilies and the way they grew. He rounded off with a rhetorical flourish that would have floored many fine orators. 'Now, whose advice am I to take, yours or Christ's?'

Whether religion shapes our views of nature or nature inspires religious feelings or neither, religion and its traditions will always have an influence on the places and people we visit. Religion can bring colour to places without the need for us to don theological waders and attempt to fathom its every meaning. Only the coldest hearts will fail to be warmed by spending a few minutes admiring the temples of Southeast Asia or clambering amongst the ruins of the Chapel in the Rock in the wild centre of Cornwall. Who, on passing through the town of San Lorenzo de Escorial, near Madrid, could honestly not feel drawn to investigate one particular ash tree after hearing about its setting as the scene of miraculous visions of astonishing regularity? On the first Saturday of each month the Virgin Mary is said to appear to the retired cleaning lady, Amparo Cuevas, at this very tree.

Beauty

> Beauty, thou wild fantastic ape,
> Who dost in every country change thy shape!
>
> Abraham Cowley

The image that would not leave my mind was of that voluptuous curve in the dry riverbed by Stoke Hazel Wood. There was something in its line, something in its radius, something in its colour that resonated. There was no single aspect of the scene that held its beauty, but the whole was powerful.

The valley spoke of the frozen rocks of long gone times, of past fast flow of water and a green that could not be beaten, but more than these things, it offered a curve that lived in the mind. Nothing dead could hold my eyes and work my heart like that, only something that was both alive and beautiful.

• • •

What are we searching for when we embark on a journey? If there is one thing we crave more than anything else, could it be beauty? If so, could it be that an eccentric eighteenth-century headmaster holds the key to finding it?

William Gilpin was born in Carlisle in 1724, married his cousin in 1751, became the headmaster of Cheam school soon after that and climbed into a boat in Ross-on-Wye in 1770. The subsequent account of his journey along the Wye Valley to

Chepstow changed the way we think about the landscapes we see.

Gilpin was following in the philosophical footsteps of the British theorist, Edmund Burke, whose book about the sublime and the beautiful had been published in 1757. Burke had tried to set out objective ideals for beauty, but he struggled. The idealism and the struggle fit well with the fact that he was a teenager when he wrote it. Burke found that fitness, perfection, virtue and proportion all fail to account for beauty in plants, animals or humans. It is strangely satisfying to read as he flounders with the flowers.

> The rose is a large flower, yet it grows upon a small shrub; the flower of the apple is very small, and it grows upon a large tree; yet the rose and the apple blossom are both beautiful . . .

It becomes less comfortable reading when he gets too close to our bones. 'The neck, say they, in beautiful bodies should measure with the calf of the leg; it should likewise be twice the circumference of the wrist.' Relief comes swiftly as he dismisses this notion with a tongue in his young cheek. 'These proportions are certainly to be found in handsome bodies. They are as certainly in ugly ones, as any who will take the pains to try, may find.' Burke does attempt to define beauty in terms of smoothness, in leaves and streams, and of gradual variation of colour, but he is never as convincing as when he is dismissing fixed notions of beauty.

William Gilpin was concerned with the aesthetic ideal in landscape that he termed 'picturesque', and he approached this topic practically and rigorously. His book, *Observations on the River Wye and Several Parts of South Wales, &c. Relative chiefly to Picturesque Beauty: made in the Summer of the Year 1770*, was conventional for the time in its choice of excessively long title, but revolutionary in its content. In it Gilpin offered instruction in the art of understanding the components that would make a scene beautiful and sublime. He was in effect trying to analyse and then condense the whole of the outdoors into a manual for appreciating beauty and wonder. It is no great surprise that he was ridiculed and satirised by some of his contemporaries, but only those who have an impact get to be satirised and his study is important and still has much to offer.

Gilpin wrestles with the challenge he has set himself as he looks out over the Severn Vale.

The eye was lost in the profusion of objects which were thrown at once before it, and ran wild over the vast expanse with rapture and astonishment, before it could compose itself enough to make any coherent observations.

But compose itself it does. For Gilpin, individual rocks were made beautiful only with the help of a 'tint' from mosses and lichens. Scattered rocks and the stones of Tintern Abbey were too bold without offsetting, and Gilpin was clearly alarmed by the Welsh habit of whitening their houses. 'A speck of white is often beautiful; but white, in profusion, is, of all tints, the most in-harmonious.' He was adamant that nature did not do white in great swathes, with the exception of chalky cliffs, which were very fortunately tempered by hanging samphire, or stained with 'various hues, so as to remove, in part at least, the disgusting glare.' (He was good enough to confess that a colleague had pointed out that snow was quite white, but his friend agreed with him that it was not a pleasing colour in a landscape.)

Small rivers or streams need 'agitation', apparently, in the form of cascades, to be picturesque, but large bodies of water are able to 'support their own dignity'. It is fine for a tree in a forest to be ordinary as its deformities will be 'lost in the crowd', but a tree standing on its own had better be something very special. Agriculture is not spared and fields that are shaped as squares and rhomboids are 'commonly disgusting' when viewed from above.

There is something vulgar about the objectifying of natural

beauty, something that makes it hard not to sympathise with the satirists who mocked Gilpin. Some beauties wend their way from his account but his attempts to cage them in universal truths is simultaneously attractive and repulsive. Perhaps this is why it comes as a relief nearing joy when he encounters a scene that snaps his approach like a twig.

At the ruins of Tintern Abbey, whilst busy assessing the effects on the scene of the ornaments of the west window, Gilpin is shocked by the poverty he encounters. One woman stood out from the squalor and she was in an appalling physical condition, 'shuffling along her palsied limbs and contracted body by the help of two sticks'. The poor woman promised to show Gilpin the monks' library, but instead led him to her own dwelling among the ruins. Gilpin moved into the middle of the damp hovel to avoid the cold water trickling down around him and felt genuine surprise that the woman was able to survive at all in her 'cell of misery'. He confesses to being fascinated by her. He presses on and continues his journey, noting the discolouration of the river's waters, but aware that this human suffering will not fit easily into his thesis. The shocking ugliness of a woman struggling to survive has more effect on him, and his reader, than any of nature's tints on the ruins.

If there is any satisfaction in seeing Gilpin's train temporarily derailed then it is not a guilty one. We can appreciate his honestly conceding that there is an outer and inner journey. Beauty is impossible without ugliness and both have a power that we cannot contain.

Gilpin shares his original ideas successfully and evocatively, allowing us to 'give a loose to the most pleasing riot of imagination'. He also demonstrates that although connection with the natural world may involve consideration of mountains, rivers, buildings, plants and animals, this will not amount to much if we do not at some point tackle the role of the human animal and the maze that is to be found between its ears.

His book probably resonated and became influential, even

among those who disagreed with him, because it appeals to our deep fascination with beauty. Fascination always contains some measure of hope and fear. We aspire, desire and long to enjoy the beautiful in our lives, whether we find it in a view from a hillside or in the face lying next to us on the pillow. Life, and therefore exploration, is a striving dance towards beauty and away from ugliness. The fully-aware explorer must suffer some insecurity though: we know that the world we see can be beautiful or ugly, but also that we may be seen as beautiful or ugly by others.

Beauty is power, it sidesteps our rational response to the world and works with something more primal. Edmund Burke knew that, 'beauty demands no assistance from our reasoning.' A man's pupils dilate when he sees a beautiful woman and he finds women with dilated pupils more beautiful. One of the consequences should not be surprising: before going out with gentlemen, the women of both the Italian Renaissance and Victorian England would artificially dilate their pupils, using eye-drops containing belladonna, a plant from the poisonous nightshade family.

Fearing the idea of an objective beauty is therefore quite rational. If someone has somehow cracked the formula, then they will understand our response to the world and the people in it better than we do ourselves and they will be able to use this to influence us. American author and naturalist Diane Ackerman has collected examples of how beauty affects our prospects and they are frightening. Those deemed to be beautiful do better in school, work, the military and even prison. In 1968 in New York a study found that prisoners with deformities who underwent cosmetic surgery fared better than those who only received counselling, and were less likely to re-offend as a consequence. About the only thing that can temper our uneasiness in the face of this base notion is the fact that we can prove that, when it comes to humans at least, beauty is definitely subjective and modish. Contemporary travellers battling to lose weight before stepping onto a beach in summer might be interested in Marco Polo's reports that the women of Badakhshan (now parts of Afghanistan and Tajikistan), tried to make themselves more attractive to men by stuffing great quantities of folded cotton cloth into their trousers to give the impression of much plumper hips.

More recent studies to establish which natural scenes we find appealing throw out dull nuggets that vary from the unsurprising to the obvious without enlightening us much: we like water, blue sky, greens more than browns and we do not like rubbish or abandoned cars. Between these broad sweeps and in the detail that may yet prove more fascinating, lies the strong likelihood that beauty in the world we experience is as subjective as beauty in the human form. As a species we crave variety in our travels, but also variety in our assessment of each experience. Homogeneity is the enemy here. Is this the truth that can be felt in the words of the American baseball star, Yogi Berra: 'If the world were perfect, it wouldn't be'?

Contemplation of beauty is not something that modern explorers have allowed themselves to indulge in, it is permitted a mention in passing at best, and then dispensed with. Is it too effete for the tastes of most? Is it too slippery to fit into grand narratives? Or too philosophical perhaps, holding up an awkward mirror that gets steamed up by the huffing and puffing to the next destination? One possibility is that it is too extreme. The human coping strategy for ideas that are too big and scary is to dodge and gloss, to duck and run. Only those who have no choice, or are crazy or brave enough to venture into the loneliest areas find themselves able to speak honestly about beauty.

Hermann Weyl was on an expedition into an unknown land as he sought to forge links between mathematics and theoretical physics early in the twentieth century. 'My work always tried to unite the truth with the beautiful, but when I had to choose one or the other, I usually chose the beautiful.'

Theoretical physicists, poets, artists and many other pioneers will give a variety of motives for their quests, but they are all metaphors for the desire to know the essence of life. Beauty can be seen as the fleeting visible face of a deeper hidden meaning in the world – if one exists. Hence our fascination and its ability to resist objective analysis.

Approaching death is another such feared land. When the playwright Dennis Potter was interviewed for the last time before dying of cancer, he chose to speak of how intense the world appeared to him.

Below my window in Ross . . . [is] a plum tree, it looks like apple blossom but it's white, and . . . I see it is the whitest, frothiest, blossomest blossom that there ever could be. Things are both more trivial than they ever were, and more important than they ever were, and the difference between the trivial and the important doesn't seem to matter. But the nowness of everything is absolutely wondrous. There's no way of telling you; you have to experience it, but the glory of it, if you like, the comfort of it, the reassurance . . . not that I'm interested in reassuring people – bugger that. The fact is, if you see the present tense, boy do you see it! And boy can you celebrate it.

In beauty we have a glimpse of the wondrous, and the wondrous is what is worth searching for. The aim is to find wonder in vast landscapes and small plants, in wild animals and the human being.

Glimpses of beauty do not guarantee joy, but they intensify our emotions, they give us the sense of being truly alive and they lift us towards the insight we crave. In seeking something during our explorations in the world, we mimic our searches in art, literature and music.

Edmund Burke is still widely read two centuries after his death and this honour is only bestowed upon those whose vision has allowed them to grapple with the most powerful ideas. He could not have written anything more powerful than the line, 'What by general consent is allowed to be a more beautiful object than an orange tree, flourishing at once with its leaves, its blossoms, and its fruit?'

Inner Time and Mood

> Learn to reverence night and to put away the vulgar
> fear of it, for, with the banishment of night from the
> experience of man, there vanishes as well a religious
> emotion, a poetic mood, which gives depth to the
> adventure of humanity.
>
> Henry Beston

*There was a moment in the afternoon when I felt the deadening
pull of lethargy, but then it disappeared as fast as it had arrived.
    The way the silverweed flashed each time the breeze caught it
made me stop and stare. I experienced a mild euphoria as this plant
danced to the tune of the wind, flipping between pale and dark green
lights. The thought occurred to me that its beauty might have been enhanced
ever so slightly by the sugar in the dried mango I had just eaten on an
empty stomach.*

* * *

Time changes the world around us with each passing season, day
and second, but even if the world remained static, our view of it
could not. Every single one of our experiences must pass through
our senses to our brain. Time toys with this process, it bends our
response and experience of the world.

Heraclitus was right when he said that we cannot step into the
same river twice: each moment of sensing the world is unique, it

is never replicated, there are too many variables. This unmatched tapestry is then projected on to a subjective observer, whose experiences, memories, mood, physical and mental wellbeing mesh with their awareness of the moment to forge something that is now subjectively as well as objectively unique.

Each of us has our own pattern of wakefulness and sleepiness during the course of an average day, we have what is known to scientists as an individual chronotype. Some of us find we have most mental energy in the morning and some in the late afternoon or evening, these are the larks and owls amongst us. But nobody is immune to the cycles of alertness and drowsiness during their day, and these cycles impact our actions, experiences and impressions. Russell Foster and Leon Kreitzman have collected some eclectic examples of the patterns of these circadian rhythms in their book, *Rhythms of Life*. The best time for proof-reading and sprint swimming is in the evening, tooth pain is lowest after lunch, women usually go into labour at night and give birth in the morning. We solve complex problems most effectively in the middle of the day and our physical coordination peaks in the early evening, as does our body temperature.

The difference between us performing at an optimum level and our worst is similar to the performance difference between an individual with no alcohol in their blood and the amount at the legal driving limit.

A worrying number of accidents occur during the troughs of these cycles. The Titanic, Exxon Valdez, Estonia ferry, Chernobyl, Union Carbide plant and Three Mile Island disasters all took place within a couple of hours of midnight. These cycles impact our mental performance partly because they reduce our alertness and therefore our awareness. It is hard for someone at the bottom of this cycle to be as finely tuned to their surroundings as someone at their peak. The world we see changes during the course of the day even if it does not change at all.

There are inner cycles that are much longer than a day. The length of night and day triggers seasonal responses in the plants around us, but it also has an impact on us. Seasonal Affective Disorder affects three per cent of people in the UK, but even those who would not recognise themselves as having a disorder would admit that it is hard to feel the same way on a cold dark morning as a warm light one. We do our best to bend the seasons with artificial lighting, but we are belching against thunder: daylight is typically between 100 and 2,000 times brighter than indoor lighting. Things grow more complex and interesting the more we think about time and light. Recent research has shown that the colours we can see change our perception of time. If we are surrounded by the colour blue, then a minute feels shorter than if we are surrounded by red.

Our perception of time also changes with fluctuations within our body, particularly with changes in our body temperature. Research has shown that thirty seconds can feel like a minute when we have a serious fever. Galileo supposedly timed the pendulous swinging of a lamp in a Pisa cathedral during a sermon, by taking his own pulse. If he really did, it would be a beautiful example of the interconnectedness of our bodies, our minds and our perceptions.

Imagine that early in the sermon, as the priest is warming up, Galieo measures the swinging lamp and finds that it swings 30 times in the time it takes his heart to beat 60 times, his best estimate of a minute. (The time it takes for any pendulum, including a swinging lamp, to swing from one side to another should not change, even as the energy in the system reduces and the length of its swing decreases. This is how pendulum clocks keep dependable time.) Ten minutes into the sermon, the priest has really got into his stride and is bellowing at the congregation with terrifying warnings about the likelihood of their sizzling in damnation. Galileo times the lamp again and finds that it has slowed down and only swings 28 times in a minute. Is it taking longer for the lamp to swing or is Galileo's pulse rising at the thought of roasting in hell?

Our changing feelings during the course of each day and year have consequences, some of which are more predictable than others. The most common time for lovemaking is 10.00p.m., but testosterone is highest in northern-hemisphere men during early afternoons in October, possibly to increase the chances of a summertime baby.

On top of the inevitable cycles dictated by our inner clocks, we have a habit of doing things that exacerbate the situation. British Airways has published warnings to its passengers that jet lag can degrade decision-making ability by fifty per cent, communication skills by thirty per cent, memory by twenty per cent and attention by seventy-five per cent. Bill Schwarz, a passionate baseball fan and neurology professor, analysed baseball league game data and found that West Coast teams did worse than East Coast teams whenever they had to travel for a game, because travelling east and against the direction of the sun has a more detrimental impact on us. We will therefore have a different experience of a place depending on whether we arrive by air from the west or the east.

There are aspects to time and its relationship to our emotions that are less simple than circadian and seasonal rhythms, or jet lag. Pierre Lecomte du Noüy, a biophysicist and philosopher, believed that men and women experience time in different ways. According to du Noüy, men are interested in the measurement of time and can become obsessed with measuring it ever more accurately, but women are interested in events. He argued that women's lives are punctuated much more dramatically by biological events than are men's: they go through not just puberty, but periods, pregnancy, childbirth and the menopause. This theory led du Noüy to propose a solution to one of the great domestic mysteries.

When a woman responds to her impatient husband as he waits to take the family to the theatre, by saying 'Coming, dear, right away,' she does not mean this literally. She means only that at that moment this is the next event she has in mind to join her husband. Meanwhile, he makes a mental note of her reply and allows her forty-five seconds to make the trip from her bedroom to the front door! Consequently, he is frustrated when, ten minutes later, he is still pacing up and down the hall . . . Neither party seems able to accept the other's sense of time. *And* children have the same problem with grown ups.

Adults and children do experience time in different ways and time does appear to accelerate as we get older. This is logical in many ways, one year is a quarter of a four-year-old's life but only two per cent of a fifty-year-old's. But as we get older we also learn ways to understand some of the paradoxes of time and this helps us to nurture our relationship with it. Only an adult could appreciate the saying of the composer and philosopher John Cage, 'If something is boring after two minutes, try it for four. If still boring, then eight. Then sixteen. Then thirty-two. Eventually one discovers that it is not boring at all.'

Age also changes our assessment of situations. Something many parents will attest to is the fact that teenagers' brains are wired differently to that of an adult's. In our teenage years our brains reward risk-taking by triggering a pleasurable sensation each time we take a risk, by the time we are twenty our brains no longer do this in the same way. One theory is that this risk-reward stage of life encourages us to experiment, to help us discover things before our behaviour settles down, at least a little, in adulthood.

There is an excellent reason to savour the present moment as we get older: we are less likely to remember it. We remember details for the first fifty years of our life, but by the time we reach our sixties we tend to remember tone and emotion, but fewer details.

As Leichhardt approached Port Essington on the northern coast of Australia and the goal of his epic overland journey, he felt a dangerous enemy growing among the expedition in the 'irresistible impatience to come to the end.' The desire for journeys to speed to a conclusion has probably robbed more travellers of gratifying experiences than any other single factor. Think of how much more frustrating a delay in the final minutes of a train journey feels than in the first minutes. If the train comes to an unexpected halt shortly after setting off, we tend to be philosophical and might well find ourselves looking out of the windows or casually inspecting our fellow travellers with skipping glances. If the train comes to a stop near our destination however, the curiosity about the world has evaporated and its place has been filled by one hundred thoughts about the pressing wants and needs of the destination itself. At such moments rare birds could court outside the window without fear of being spied on, as everyone onboard the train is desperately trying to force their ticket through a barrier that is still two miles away. It is at these moments that Time himself likes to walk alongside the tracks, peer in and smile with a finger touching his black felt hat, before noting in his pocketbook another fine trick he has played on us.

If it is a male trait to want to measure time, then both sexes are keen to mark it. Leichhardt and the rest of the expedition celebrated the Queen's birthday on 24 May 1845 by eating a cake made of flour and suet, washed down with tea with sugar in it. Leichhardt savoured his first sugar for several months, before noting the need in human nature to, 'interrupt the monotony of life by marked days, in which we indulge in recollections of the past, or in meditations on the future.' No other animal has this habit of punctuating the string of time with these celebratory knots, and even less to feel dewily back along the string or anxiously along it into the future.

We recall the world around us through our own birthdays, those close to us or the big names, like Christ's. We remember birthdays that fell during heat waves or under inches of snow. We also come to associate these points in time with places. Most people can remember where they were on the eve of the new millennium, even if not everybody can recall every detail of the evening. Gerard Manley Hopkins decided that spring was running at least a fortnight late in 1866, because he could remember crowning a bust of Shakespeare with bluebells the year before on Shakespeare's birthday, 21 April, but it was already the 4th of May and the bluebells had failed to arrive in numbers. The more connected we become with our surroundings, the more time, climate, light, events and mood swirl together and then hang from the same periods in our memory. Author and pioneer wild swimmer Roger Deakin remembered the winter of 1963 as one of perpetual grey and the death of Sylvia Plath.

Nature occasionally seems to conspire to make things appear gloomy, and some have commented that this perception increases as we age. We come to realise that everything perishes, the animals, the plants, the bugs in the soil and even the rocks crumble to dust. If we live to a ripe age then, as Italo Calvino observed, there is going to come a point when we know more people who have died than those who are still alive. Hopefully, before we reach this moment we will have garnered enough wisdom that time ceases to frighten us. For those who worry obsessively about ageing, a spell with the Amazonian Amondawa tribe might alleviate things. The Amondawa, who had no contact with the outside world until 1986, have no words for time, no words for month or year and do not refer to age at all. Instead each person assumes a different name to reflect each stage of life.

By accepting that our inner clock means our awareness of the constantly changing world fluctuates with each hour, we befriend time. That is after all the only sensible way ahead. We can measure it, but we will never master it. This acceptance may be the moment when we recapture some of the joy of our carefree days, when each place we find feels more like the first beach, the first woodland, the first river and the first town we loved in our youth. Sometimes all it takes is one breath of air. While standing in the palmy woods in Florida, the rocky coasts of Dunbar came back to John Muir. He had felt as though his whole childhood had 'utterly vanished', but he found it restored in one gulp of salty sea air.

Time can sharpen or dull our awareness with its circadian clock, but it also likes to spin our experiences beyond our control by leading our moods on a dance with other clocks. The finer details of the mesmerising water gardens of the Alhambra palace in Granada might find themselves drowned out by the tsunamis caused within us by hormones, blood-sugar levels and tiredness, to name only a few of the physiological mood-bullies. The hormonal onslaught that women endure once a month in menstruation, or once a life in the menopause, are storms that rage and at times do their best to obscure any beauty in a landscape.

It is not all bad news though, our minds and bodies can receive boosts from small stimuli: the smell of spiced apples can make us feel relaxed by lowering our blood pressure, or we might feel energised by the smell of lavender, which kick-starts our metabolism. In one experiment, women who sniffed musk regularly found it easier to conceive.

Colours also like to tinker with our feelings. Red excites the brain; in experiments where people were asked to grip something while they were shown different colours, their grip strengthened by 13.5 per cent when the colour red appeared. People perform less well in IQ tests if they are shown the colour red just before they take them, and footballers who wear red shirts when taking penalties are less stressed than those who wear blue ones. Pinks and greens have a calming effect, hence the 'green rooms' that are the holding cages for those about to face the TV cameras.

It has been traditional for restaurants to decorate with lots of browns and reds as these are the colours that are supposed to make us hungrier, but recent experiments have shown that our wakefulness is influenced by cells in our eyes that are only sensitive to blue light. One restaurant noted this research and bathed its diners in blue light: they found that everyone perked up at 10.00p.m., when energy levels usually tailed off.

Moods change the world we see. Even if we all looked at the same world the same way with the same eyesight, we would not all see the same thing. Our perception is affected by our experience and psychology. The way we perceive colours is also influenced by our age, sex and status. Women are more sensitive to colour difference than men, but both men and women are more sensitive to colour difference when they are feeling powerful.

Colours can impact our judgment too. A study of the martial art Tae Kwon Do in the 2004 Olympics made an extraordinary discovery. Each competitor had to wear either red or blue clothing and these were allocated randomly. However, researchers found that the competitors who wore red won nearly two-thirds of the bouts. This posed the following question: was the red influencing the competitors or the judges? An ingenious piece of follow-up research answered the question. Video of the bouts was digitally edited to swap the colours of the competitors, so that red now appeared blue and vice versa. These videos were then shown to Tae Kwon Do judges, and they were asked to judge these fights. Red still won. Even though it was actually blue. The red clothing had dramatically influenced the judgment of those who were, in theory, impartial. This research taken into a broader context should play on the thoughts of the aware traveller. It is now hard to believe that we will feel exactly the same about a stranger we meet who is wearing blue as one who is wearing red, particularly if we are involved in a meeting of any intensity.

Some sounds can break us, like the 'white noise' favoured by interrogators, but there are many kinder ones. There are specialist recordings of the sounds of nature to be used for meditation, but it is a fine line between the sounds of running water that make us feel relaxed and those that make us want to relax our bladder.

From waking up to the sounds of birdsong entering an open window versus the sound of the pneumatic drill of roadworks, our feelings during the course of each day are nudged with greater or lesser strength towards tension or relaxation. We are trying to manipulate this effect each time we choose to listen to music. We are lifted up by major chords and pop music, we are worked into a lather by heavy metal, relaxed by classical music and then depressed by minor chords or Leonard Cohen.

The absence of sound can also have an effect on us. Silence

can be frightening and total silence bizarre: those who have been in an anechoic chamber, a room where all sounds are excluded and dampened to achieve as close to perfect silence as possible, report hearing the rushing of their own blood. One volunteer found perfect silence so dreadful they asked to be released after only one minute.

If our health deteriorates or ameliorates it will have a dramatic impact on our mood and consequently our impression of any new place. Who has not felt the almost intoxicating euphoria of a heavy flu lifting, when suddenly every colour, smell and sound seem to vibrate with a new energy?

Immersing ourselves in nature can be calming or uplifting. It was almost a Romantic creed that the harmony of nature could restore balance to our minds and Humboldt wrote to his older brother, Wilhelm, that nature could 'be soothing to the tormented mind' and that it 'lends wings to our feelings and thoughts'. Later in his travels Humboldt wrote of the powerful effect that the contemplation of trees can have on our feelings.

Conversely, the town has long been suspected of engendering unnatural and unhealthy moods and states of mind. An excess of asphalt and concrete is so often silently blamed for many inner city problems, including violence. There are many who believe that a course of walking amongst nature should be prescribed before the many pills that are now so commercially successful. Sometimes it seems that those who are unhappy cry out for nature, even if these cries are hard to understand. A fifteen-year study of psychiatric patients in Sweden found that the patients often complained about the art on the walls and even damaged a lot of it. Researchers discovered that the patients only ever vandalised the abstract pictures, there was not a single case of a painting of nature or landscapes being damaged.

In another study, twenty people were put on a treadmill and then shown different images as they exercised. Their blood pressure was measured before and after viewing the images. The blood pressure of those who had been shown pleasant rural images dropped; amongst those who had been shown images of urban landscapes, it rose.

Our mood and feelings will be set into turbulent fluctuations by any sense of imminent danger. This is a large part of the draw of mountain climbing. Like the fugu-eaters of Japan, mountain climbers find a piquancy in their journeys through the dance with risk. When the English literary critic of the latter years of the seventeenth century, John Dennis, found himself on a narrow path high up in the mountains his emotions became super-charged.

> The sense of all this produc'd different motions in me, viz.,
> a delightful Horrour, a terrible Joy, and at the same time,
> that I was infinitely pleas'd, I trembled.

The greatest risk we seek out though is not in the mountains, but in each other. Our moods can be more dramatically spun by thoughts triggered by our relationships with each other than by any amount of hormones, food, smells, colours, sounds, exercise, images or precipitous paths.

James Holman had been suffering from insomnia and headaches and these compounded the stress of losing his vision completely. During his travels he decided to try to get better through eating healthily and exercising lots, both activities which sound sensible to the point of being obvious today, but which would have been unorthodox to the point of being almost perverse at the start of the nineteenth century. Holman ate fresh fruit rather than the bread and brandy that his fellow travellers preferred for breakfast and he used a long piece of string to allow him to walk briskly behind the horse-drawn carriage. Unsurprisingly, his regimen did him a lot of good, the headaches lifted and he slept well.

It was while walking behind the carriage that one of his companions, known to us now only as the 'bootmaker's wife', decided to join Holman. This lady, who had taken to flirting with the fascinating and handsome blind man, offered her hand in place of the string. Holman walked with her as she let slip that her marriage was not all that she might hope for in a relationship. They paused together and the wife described the beautiful view to her new crush. He records the moment in this way. 'The air at this spot I found so soft, balmy, and exhilarating, that I felt assured that I had now reached the south of France.'

Was it really the balmy air that made him feel like this? Holman is more orthodox in the repression of his emotions than his diet, but anyone who has ever felt that intoxicating surge of sensations from a nascent romantic bond will recognise the giddiness of the moment, even in those carefully chosen words. It is a feeling that can lend a tint of paradise to the plainest landscape.

Imagination and Wonder

> How strangely mobile is man's imagination, eternal source
> of his joys and pains!
>
> Alexander von Humboldt

A t various moments on my journey I was joined by those from other times. The quarry workers, the first farmers, the congregation of the church in North Stoke almost a thousand years ago, they all walked a section with me.

I had stepped into many of the buildings, eaten a cream tea and paddled a kayak along the River Arun. I had imagined for a moment being on the yacht whose white sails I could just make out in the band of blue. One walker passed me and the smell of their suntan lotion took me to a Greek beach for about three seconds.

It was no surprise then that by the end of my walk, my legs were less exercised than my mind. There had been the odd moment when I had felt a mental weariness. But it always passed and it was usually when, noticing some small ripple, cloud or leaf, I was left with a sensation of ecstatic curiosity. My energy levels would soar as thoughts of the extraordinary richness before me emerged.

* * *

Humboldt compared the coasts to clouds, observing that they both assume new forms in each of our imaginations. One night while stargazing in Venezuela, he felt himself transported back from the southern stars and away from the luminous insects that danced in the air. Humboldt was for a moment returned to his homeland of Germany, whisked there in an instant by the sound of a cowbell.

An awareness of every aspect of the land and sky, the colours, sounds, smells and feel of our surroundings and their interconnections, helps to build a rich picture of the world around us. However, even when we have accepted that this is formed from our own unique perspective and that it may be tainted by our moods and prejudices, the impression we form is barely complete, because it is at this point that our imagination seizes the canvas we are working on and starts to throw paint at it like a wild child.

Our imagination sculpts the world around us, it gives nature's shapes new forms, but it also transports us across the globe in fractions of a second. We only need think of the areas where our desires grow most strongly to witness the power of our imagination. The slightest scent of food on an empty stomach conjures up long baronial banquets. The merest hint of mutual attraction will lay on a story of romantic developments with a Hollywood budget, handholding on a beach walk becomes perfect lovemaking before we are swept together instantly, and without the need for a passport, to an Italian villa with exquisite views over the lake. Our imagination is a more powerful aphrodisiac than any herbs, potions or pills available over a counter. It can also be enlisted to suppress such thoughts and we use it both to ignite passions and to douse them. Who can feel either hungry or sexually aroused whilst thinking of a naked grandparent eating a pork sandwich that has fallen into an ashtray?

Our imagination can help us leap huge cultural divides as it offers us the gift of empathy. Cannibalism lost some its abhorrence for Humboldt once he had witnessed the Indians eating the arms and legs of roasted monkeys. His mind was able to cross the bridge at that point.

Sounds take us to new, sometimes dangerous and always creative worlds, the creak of the eucalyptus in the wind is the ship's hull about to cede, pines hit with a gust are a vehicle on the track behind, suddenly bearing down on us. Among the Scottish Highlands, Mary Ann Hathaway felt her imagination expanding. Listening to the sounds of water flowing, the 'cadence of a cascade', gave her the urge to write poetry.

Our inner longings must dictate the direction that our imagination takes us, but it is a mysterious process, full of surprise. While most feel themselves pulled from the wan and routine towards the wild and remote, Vaughan Cornish found the lava of Vesuvius took his thoughts back to the flow of molten iron that ran from the blast furnaces of Middlesbrough. Thoreau was a firm believer that wildness was not an objective quality, it was something to be found within us which we then bring to a place. 'I shall never find in the wilds of Labrador any greater wildness than in some recess of Concord, i.e. than I import into it.'

There are many who suspect the old type of explorer of working against the joys of our imagination, those who believe that the addition of places to a map in some way fences them off from the liberal wanderings of our mind. The poet Francis William Bourdillon expressed such fears.

Already it is more difficult to find sustenance for our imaginations than in the days when Herodotus or Ulysses roamed in worlds all romantic and unknown, more difficult even than in the spacious times of great Elizabeth.

Bourdillon has struck upon one of the cords that simultaneously ties the new explorer to the old, and divides them. It is becoming more difficult in one sense, but then exploration has always grown more difficult. The old explorer is used to the one-way arrow of growing expeditionary challenges: physical exploration has always progressed from the easily achievable goals through the great challenges towards the near-impossible. But Bourdillon is describing something different here, he is saying that it becomes harder for our imagination to work as the blanks on the map are filled. Imagination adores uncertainty and so, as the white spaces become crowded with detail, the task becomes tougher. There are individuals for whom finding sustenance for the imagination in new and challenging environments is what the job is all about: this is the grist of the writer, artist and thinker. When it becomes tough to use our imagination we are looking at the north faces that draw the creative individual.

We are now closing in on the role of the Natural Explorer. The task of the explorer will always be to search in the places that remain unknown and share what they find. It is just that we may have reached the point where our powers of imagination, combined with the pen and the brush, become more relevant to the task than the sledges and camels preferred of old.

Once every glacier and desert wadi has a name, it is the job of those who work with their imagination to find the places where ignorance still prevails. This may require vast journeys or short walks. There are mountains in these places where we have barely touched the foothills, let alone viewed the summits. It only takes our imagination to find them. The author, Robert Macfarlane, wrote, 'To a child, a back garden can be an unknown country.' To even the oldest of Natural Explorers, one small corner of it will be.

We will always know when we are getting close to virgin territory, because we will share with all explorers of the past the emotions that confirm a goal may be nearby: excitement, fear and awe. The questions that drew the old explorers to great feats, like 'Where is the source of the Nile?' are being replaced by very different ones. 'Are we capable of falling in love more quickly in an urban landscape or a rural one? Why?'

A sense of awe is important because this is the emotion that so often precedes wonder, and there can be no greater ultimate goal for explorers, old and new, than that. As Goethe once said, wonder is the highest response we can attain. Beauty and awe are the scents that draw us towards it. If something is incapable of creating awe in us then it will be harder for us to experience wonder. We may be looking in the wrong place, or much more likely, looking in the wrong way.

Laurens van der Post needed a cameraman for his expedition into the Kalahari. A man called Eugene Spode got the job, but it was not to prove a happy arrangement. Van der Post had reservations about Spode from the outset; he appeared an unhappy type, but van der Post forgave him this and ascribed his dour demeanour to the various ordeals he had endured under the Nazis, Communists and Fascists. He preferred to dwell on Spode's reputation for heroism in the Resistance and his love of Africa. The relationship became strained early on in the expedition and van der Post feared for its future. Spode clearly had his demons and they were gathering at the forefront of his mind, clouding his view of the Africa he loved.

One night, whilst camping together, Spode did lighten for a moment. He then fetched his violin and moved away from the circle at the heart of the camp and stood with his back to his colleagues. He began to play his instrument, all the time facing outwards, towards the bush itself. Everybody stopped talking around the fire and listened for half an hour as Spode played passionately. Then he stopped, turned and stumbled back to the camp. He put his arms around van der Post, who realised he was crying. Spode explained that he had lost himself as he thought of nothing except the music to play to the forest. Van der Post was delighted and suggested that the emotion he had just experienced should remain at the heart of his attitude. It was central.

Spode had experienced a moment of wonder, the euphoria of mentally coming up from a suffocating place to an oxygen-rich environment. In his case it appears it was borne from a release of oppressive and negative thoughts from his past, but for many more it is stirred by emergence from a thick blanket of unawareness.

There is a progression amongst Natural Explorers, from the need for staggering natural beauty to the ability to make more of modest opportunities. On seeing Mont Blanc for the first time, Percy Bysshe Shelley described his reaction as, 'a sentiment of ecstatic wonder, not unallied to madness.' Like Shelley, we should experience wonder on seeing Mont Blanc, but this lies at the beginner's end of understanding the potential of wonder in our travels. We learn what it feels like to experience wonder by being spoilt by incredible and fantastic sights of geographical awe, but as we get practised at immersing ourselves in a landscape it becomes possible to experience this with less dramatic prompts. It is a more daunting challenge to find wonder in a hill than a mountain, and a great achievement to find it in a molehill.

The progression from the need for bold statements to subtler ones is characteristic of all artistic immersion: there is a maturity to be gained in the appreciation of music, art or literature. The wonder in some of the finest works will be lost on those who are new to the art, its subtleties will pass them by, but they will appreciate blunter works.

The relationship between artistic appreciation and maturity is a little simpler than that between the sense of wonder and age. We learn to develop our sense of wonder with age in some ways and lose it in others. Children find many journeys that adults enjoy boring, but they show a remarkable ability to find wonder in the smallest things in a way that adults lose through the attritional nature of the lives we lead. A child may not get much joy from a walk around a ruined church, but we are reminded of what we have lost when we see a child experience ecstasy while playing with a feather in the breeze. The Natural Explorer is tasked with finding wonder in both.

The feeling of wonder can be so rapturous that it is closely associated with the joyous emotions of spiritual enlightenment. This is exactly the sentiment that Aristotle described in an allegory.

If there were men whose habitations had been always underground, in great and commodious houses, adorned with
statues and pictures, furnished with everything which they
who are reputed happy abound with; and if, without stirring
from thence, they should be informed of a certain divine
power and majesty, and, after some time, the earth should
open, and they should quit their dark abode to come to us;
where they should immediately behold the earth, the seas,
the heavens; should consider the vast extent of the clouds
and force of the winds; should see the sun, and observe his
grandeur and beauty, and also his creative power, inasmuch
as day is occasioned by the diffusion of his light through the
sky; and when night has obscured the earth, they should
contemplate the heavens bespangled and adorned with
stars; the surprising variety of the moon, in her increase
and wane; the rising and setting of all the stars, and the
inviolable regularity of their courses; when they should see
these things, they would undoubtedly conclude that there
are Gods, and that these are their mighty works.

Although wonder can lead to religious feelings, enlightenment
need not be religious in its nature. The most secular of descrip-
tions of extreme wonder could be that of one explorer and former
president of the Royal Geographical Society, Sir Francis
Younghusband. In his book, *The Heart of Nature*, Younghusband
described a feeling of being in love with the world and in touch
with the universe beyond the Earth. It was a sensation he likened
to feeling a patriotism not just for one's country, but for the whole
universe.

Wonder, as the emotion of enlightenment, can be defined in a
secular way, by reference to a sense of perfect awareness. This
awareness is an intellectual condition that can remain distinct from
religious notions even if it will inevitably run close to our understanding of the spiritual, since omniscience is synonymous with the

mind of god for many. Buddhist thought is dominated by the idea of enlightenment, but without any specific god associated with it. In Zen Buddhism 'satori' means the sudden awakening that is an important step towards full enlightenment. Satori is usually triggered by the small and ordinary, the sound of a raindrop landing in a puddle perhaps. It is a profound moment that combines awakening and self-realisation.

There are some scintillating similarities in the senses of euphoric enlightenment reported by very different searchers, from philosophers and the religious to naturalists inspecting a leaf. This may be why there has recently been a renaissance of interest in two seemingly unrelated areas: reconnection with the natural world and meditation. Andy Puddicombe, a clinical meditation consultant, asks a pertinent question. 'When was the last time you actually tasted a glass of water?' Imagine the potential of carrying this awareness into every travel experience.

When St Augustine declared that we have 'restless hearts', he was acknowledging that we are searchers. Physically, mentally and spiritually the human race has always been hunting for 'better'. The answers we long for need not be in the form of religion or dogma, but the ones that have resonated over the years have often been found with nature's help. The moments of exhilaration that are possible when feeling a connection with our surroundings allow the experience of something more profound than what we habitually find rattling around in our skulls. This is particularly true when we have viewed the world through the prism of striving and self-gratification.

The German philosopher, Schopenhauer, believed that this striving could only result in alternating pain and boredom. He advocated only two ways out of this problem. One was to lead the ascetic life of a saint, the other was 'through art, through the pure, disinterested contemplation of beauty.' If Schopenhauer is right and we take the natural world to be the greatest artwork there is then its contemplation will offer us something extraordinary and very worthwhile.

Sharing the Experience:
Towards a New Explorer

> The beauty of nature re-forms itself in the mind, and
> not for barren contemplation, but for new creation . . .
> The creation of beauty is Art. The production of a work
> of art throws light upon the mystery of humanity.
>
> Ralph Waldo Emerson

Al-Masudi was ahead of his time when he observed that 'even the cleverest and most judicious minds have neglected extensive areas, each one specialising in a particular field.' The days of the great polymaths are gone; in order to push back the frontiers of academic knowledge, the need for specialisation grows each year. Once there was geography, now there is biogeography, geodesy, glaciology, cultural geography, economic geography, urban geography, political geography and the branches within these, to name a few. Nobody is doubting the wisdom of these developments in the desire to build human knowledge, it is just there comes a point in specialisation where it takes our senses away from the beauty of the whole.

Leichhardt discovered an unknown fossil in Queensland and he passed it on to a specialist, receiving a full description of it in return. The fossil was apparently 'concavely cylindrical, not dichotomous . . . laterally if at all proliferous. Corallum beautifully stellular . . . radiating lamellae . . . latitudinal axial line . . . convex and oblique dissepiments . . . surface longitudinally striated . . .

formed by the coalescing lamellae . . . occasionally dentriculated . . . broken transverse septa.' It is very hard for most of us to tell what it was like to see or feel the fossil from this description, but that is unlikely to have troubled Leichhardt himself. The specimen was named C. Leichhardti in his honour.

We may understand the sun, sky, land, meteorology, thermodynamics, light refraction and diffraction . . . and still not quite *know* a sunset. Vaughan Cornish believed that thanks to our love of the phenomena we see in the sky, we had come to understand their science well, but it was 'only the source of their influence on our emotions which has not yet been fully explored.'

One of the things that separates humanity from the rest of the animal kingdom is our ability to communicate complex ideas to each other. Bees, whales, birds and many other animals succeed in passing simple messages via movements and sounds, but there is no evidence of animals' ability to communicate abstract ideas. It is likely that an ability that helped us emerge from a lower state of consciousness to a higher one is the key to further progress along that road and exploration can play its part.

The hope must be for a new generation of explorers to emerge. We need explorers who are capable of matching the species' vast physical bounds with fresh mental ones. The potential and challenges for new discoveries in the areas that will never find their way onto maps is exciting. And there are equally tantalising possibilities in the way that these are shared.

We already know one of the channels that is available for communicating fresh insight into holistic ideas: this is the role played by the arts. Expression through artistic production can be seen as the passionate attempt to both hold onto a new insight and share it simultaneously.

It is the ability of this creative endeavour to crystallise insights that unites those who prize art and literature and those who feel drawn to explore. Van Gogh is forever taking us to a moment in Arles. Dostoyevsky walks with us in St Petersburg whenever we choose. The most powerful art encapsulates places, it becomes part of those places, the divisions crumble.

These are the greatest moments and there are millions of less great ones, but the challenges that lie before all of them are serious. The Swiss physicist and Alpine explorer, Horace-Benedict de Saussure knew this. 'But what language can reproduce the sensations and paint the ideas with which these great spectacles fill the soul of the Philosopher?' De Saussure was writing about mountains in the late eighteenth century, but these words could apply to all scenes at all times. Art suffers the same daunting task as literature. In the words of the cannabis-eater and American explorer, Fitz Hugh Ludlow, 'You paint a Big Tree and it only looks like a common tree in a cramped coffin.'

Some of the greatest artists hint at a transcendental experience behind their work. Cézanne strove hard to convey as much as he could through the medium of paint – not just the light, shades and textures of objects, but even their smell. He was straining to offer not an object for view but a sense of the whole, an insight into the unity of what we apprehend. To achieve this he allowed the boundaries between himself and the landscape to melt, as he explained in a letter he wrote to a friend. 'The landscape thinks itself in me . . . and I am its consciousness.'

The French philosopher, Maurice Merleau-Ponty, analysed Cézanne's approach and thought along similar lines. Merleau-Ponty felt that vision and the art of looking were not defined by objects and a subject, but by a process that brought the two together. 'As I contemplate the blue of the sky I abandon myself to it and plunge into this mystery, it thinks itself in me.'

Part of the challenge lies in the fact that a heightened sense of natural awareness generates an abundance of observations and sensations, which do not necessarily make the task of representing a scene or experience any easier. A little detail is essential in all art, to facilitate the suspension of disbelief, but it is a fine line and once crossed becomes a problem. We do not like to have our enjoyment of narratives or artworks interrupted by the jutting beak of a curlew.

There are obstacles in our own experience, our perspective can be seen as the culmination of the art we have experienced. There are analogous obstacles in each era and medium. Renaissance landscape art became Arcadian through convention, and conventions, if followed too closely, tend to dampen fresh insight. Richard Long and other land artists have attempted to free art from the constraints of the gallery altogether and their works appear, if they appear at all, on hills and by rivers.

There are challenges in our own nature. There appears to be only a weak correlation between those who enjoy scrambling about in the world and those who like to press at cerebral frontiers. Rebecca Solnit describes this conflict well: the 'combination of a silver tongue and iron thighs seems to be a rare one.' So often we are built to excel only in one area. It is easy to find shortcomings in the physical abilities of great writers and the muse-lessness of the tough heroes. Both fail to achieve perfect awareness. The truth, and it is a happy one, is that this will always leave room for fresh exploration. Paul Bowles had few superiors in the field of travel writing, his ability to evoke scenes was wondrous, but he was human and his powers of awareness fell short of perfect. He wrote of seeing a star cast a shadow through his bedroom window in Cape Cormorin and described it painting a silhouette of his head and the fingers of the hand he held up on the opposite wall. He was clearly unaware that he must have been looking at the planet Venus, since no star could have cast such a shadow.

A further challenge is that we are driven to the creative process by some purpose, the desire to share some particular idea, viewpoint, experience or sensation, but the more we feel driven by this one aspect, the greater the risk that the purpose mars the work in question. Art is not advertisement.

An understanding of the challenges in order to overcome them is part of the transformation from traveller to Natural Explorer and there is no escaping them. Samuel Johnson once wrote, 'Sir,

if a man has experienced the inexpressible, he is under no obligation to express it.' This remains true for the traveller, but has
never been true for the explorer. The explorer who makes discoveries is obliged to at least attempt to share them, otherwise they
cease being an explorer and resume life as a traveller. However
hard it is, there must be a way.

James Holman left his mark by detecting and reporting a
sensuous richness that full-sighted travellers would have overlooked, but he sensed more than he could reveal. Holman knew
the real challenge.

> On the summit of the precipice, and in the heart of the
> green woods . . . there was an intelligence in the winds of
> the hills, and in the solemn stillness of the buried foliage,
> that could not be mistaken. It entered into my heart, and I
> could have wept, not that I did not see, but that I could not
> portray all that I felt.

The rewards for overcoming the challenges are great. In dealing
with them it is best to be honest: most of us hold at least some
small fear of dying without having left a mark of any kind. Many
feel the calling to leave one of the most dramatic marks in our
desire to pass on our genes and have children. There is also a
desire that sits apart from procreation, a desire for our experiences not to be washed away altogether with one more revolution
of the Earth. Why do diaries exist, if not to fight the silent dread
of our inevitable trajectory towards gas and dust? There was graf-
fiti on the Egyptian pyramids by 1500 BC: we all like to leave a
mark of some kind.

David Livingstone scratched his initials and the date 1855 into
a tree – the irony of his admitting the vanity of this in his account
of his journey was perhaps lost on him. Vanity has a long and
strong tradition in the arts of course, the Roman poets used to
encourage support from those in power by pointing out that the
deeds of great men would be forgotten if it were not for their

having been immortalised in poetry. Everyone is vain, even to declare oneself totally without vanity is to attempt to set oneself apart as special in some way. An explorer is a vain traveller, one who is unashamed of the idea that they do not wish their time travelling to be worthless or disappear forever. But there is a difference between openly possessing a desire to express our deeper experiences and trying to prove ourselves better than everyone else. The hope must be that we can accept a level of vanity, without it becoming the goal itself. Vanity, if properly understood, becomes a rock we carry in our rucksack, not a summit to strive for.

Shelley's sonnet 'Ozymandias' uses the metaphor of a once great king's crumbling statue to illustrate the inevitable decline of power and empire. It is a poem that will live for as long as the English language, unlike most statues or buildings. This is the prize of great art and it is available to explorers, but only those who value the goals of insight and expression.

The arts are the only effective means available to share with others the experience of lying by a river at a particular moment. They are the only weapons that the traveller can use to overcome the eerie footsteps of passing time. One short walk, shared, can live long after our longer stroll on the planet has come to an end.

There are forces that will further unite explorers and the creative community. The two come from a similar place, a restless place. Explorers and creatives have both rebelled, both find the 'normal life' insufferably claustrophobic. The adversity that comes from rebellion is likely to draw these two passions closer over time, but the price of rebellion is the same for both, it is to be ostracised.

For all the explorers that found themselves etched in pink granite in parks around the world, there are many more that were written off by their friends and their family, before dying lonely and forgotten. This is the lot that so often confronts the writer, and the artist too: for every Shelley there are millions who fail nobly and ignobly. It is a wonder the two worlds have not come together more frequently to console one another on the rum life they have chosen. There lies the problem and the bond: these are not chosen lives.

True explorers, writers and artists so often feel they are allergic to the life that makes most people content; they feel bounced from the bourgeois. There is something in the great soup of human genes and experience that turns out individuals in each generation who feel driven towards these lives despite the impracticality and unfavourable odds. Explorers, artists and writers feel they have a compulsory vocation, few consider it a lifestyle choice.

One of the things that forced such a stark calling on previous generations was the barrier to expression. Not even the political barrier of censorship, but the logistical one, the fact that for most of human history it has been almost impossible to spread ideas or experiences without overcoming a great inertia of cost, approval and access. Recently it is the cruel cold bottleneck of the front door of the publisher or the gallery that has been the problem.

However, the barriers to publication have now evaporated altogether with the Internet; the front door has been tunnelled-under, if not blown off its hinges. The Internet allows a writer or artist to share their work with millions for the cost of a day's living. There is an entirely separate debate concerning the economic impact of these developments on the creative industries, but little debate in terms of the potential it offers for sharing ideas and experiences.

The speed of the communication and the speed of change in this area are currently too fast for us to fully comprehend, but we gain some perspective by contemplating the fact that this level of mass communication has been possible for less than 0.01 per cent of the history of modern humans. If the life of Homo Sapiens so far can be thought of as lasting a day, then the Gutenberg printing press started working about four minutes ago and the Internet entered widespread use four seconds ago.

The traveller who makes a discovery, however small, can now share it easily. The individual who uses a small discovery to forge a deeper insight can share this with equal abandon. However hard either of these steps are, they will not be thwarted by lack of access to dissemination and at this moment the traveller becomes an explorer.

The awareness of travellers is rising steeply in tandem with a fusion between the worlds of exploration and the arts and a new golden age of exploration is being born. In this new age neither physical extremes nor those of vainglory are a prerequisite, only heightened awareness and honest expression.

In this new age, the individual who chooses to travel to the South Pole will have to compare discoveries with the backpacker on the beach of Bognor Regis. The motives for each will become clear in the work they produce afterwards, their courage and determination will be judged by the way they create and share, not by their destinations.

Humboldt believed that a traveller could be considered lucky if he added facts to the canon of human knowledge, but his passion did not lie in the accumulation of dry facts. He insisted that, 'modern civilisation can be characterised by how it broadens our ideas, making us perceive the connections between the physical and the intellectual worlds.' Humboldt did not discuss whether our emotions lie between these connections, but he would surely agree that these are arousing times.

The End of the Journey:
An Epilogue

I reached the car a little more than four hours after setting off and rested for a moment by leaning against it.

Before me I could see where the river had carved its low pass through the crumbly chalk. I saw the shades in the crops on the hills as their gradients waxed and waned and I could almost feel the chalk softening on the shallow slopes. My mind moved to thoughts about the stone in Arundel Castle, then onto the beach in the distance and then back to the stones I had held in my hand that afternoon. The shapes of the clouds had shifted and yet, in some comforting way, the sky had not. The tails of cirrus above me still suggested change may be on its way, but it had not beaten me back to the car.

I looked and laughed at the range of colours, but I felt no need to count them. It was enough to know they were there. They were now as easy to feel as the breeze, which had died a little. The warmth of the sun was ebbing away too as it headed north west, altering the shades of the land beneath it on its way. The village of South Stoke appeared different, now that it was deprived of direct sunlight, but its name remained. Things seemed quieter.

I popped the second blackberry of the day into my mouth, as I opened the car door, and didn't hesitate to squeeze the juice from it with my tongue. In the car I pulled out a piece of paper from the glove compartment and glanced at the handwritten lines. Before reading them, I looked up at the chimney by the road. There was no pigeon perched on it, the bird had moved on. As I read the words out loud, I thought of home. The walk had taken four hours. The walk had taken thirty-seven years. I bit my lip and then turned the key.

We shall not cease from exploration
And the end of all our exploring
Will be to arrive where we started
And know the place for the first time.

T. S. Eliot, The Four Quartets

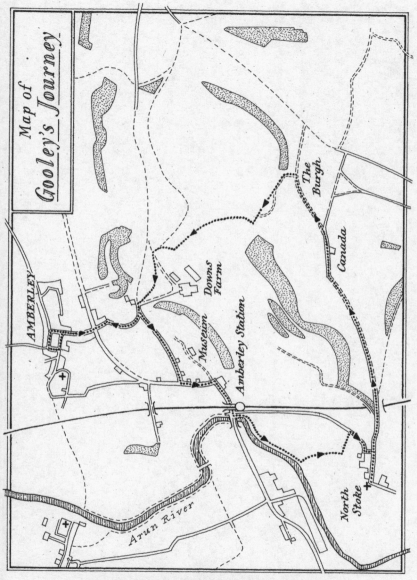

Map of
Gooley's Journey

AMBERLEY

Downs
Farm

Museum

Amberley Station

The
Burgh

Canada

North
Stoke

Arun River

Tristan Gooley's Sussex Expedition, 6 August 2011

The Cast

Ibn Battuta 1304–1368

Ibn Battuta was the greatest medieval Islamic traveller. He travelled over 75,000 miles and his most famous book, the *Rihlah* or *Travels*, remains a classic.

Vaughan Cornish 1862–1948

Vaughan Cornish was a successful British geographer who branched out into the appreciation of scenery, going on to describe himself as a 'Pilgrim of Scenery'. His zealous appreciation of the natural landscape was encapsulated in his 1943 book, *The Beauties of Scenery*.

Francis Bond Head 1793–1875

Francis Bond Head was a Battle of Waterloo veteran, businessman, colonial administrator, traveller and author. He was known as 'Galloping Head' for his feats of riding vast distances across South America and his exploits became popular through his colourful written accounts of these journeys. He also earned a reputation for impulsiveness, a love of nature and an interest in indigenous cultures.

Bond Head's observations in this book are all from his rich account, *Rough notes taken during some rapid journeys across the pampas and among the Andes,* published by John Murray in 1826.

Charles Darwin 1809–1882

Although best known as the originator of the theory of natural selection, there is so much more to celebrate about Charles Darwin.

Darwin first expressed his big idea privately, following a circumnavigation aboard HMS *Beagle*, and then went on to shock the world by expounding it publicly in his book, *On the Origin of Species*, in 1859. The power of the idea of evolution was such that Darwin's extraordinarily beautiful account of his travels during that journey aboard the *Beagle* often gets overlooked. In his journal of his experiences, better known as *The Voyage of the Beagle*, Darwin displayed a stunningly broad curiosity in and fascination for the lands he visited. He came to know places through a scintillating prism composed of disciplines ranging from geology to anthropology, taking in huge sweeps of natural science in between.

It transpired that from a philosophy of finding no observation too small or unworthy, grew an idea big enough to change the world.

William Gilpin 1724–1804

William Gilpin was a traveller, writer and headmaster. He travelled widely in the UK and was always on the hunt for scenery that he deemed 'picturesque', in other words, landscapes that would make good pictures. He was a pioneer in this field and started a trend for picturesque tourism. The best introduction to his thinking and view can be found in *Observations on the River Wye*, published in 1782.

James Holman 1786–1857

James Holman, who became known as 'The Blind Traveller', was an extraordinarily ambitious and perceptive traveller and author. Holman's blindness never deterred him, even from climbing mountains, and his lack of sight spurred him to become acutely aware of and sensitive to his surroundings using his other senses.

Jason Robert's biography of Holman, *A Sense of the World* (2006), is the best place to get to know him.

Alexander von Humboldt 1769–1859

Humboldt was a German naturalist and explorer whose written works are staggering in their ambition and beauty. Like Charles Darwin, who was heavily influenced by him, Humboldt resisted the temptation to view the places he travelled to from a single perspective and delighted in an approach that was simultaneously scientific and holistic.

Humboldt was particularly interested in the 'unity of nature' and in 1845 he published the first volume of his massive work, *Kosmos*, which attempted to unite the branches of science. His account of his travels in South America has served to illustrate so many points in this book and remains an informing, entertaining and inspirational read.

Humboldt's ability to combine the approach of a scientist, the ambition of a philosopher and the passion of a poet have endeared him to the broadest spectrum of curious travellers.

Ludwig Leichhardt 1813–1848

A Prussian explorer and naturalist, Ludwig Leichhardt undertook an expedition in Australia that made his name. Travelling from the east of the country to Port Essington on the north coast, Leichhardt's journey was remarkable for the determination he showed and hardships his team endured. But as an explorer he deserves the greatest credit for his ability to remain sensitive to and curious about the natural world around him, despite the extreme conditions that would have snuffed out any inquisitive spirit in most people.

Leichhardt embarked on a subsequent expediton in 1848, this time aiming to travel from the east to the west coast of Australia. He and his party were seen for the last time on 3 April 1848 on the Darling Downs. He is believed to have perished somewhere in the deserts of the Australian interior, but despite numerous searches and inquiries, his final resting place remains unknown to this day.

John Lubbock 1834–1913

A rare combination of banker, politician and naturalist, John Lubbock's scientific interests ranged from entomology to archaeology. He drew from his wide experience of the natural world to lay out a popular approach to gaining the most from appreciating our surroundings in *The Beauties of Nature,* published in 1896.

Al-Masudi Late ninth century to 957

Abu al-Hasan Ali ibn al-Husayn ibn Ali al-Mas'udi, abbreviated to Al-Masudi, was a historian and traveller whose epic works earned him the nickname 'Herodotus of the Arabs' in the West. The scale of Al-Masudi's itinerancy and works was matched by the originality of his approach. He focused on areas that would have seemed beneath most other travellers of the time and took a keen interest in the culture of the places he visited, as well as their social, economic and religious idiosyncrasies.

His work is accessible, most easily via edited and abridged editions of his great work, *The Meadows of Gold and Mines of Gems.*

John Muir 1838–1914

Born in Dunbar, Scotland, John Muir emigrated with his family to Wisconsin in the United States in 1849. He built a career as a successful mechanical inventor, but temporary blindness caused by an accident led Muir to reassess his life. He became much more interested in God's inventions, as he saw nature, rather than his own or any other person's.

Muir's sight returned in one eye and he went on to become a legendary naturalist. He was largely responsible for the formation of Yosemite national park.

John Muir's account of his epic trek from the mid-west to the Gulf of Mexico was published posthumously as *A Thousand-Mile*

Walk to the Gulf. It is a wonderful exposition of the ability of nature to enrich a journey.

Pliny the Elder 23–79

Pliny was a Roman scholar and author of the incredible *Natural History*, which aimed at the broad target of describing the 'nature of things' and 'life'. The 37 books of his epic take in cosmology, botany, humans, animals, medicine, agriculture, minerals and mining and many more topics besides. Although daunting in its scope, the selected excerpts that can be found in most modern editions are very readable and enjoyable.

Marco Polo circa 1254–1324

The Venetian merchant and explorer is famous for the scale of his journeys to Asia and in China in particular, but it was his habit of noticing the smallest and most diverse details that makes him of greater interest. *The Travels of Marco Polo* will remain a travel classic.

Nan Shepherd 1893–1981

Anna 'Nan' Shepherd was a Scottish author and teacher. A successful novelist and poet, her love of hill-walking and the highland mountains infuse all her work. However it is in the non-fiction book, *The Living Mountain*, that fellow explorers will find the most abundant clues to enrich their own journeys. *The Living Mountain* was written in the 1940s and anyone who takes the time to read this beautiful work will be aghast to learn that it was declined by a publisher at the time and left in a drawer until 1977.

Wilfred Thesiger 1910–2003

Declared by many to be the last of the true old school of explorers, Sir Wilfred Patrick Thesiger combined extreme toughness with a delicate eye. His power of observation was translated into stark and sublime prose and photography.

Thesiger's best known work and, in his own opinion, his best book, is *Arabian Sands*, which chronicles his time with the Bedouin in the Empty Quarter.

Henry David Thoreau *1817–1862*

An American writer and naturalist, who may best be thought of as a philosopher of the outdoors. Thoreau was a subscriber to many of the ideas of Transcendentalism and his philosophy is regularly simplified unfairly as: nature good, civilisation bad.

A thorough rebel, Thoreau lived his philosophies and enjoyed resisting almost all attempts by society to make him conform, from being jailed for refusing to pay taxation to spending two years living apart from the world in a self-built house at Walden Pond. His best-known work is appropriately titled, *Walden*, but an excellent introduction to the outdoors philosophy of Thoreau can be gained in *Walking*, published in 1861. Fortunately there is no need to sign up to all of Thoreau's opinions to derive a lot of benefit from the energy and originality of his writing.

Laurens van der Post *1906–1996*

Sir Laurens Jan van der Post was an explorer, writer and conservationist, born in South Africa. His extremely colourful, sometimes controversial life included military service during the Second World War and time in a Japanese prisoner of war camp, where he established a university for prisoners. His friendship with the psychologist Carl Jung lasted until Jung's death.

In *The Lost World of the Kalahari*, van der Post mixed a unique insight into the lives of Kalahari tribesman with the environment they lived in. He also gave an insight into the challenges of travelling with others. He became an influential friend of Prince Charles and was knighted in 1981.

Gilbert White *1720–1793*

The clergyman and naturalist, Gilbert White, wrote about his local area of East Hampshire in *The Natural History and Antiquities of Selborne*. Published in 1789, it was a title that promised very little and delivered so very much. The book became a classic by illustrating, through a series of letters, how much satisfaction there is to be derived by doing our best to understand the world we see around us, however small it seems. Mr White was an explorer if ever there was one.

Dorothy Wordsworth *1771–1855*

Dorothy was very close to her famous brother William and a talented writer in her own right, but with little desire for fame. In fact she seemed relieved in 1803 when a publisher could not be found for her travel book, *Recollections of a Tour Made in Scotland*. It would not be published until seventy-one years after she wrote it and two decades after she died.

Dorothy lost both her parents young and experienced poverty in her early life, but was blessed in many ways later. She spent much of her life in the beautiful surroundings of the Lake District and could count as friends some of the most interesting literary minds of the time. Alongside her brother, she knew Samuel Taylor Coleridge, Thomas de Quincey and Robert Southey. Dorothy's appreciation and taste in landscape was described by Coleridge as being 'like a perfect electrometer'.

Acknowledgements

The worlds of exploration and book writing have the potential to be daunting, lonely, exhausting and not perfectly sensible. Both occupations also attract those who find themselves believing from time to time that they are capable of achieving things as individuals, which in truth require a team effort of highly skilled people. This book would not exist without the hard work and talents of many to whom I am very grateful. So, through the ice on my moustache, which may on this occasion be the foam at the top of a cappuccino, I would like to take this opportunity to sincerely salute the following.

I would like to thank those present in the first meeting where this book was discussed: Sophie Hicks, Rupert Lancaster and Carole Welch. In that meeting I gave this small group little more to base their faith on than a story about Mungo Park (which has made it into the 'Plants' chapter) and a lot of enthusiasm. If they did not have such experience and confidence in what they do, it is unlikely they would have allowed me to embark at all.

My thanks to the whole team at Hodder & Stoughton, who have been a joy to work with throughout. The following have combined great enthusiasm with copious experience to assist me at each turn: Kate Miles, Lyndsey Ng, Sarah Christie, Amanda Jones and Juliet Brightmore.

The writing of the book was made possible by the experiences of those who are no longer with us, especially those listed in 'The Cast' section, but also many contemporaries, including the writers, Philip Ball, Patrick Whitefield, Rebecca Solnit, Diane Ackerman, Roland Huntford, Jason Roberts, David

Abram, Robin Hanbury-Tennison, Colin Tudge, Desmond Morris, Simon Schama, Robert Macfarlane, Russell Foster & Leon Kreitzman. I would also like to thank Colin Thubron, Lord Bragg and Sir Ranulph Fiennes for their time in responding to my personal correspondence and Lord Bragg and Felix Dennis for granting permission for me to reproduce material.

Neil Gower has done a superb job with the illustrations for this book and I cannot thank him enough for exceeding his tough brief, by some way. Helen Coyle showed an equal disregard for normal standards with her copy edit: brilliant, thank you.

The sections of the book that comprise 'Gooley's Journey' were written by building layers and there are many who have added to this process through their writing, but others who have helped in more practical ways. There are a few who have my deepest gratitude for donning boots last summer and joining me as we explored one small corner area of West Sussex together. Before setting off, I explained that volunteers were wanted for . . . non-hazardous journey, wages non-existent, no darkness, inconstant danger, safe return was likely, honour in case of success was doubtful . . . but the closest to recognition would be found here: Richard & Ollie Webber, David & Anne Bone, Tracey Younghusband, Anna Richardson and John Pahl, I thank you.

A second thank you is owed to my editor, Rupert Lancaster, and my agent, Sophie Hicks, who have helped shape the book through their input, guidance and that hard-to-pin-down, quasi-British quality that is required in all endeavours that are both literary and exploratory. I'm thinking of that rare ability to keep smiling, even under the weight of the seventh version of the cover . . . that gritty will to edit on the beaches, to edit in the fields and in the streets, and to fill the inbox with our subtitles dead!

Thank you all.

Tristan.
January 2012

Notes on Sources

The Lost Explorer: An Introduction

'And that, in brief, is all there is to tell about the South Pole . . .' Byrd, R., 'The Flight Over the South Pole 1929', from Hanbury-Tenison, R., p. 520.

'Others considered the undertaking exceedingly dangerous . . .' Leichhardt, L., p. 6.

Shackleton refers to Amundsen as fortunate four times: *New York Times*, 11 March 1912.

'The discovery of the South Pole will not be the end of Antarctic exploration . . .' *Daily Mail*, 11 March 1911.

'astounded at the absurdity of Shackleton's plan . . .' This and subsequent quotes referring to Shackleton in this chapter are sourced from Huntford, R., *Shackleton*, pp. 365–6.

'What a man he is! I have known him so long and yet he amazes me all over again.' Von Humboldt, A., Introduction by Jason Wilson, p. xxxvii.

The Senses

'Earth, however, is kind, gentle, indulgent . . .' Pliny, p. 30.

Ishi, see Kroeber, T., p. 111 et al.

'Every new moon also was hailed . . .' Leichhardt, L., p. 126.

Wilfred Thesiger had similar experiences: Thesiger, W., p. 42.

'If they had been Arabs you would have sat there . . .' Thesiger, W., p. 78.

'The impressions on their retina seem to be naturally more intense . . .' Leichhardt, L., p. 59.

'The fundamental event of the modern age . . .' Heidegger, Martin, quoted in Pallasmaa, J., p. 21.

'I am constantly asked, and I may as well answer . . .' Holman, James, quoted in Roberts, J., p. 224.

'as a compressed definition of ambient space.' Roberts, J., p. 76.

'I see things better with my feet.' Holman, James, quoted in Roberts, J., p. 2.

'Everything is very ordinary in Llangollen . . .' Thomas, D., 'Quite Early One Morning', quoted in Perrin, J., p. 31.

The Plants
'Flower in the Crannied Wall': http://en.wikisource.org/wiki/Flower_in_the_Crannied_Wall, accessed 22 October 2011.
'to have a better view of what had happened.' Park, M., p. 223.
'Whichever way I turned, nothing appeared but danger and difficulty' and 'At this moment, painful as my reflections were . . .' Park, M., p. 225.
'descend towards the plains in proportion as their distance from the equator . . .' Humboldt, A., p. 139.
'The pines of Mexico are absent in the Peruvian Andes . . .' Humboldt, A., p. 139.
'white man's footprint': Whitefield, P., p. 84.
'preserve physical charm' and 'a kind of aura of attractiveness and sex appeal': Pliny, pp. 230, 235.

The Changing Mountain
'The wilderness has a mysterious tongue': Shelley, P., http://www.gutenberg.org/cache/epub/4800/pg4800.html
'knowledge of the anatomy of mountains contributes to the recognition of their beauty': Cornish, V., p. 43.
'Here it comes again!' Darwin, C., p. 326.
'adolescents with sharp punkish ridges': Macfarlane, R., p. 64.
'It is easy to see why the inhabitants of beautiful climates . . .' Humboldt, A., p. 25.
'From up here the island becomes an immense heap . . .' Humboldt, A., p. 31.
'Everything here betrays a deep solitude.' Humboldt, A., p. 31.
'There is a saying that a mountain is high enough to reach the rhododendron . . .' Humboldt, A., p. 139.
Pedro III of Aragon: Schama, S., p. 411.
Scheuchzer made an extensive collection of dragon sightings: Schama, S., p. 412.
'We of the Orient have never conceived Nature . . .' Suzuki, D. T., p. 334.
'The whole scene around us in every direction was devoid of vegetation . . .' Bond Head, F., p. 221.
'the mountain gives itself most completely . . .' Shepherd, N., p. 11.
'Each time I see Fuji . . .' Masamune, quoted in Suzuki, D. T., p. 332.

'The blessing of my life – the gift is yours . . .' Wordsworth, W., http://
www.bartleby.com/145/ww288.html, accessed 20 June 2011.
'even though I should read Homer': Keats, John, quoted in Solnit, R.,
Wanderlust, p. 117.
As Rebecca Solnit has pointed out in her book: Solnit, R., *Wanderlust*,
p. 113.

The Coast
'The reflections in the water were more beautiful than the sky itself . . .'
Wordsworth, Dorothy, quoted in http://www.guardian.co.uk/
news/2011/jul/29/weatherwatch-summer-wordsworth-calais,
accessed 1 September 2011.
'Very quickly we saw that these "stones" are the thin and porous
valves . . .' Humboldt, A., p. 74.
'For man, nature seems more grand the more it is mysterious . . .'
Humboldt, A., p. 74.

Valleys of Ice
'A glacier may be considered as a vast instrument of friction . . .' Ruskin,
J., p. 178.
William Buckland: *Oxford National Dictionary of Biography*, accessed 18
March 2011. http://www.oxforddnb.com
Milankovitch cycles: *Encyclopedia Britannica 2009 Ultimate Reference
Suite*.
1,000 tons per square foot: Reader's Digest, *Joy of Nature*, p. 74.
The rock 'scratches its own face': Fortey, R., p. 55.
'Here lyes The body of John Hunter . . .': http://www.ajbhope.net/
listed-buildings-in-tweedsmuir/

The Earth
'Though these two forests are only parted . . .' White, G., p. 29.
'hog-backed', 'an immense skein of silk agitated and disturbed
by tempestuous blasts' and other Borrow quotes: Borrow, G.,
pp. 345–6.
'perfectly horizontal white band' and other Darwin references here:
Darwin, C., p. 9.
Limestone can form marble, granite: Fortey, R., pp. 14–17.
'who has either sense of danger or delight in rarity.' Johnson, Samuel,
Journey to the Western Isles of Scotland, http://www.readprint.com/
chapter-33191/Journey-to-the-Western-Isles-of-Scotland-Samuel-
Johnson
'The difference between the sandstone country . . .' Leichhardt, L.,
p. 65.

'We were encamped in the shade of a fine Erythrina . . .' Leichhardt, L., p. 38.

Ben Lawers: see www.nts.org.uk

'The oaks of Temple and Blackmoor stand high . . .' White, G., p. 9.

The wood of trees may be given colours: Tudge, C., p. 90.

'In the bed of the river, I still found pebbles . . .' Leichhardt, L., p. 100.

'The nature of the soil was easily distinguished . . .' Leichhardt, L., p. 73.

Wilfred Thesiger recognized: Thesiger, W., p. 77.

Patrick Whitefield highlights: Whitefield, P., p. 2.

This can be used to spot the granite mountains: Whitefield, P., p. 27.

After the Pilgrim Fathers had shown the way: Tudge, C., p. 114.

The county of Surrey has sandy soils: Whitefield, P., p. 29.

'The penetrating sweet smell and beautiful colour . . .' Mas' Udi, p. 47.

'To see a world in a grain of sand.' Blake, William, 'Auguries of Innocence', http://en.wikiquote.org/wiki/William_Blake

As Gilbert White discovered in Selborne: White, G., p. 9.

The Animals

'The essential quality of an animal . . .' Henry Mayhew, http://www.uoguelph.ca/englit/victorian/HTML/taxonomy.html, accessed 13 November 2011.

'They have the prettiest hens to be seen anywhere . . .' Polo, M., p. 307.

There are 750 different species of fig tree: Tudge, C., p. 4.

In 1995 a study of 19 trees in Panama counted 1,200 different beetles: UNEP, 1995, cited in Foster, R. & Kreitzman, L., p. 121.

'I've more than once involuntarily dropped to my knees under them.' Mabey, R., p. 49.

'lamb is innocence . . .' Emerson, R. W., p. 49.

'I am perfectly aware that the mosquito . . .' Pascoe, J., ed., *Mr Explorer Douglas*, Wellington, 1957, quoted in Hanbury-Tenison, R., p. 462.

In April 2011 staff at a bank in Uttar Pradesh in India: BBC website, http://www.bbc.co.uk/news/world-south-asia-13194864, accessed 1 May 2011.

'honesty, good sense, justice and also respect for the stars . . .' Pliny, p. 108.

'a single green leaf can scarcely be discovered.' Darwin, C., p. 6.

'How doth the Banking Busy Bee . . .' *Punch*, from http://en.wikipedia.org/wiki/John_Lubbock,_1st_Baron_Avebury

'Their ideas of the rights of property are far stricter than those of some statesmen.' Lubbock, J., p. 74.

'Sea-gull, sea-gull sit on the sand . . .' Binney, R., p. 106.

'When the glow-worm lights her lamp . . .' Binney, R., p. 108.

'Wet weather seldom hurts the most unwise . . .' Virgil, quoted in Binney, R., p. 133.
'After having grazed, he returns . . .' Mas' Udi, p. 49.

The Shape of Nature

'Compared to this what are the cathedrals or palaces built by men . . .' Banks, J., quoted in Ball, P., *Branches*, p. 71.
'This grand book the universe . . .' Galileo Galilei, cited in Jones, E., *Reading the Book of Nature*, Athens: Ohio University Press, 1989, p. 22, quoted in Abram, D., p. 32.
'The stiff soil of these plains was here and there marked by very regular pentagonal . . .' Leichhardt, L., p. 134.

The Light

'As the red disk sank behind the west . . .' Lummis, C. F., p. 48.
'served just to let in light enough . . .' Gilpin, W., p. 45.
'glides from her lair' Heine, H., London, excerpt from *Poetry of Heinrich Heine*, London: Citadel, 1969, quoted in Davidson, R., p. 23.
George Mallory: Macfarlane, R., p. 214.
'Death is darkness. But are we not conceived and nurtured from the egg in darkness?' Jamie, K., p. 3.
'Why, he wondered, Orientals seek beauty in darkness . . .' Tanizaki, J., p. 47.
'Light in Scotland has a quality . . .' Shepherd, N., p. 2.
'We felt meditative, and fit for nothing but placid staring . . .' Conrad, J., p. 6.
'scarcely any landscape will stand the test of different lights.' Gilpin, W., p. 50.
'Old towns are more mysterious . . .' Pallasmaa, J., p. 46.
'Twilight holds us between being focused and unfocused on our surroundings . . .' Pallasmaa, J., p. 46.
Edvard Munch's *The Scream*: *The New York Times*, 8 February 2004.
'Many children, their eyes no longer blocked . . .' Abram, D., p. 63.

The Sky

'The moon is at her full, and riding high . . .' Bryant, William C., *The Tides*, http://www.gutenberg.org/files/29700/29700-h/29700-h.htm, accessed 17 November 2011.
'Humboldt, "the first of travellers," but not . . .' Byron's *Don Juan*, http://www.gutenberg.org/files/21700/21700-h/21700-h.html
'The heavens of America appear infinitely higher . . .' Bond Head, F., quoted by Thoreau, H. D., *Walking*, p. 23.
'delicate china blue that's unique to the Hebrides' Whitehead, P., p. 69.

'like some crystal of an unknown water'. Professor Colvin, quoted by Lubbock, J., p. 31.

'triumphal arch'. From Campbell, Thomas, *To the Rainbow*, http://books. google.co.uk/books?id=JcAsAAAAYAAJ&printsec=frontcover&dq= inauthor:%22Thomas+Campbell%22&hl=en&sa=X&ei=FS_ vTonWKIqc-waot8WJAg&ved=0CDKQ6AEwAA#v=onepage&q= inauthor%3A%22Thomas%20Campbell%22&f=false

Cezanne painted the same view sixty times: Wylie, J., p. 1.

'Even those with no inkling of astronomy know . . .' Humboldt, A., p. 42.

'And those long gentle lines of the dip-slope of the Cotswolds . . .' Hoskins, W. G., quoted in Wylie, J., p. 31.

'The Pico de Teide is not situated in the Tropics . . .' Humboldt, A., p. 36.

'air-conditioned, bright canteens . . .'; 'tinned minds, tinned breath'. Betjeman, J., 'Slough', passim, http://www.bbc.co.uk/berkshire/ bigread/bigread_betjeman.shtml/

Charles Darwin also remembers the coldness of the air: Darwin, C., p. 319.

'The sky was perfectly delicious, sweet enough . . .' Muir, J., pp. 188–9.

The Navajo Indians see the air as providing awareness, thought and speech: Abram, D., p. 237.

'On this hot morning stripped of leaves and tartar . . .' Van der Post, L., p. 108.

Cities, from the ancient Teotihuacan in Mexico to the modern Washington DC: Aveni, A., pp. 129–57.

The Weather

'A powerful force was working within this vast assembly . . .' Wainwright, A., *A Pennine Journey*, 1986, quoted in Minshull, D., p. 88.

'Among other wonders they bring on tempests and thunderstorms . . .' Polo, M., p. 174.

'I notice first a throb of expectancy, a slight quiver, a concentration . . .' Keller, H., quoted in Herrman, D., *Helen Keller: A Life*, Google Books, p. 159, http://books.google.co.uk/books?id=VUp4uh87_ eUC&pg=PA156&source=gbs_toc_r&cad=3#v=onepage&q&f=false, accessed 26 September 2011.

'They no longer came with the old home music gathered from open prairies . . .' Muir, J., p. 176.

The average cloud weighs about one billion kilograms. For the calculation behind this estimate see http://greenearthfacts.com/ weather/how-much-does-a-cloud-weigh/, accessed 17 November 2011.

'eager gobbling'. Meredith, G., *The Egoist*, 1879, Google Books, http://books.google.co.uk/books?id=kYrUIMicHaUC

'the deep murmur of the earth taking the rain into her . . .' Van der Post, L., p. 243.

'There is a light cascade as it drips from step to step'. Hull, John, quoted in Whiston Spirn, A., p. 36.

'vitrified, siliceous tubes, which are formed by lightning entering loose sand.' Darwin, C., p. 59.

'called into life thousands of small frogs . . .' Leichhardt, L., p. 45.

'the god of the English firing his great guns . . .' Byrd, William, *History of the Dividing Line betwixt Virginia and North Carolina Run in the Year of Our Lord 1728*, 1841, in Bohls, Elizabeth A. & Duncan, Ian, p. 347.

'The Muslims say that Solomon imprisoned the wind here . . .' Mas' Udi, p. 44.

'well fitted for the abode of invalids in winter.' Roden FRCS, T. C., 'Topography and Climate of Llandudno, North Wales', *British Medical Journal*, 8 May 1958.

'The fog appears to owe its origin to the difference of temperature . . .' Lewis, Meriwether & Clark, William, p. 2.

'It appeared to me, that a strong dose of British wind . . .' Bond Head, F., p. 194.

Still Waters

'At that time the idea became fixed in my mind . . .' Jung, C. G., p. 26.

'A cluster of trees with greener foliage . . .' Leichhardt, L., p. 85.

Gilbert White noticed that all the kine: White, G., p. 27.

'A river which rushes down the hills between woods and fields . . .' Whitefield, P., p. 259.

craquelure: Ball, P., *Branches*, p. 90.

'Of all inorganic substances, acting in their own proper nature . . .' Ruskin, John, quoted in Lubbock, J., p. 248.

Colour

'Every spot of colour . . .' Jefferies, Richard, *The Open Air*, Google Books, accessed 20 November 2011, http://books.google.co.uk/books?id=keD8A5ZWjE4C&printsec=frontcover&source=gbs_ge_summary_r&cad=O#v=onepage&q&f=false

'I know nothing in the visible world that combines splendour . . .' Gilbert Hamerton, Philip, *Landscape*, quoted in Lubbock, J., p. 26.

'beautiful pearls'. Wainwright, A., *The Pennine Way*, 1986, quoted in Minshull, D., p. 124.

Millais: Lee, Raymond L. & Fraser, Alistair B., *The Rainbow Bridge: Rainbows in Art, Myth, and Science*, Google Books, p. 91, http://books.google.co.uk/books?id=kZcCtT1ZeaEC&printsec=frontcover&source=gbs_ge_summary_r&cad=O#v=onepage&q&f=false

No vertebrates contain blue pigments: Ball, P., *Bright Earth*, p. 30.

'How could anyone who sees the peacock . . .' Maguire, H., *Earth and Ocean: The Terrestrial World in Byzantine Art*, 1987, p. 30, quoted in Ball, P., *Bright Earth*, p. 31.

'convulsed orange inch of moon': cummings, e.e., quoted in Ackerman, D., p. 276.

'The light in Japan is often green.' Whiston Spirn, A., p. 98.

The City

'This City is what it is . . .' Plato, passim.

'I had hurt my right arm by my horse falling; however . . .' Bond Head, F., p. 59.

In Edinburgh the lack of saints and heroes: Jamie, K., p. 151.

'The streets of Havana are crooked, labyrinthic . . .' Muir, J., p. 155.

'at any price': Thoreau, H., *Walking*, p. 26.

'At first, some of them cry at the thought of going into the woods . . .' Jones, Sian, quoted in Pretty, J., p. 37.

'solitary mortal endowed with an active imagination . . .' Baudelaire, Charles, quoted in Nicholson, G., p. 26.

'goes botanizing on the asphalt.' Benjamin, Walter, *Charles Baudelaire: A Lyric Poet in the Era of High Capitalism*, translated by Zohn, Harry, London: Verso, 1973, quoted in Solnit, R., *Wanderlust*, p. 199.

We hear different echos in a Renaissance city: Pallasmaa, J., p. 51.

Ruskin: Pallasmaa, J., p. 59.

'And if you wish to know even for once the fine intoxication . . .' Bain, James Leith Macbeth, *The Barefoot League*, 1914, http://www.barefooters.org/key-works/barefoot_league.html

'A town of red brick, or of brick that would have been red . . .' Dickens, Charles, *Hard Times*, quoted in Willams, R., p. 153.

'Not to find one's way in a city may well be uninteresting and banal . . .' Benjamin, W., *Walter Benjamin, Selected Writings 1931–34*, Google Books, http://books.google.co.uk/books?id=7M0x5svvwyEC&dq

Hardy: Williams, R., p. 215.

'I'm a lover of learning, and trees and open country . . .' Plato, quoted in Abram, D., p. 102.

The Trees

'The treasures within the earth were long hidden . . .' Pliny, p. 164.

'To them the sight of a wheat field or a cabbage garden . . .': Weld, Isaac, *Travels through the States of North America . . .*, from Bohls, Elizabeth A. & Duncan, Ian, p. 390.

The podocarps of New Zealand . . . kahikateas: Tudge, C., p. 118.

'Whether rocking and rustling in the wind . . .' Muir, J., p. 92.

Gilbert White: White, G., p. 11.

Walleechu: Darwin, C., p. 67.

'zamang de Guayare': Humboldt, A., p. 146.

Farms in Wales that were happy to offer hospitality to these drovers would plant a clump of Scots pines: Whitefield, P., p. 305.

'displaying a spirit of restless selfishness, eager emulation and craftiness.' Bates, Henry Walter, on Burmeister, Hermann, quoted in Hanbury-Tenison, R., p. 362.

'slash and burn, plant and earn': Schama, S., p. 46.

In the UK there will be woodruff, wood anemones and wood spurge: Rackham, O., *Woodlands*, p. 250.

'Palms grow in light sandy soil – usually one containing alkaline salts . . .' Pliny, p. 174.

'I am marked to fell . . .' Dennis, F., 'Sylva Anathema', from *Tales from the Woods*, p. 67.

Eucalypts: Tudge, C., p. 278.

In the UK freestanding trees will have an age in years: Whitefield, P., p. 165.

Firs, pines, spruces, rimus . . . umbrella pines: Tudge, C., p. 278.

'spread themselves like a Persian cat on a feather bed . . .' Tudge, C., p. 89.

The Human Animal

'A white man bathing by the side of a Tahitian . . .' Darwin, C., p. 384.

'The forms of the mountains did not melt so exquisitely into each other . . .' Wordsworth, Dorothy, quoted in Bohls, Elizabeth A. & Duncan, Ian, p. 167.

'There was so much obscurity and uncertainty about her . . .': Wordsworth, Dorothy, quoted in Bohls, Elizabeth A. & Duncan, Ian, p. 168.

'other fellow'. Guest, Edgar, *The Other Fellow*, http://books.google.co.uk/books?id=86KngJwy4PAC&pg

Caucasians and blacks are hairier than Asians: Ackerman, D., p. 22.

body odour was once so rare in Japan: Ackerman, D., p. 22.

'cramped, contracted and buttoned up . . .' Hurd, Richard, in Bohls, Elizabeth A. & Duncan, Ian, p. 18.

'Thus does sensuality triumph . . .' Humboldt, A., p. 86.

'smooth tongue of deceit' and 'open expression of kind and friendly feelings'. Leichhardt, L., p. 220.

'A cheat, who knows his gold is false and counterfeit . . .' Barbot, John, quoted in Bohls, Elizabeth A. & Duncan, Ian, p. 184.

People-watching: for this section I am heavily indebted to Prof. Desmond Morris' excellent book, *Manwatching*.

'All savages appear to possess . . .' Darwin, C., p. 197.

Mas' Udi on chess and backgammon: Mas' Udi, pp. 19–80.

'It is nowhere more bitter than between Marseilles and the Provençal . . .'
  Benjamin, Walter, *Marseilles*, from Denkbilder Gesamelte Schriften
  Vol IV I pp. 359–364, © Suhrkamp Verlag Frankfurt am Main 1972
  and Harvard University Press, quoted in Davidson, R., p. 32.
'Fill this place with people. . .' Disney, Walt, quoted in Whiston Spirn,
  A., p. 146.
'Well I have precious little sympathy for the selfish propriety of civilized
  man . . .' Muir, J., p. 122.
Maeshowe: Jamie, K., p. 17.
'greatest refreshment to the spirits of man . . .' Francis Bacon, http://
  www.library.utoronto.ca/utel/criticism/baconf_ess/ess_ch46.html

Worldly Goods
'Among the mulattos whose huts surround the salt lake . . .': Humboldt,
  A., p. 71.
'This rage for searching for mines amazed us . . .' Humboldt, A., p. 93.
'Money means less the further from the coast you go . . .' Humboldt, A.,
  p. 169.
'If only gold could be completely banished from life . . .' Pliny, p. 287.
'the mineral productions of every kind; but more particularly metals,
  limestone, pit coal & saltpetre'. Lewis, Meriwether & Clark, William,
  p. xxix.
By 1994 an academic study estimated that each year in the USA, 0.8
  billion metric tons: le Hooke, Robert B., cited in Goudie, Andrew &
  Viles, Heather, p. 70.
Bingham Canyon Mine: Wired.com, http://www.wired.com/
  wiredscience/2009/10/gallery_mines/3/, accessed 4 April 2011.
'The smell of rotting eggs overlaid with the cloying scent of boiling birch
  tar . . .' Schama, S., p. 46.
The Cork Oaks provide a perfect habitat: Tudge, C., p. 198.
'Doggies catch otters, old women no.' Darwin, C., p. 204.
'I passed through the jewellers' bazaar, and my eyes were dazzled . . .'
  Battutah, Ibn, quoted in Mackintosh-Smith, T. pp. 79–80.
Colin Thubron: personal correspondence.
'Are they unhappy? No, there is no unhappiness . . .' Seneca, quoted in
  Schama, S., p. 87.
'After about fifteen minutes we came across another shepherd boy who
  was yodeling . . .' Twain, M., p. 192.
John Dundas Cochrane: Roberts, J., p. 178.
A 2010 survey found that only 6% of the French strongly support the
  concept of the free market: Globescan survey quoted in *The Economist*,
  9 April 2011, p. 68.
'the poorest know, and the richest have forgotten.' Pretty, J., p. 164.

Food and Drink

'Hunger is insolent, and will be fed.' Homer, *The Odyssey*, p. 43, http://books. google.co.uk/books?id=zDkRAAAAIAAJ&pg.

'void your bowels ten times over.' Polo, M., p. 68.

The Bantu . . . 'clanship of porridge': Ackerman, D., p. 127.

Eric Newby: *Oxford Dictionary of Natural Biography* and quoted in Archer, J., p. 200.

'Like the Italian, the Anglo-Catholic, and the Greek fasts . . .' Burton, Sir R., *To the Holy Shrines*, London: Penguin, 2007, p. 23.

The Greeks and Romans could tell which waters: Ackerman, D., p. 140.

'I went to the door of the Maestro de Posta . . .' Bond Head, F., p. 57.

'an excellent ant pâté.' Humboldt, A., p. 238.

Contrasting Lines

'The same impression repeated again and again . . .' Hugo, Victor, quoted in Guerlac, Suzanne, *The Impersonal Sublime: Hugo, Baudelaire, Lautréamont*, Google Books, accessed 21 November 2011, http://books.google.co.uk/books?id=Arod5ESDUlcC.

Francis Bond Head: Bond Head, F., p. 75–6.

Colin Thubron: 'Travel and the Writer', talk at the Royal Geographical Society, 1 March 2011.

'It is grander than anything left to us by Greece or Rome . . .' Mouhot, Henri, *Travels in the Central Parts of Indo-China*, 1864, quoted in *The Faber Book of Exploration*.

'The island would generally be considered as very uninteresting . . .' Darwin, C., pp. 5–6.

'embedded like a precious object on a dark velvet background.' Pallasmaa, J., p. 47.

David Thompson: Bohls, Elizabeth A. & Duncan, Ian, p. 387.

'I love the open Down most, but without hedges England would not be England . . .' Lubbock, J., p. 195.

There are very few stone walls in chalk country: Whitefield, P., p. 29.

Rousseau 'decided to abandon his birthplace, his apprenticeship . . .' Solnit, R., *Wanderlust*, p. 18.

Gontran de Poncins: de Poncins, G., *Kabloona, Among the Inuit*, quoted in Davidson, R., pp. 159–60.

The River

'The face of the water, in time, became a wonderful book . . .' Twain, M., *Life on the Mississippi*, http://en.wikiquote.org/wiki/Life_on_the_Mississippi, accessed 21 November 2011.

Caesar: Connors, Catherine, *Lucan's Nile: A Geography of the Unknown*,

Politics, Violence and the Republican Imagination: Lucan and His Legacy, Princeton University, 3–5 October 2003.

Flight in Exodus can be seen: Schama, S., p. 264.

The Rocky Mountains separate the flow of water: Whiston Spirn, A., p. 144.

Twelve cubits meant famine: Hibbs, Vivian A., *The Mendes Maze: A Libation Table for the Inundation of the Nile*, London, 1985, cited in Schama, S., p. 260.

'Dull echoes high up in the mountains warned us of its approach . . .' Przhevalsky, Nikolai, *Mongolia, the Tangut Country and the Solitudes of Northern Tibet*, 1873, quoted in Hanbury-Tenison, R., p. 63.

As the speed of the water increases, the size of the particles a river can carry goes up by a factor of sixty-four: Reader's Digest, *Joy of Nature*, p. 192.

During a rainstorm in the Tehachapi Mountains: Reader's Digest, *Joy of Nature*, p. 192.

'For the most appalling quality of water is its strength . . .' Shepherd, N., p. 21.

The Roman Emperor Justinian prohibited paganism: Schama, S., p. 265.

The Jordan was the sacred river: Schama, S., p. 264.

All Harkhuf: Carpenter, R., pp. 9–10.

On 5 August 1804 Lewis Clark: Lewis, Meriwether & Clark, William, p. 47.

The medieval Arabic scholar, Ibn Juzayy: Mackintosh-Smith, T., p. 61.

A citron here amongst us shows: author unknown, quoted by Ibn Juzayy in Mackintosh-Smith, T., p. 62.

'a necklace between two breasts': Ibn Battutah, in Mackintosh-Smith, T., p. 75.

Jean Leray and Reynolds number: Ball, P., *Flow*, p. 27.

Braided rivers: Ball, P., *Branches*, p. 116.

Susan Derges: Ball, P., *Flow*, p. 20 and http://www.susanderges.com

'Sometimes, if you stand on the bottom rail of a bridge . . .' Milne, A. A., *Winnie the Pooh*.

Lines in the Earth

'Sehnsucht – the passion for what is ever beyond . . .' Stevenson, R. L., *Travel*, p. 236, Google Books, accessed 21 November 2011.

H. G. Wells, Jim Harrison, Edward Thomas: Minshull, Douglas, pp. 103–35.

Carl Andre: Moran, J., p. 1.

'To the mind which pursues every road to its end . . .' Watts, A., p. 84.

Does the road wind up-hill all the way?: Christina Rossetti, 'Up-Hill', 1858, http://www.poetryfoundation.org/poem/174268, accessed 21 November 2011.

Saunter, 'idle people who roved about the country': Thoreau, H. D., *Walking*, pp. 7–8.

In Venezuela Humboldt witnessed an interesting moment in the adolescence of a path: Humboldt, A., pp. 136–7.

The relationship between the directness of a route . . .: Whitefield, P., p. 303.

Claude François Denecourt: Schama, S., pp. 554–60.

Tourists who visited Niagara Falls in the 19th Century: Whiston Spirn, A., p. 224.

'gentle chirping noise': Darwin, C., p. 27.

'between Sheffield Place and East Grinsted . . .' Gibbon, Edward, quoted in Moran, J., p. 9.

James Holmann: Roberts, J., pp. 118, 189.

'The roads are steep and dangerous . . .' Tsang, Hsuan, quoted in Hanbury-Tenison, R., p. 6.

In the UK we might find pineapple weeds and greater plantains: Whitefield, P., p. 311.

Patrick Whitefield reports that in Wales the best blackberries: Whitefield, P., p. 305.

Sir Joseph Dalton Hooker: Hanbury-Tenison, R., p. 45.

coastal plants like the Danish scurvygrass which lines motorways with small white flowers in spring: Whitefield, P., p. 309.

There are young apple trees: Whitefield, P., p. 309.

'We did so, and the moon was now behind us!' Standing Bear, Luther, *My People and the Sioux*, 1928, Google Books, p. 131, accessed 21 November 2011.

Time

'Nobody sees a flower, really . . .' O'Keeffe, Georgia, quoted in Ackerman, D., p. xvi.

'What then is time?' Augustine, http://en.wikipedia.org/wiki/Time

Pliny the Elder noticed that thyme flowered: Pliny, p. 229.

Pliny noted that bees went into hibernation: Pliny, p. 149.

'When the Pleiades, daughters of Atlas, are rising . . .', Hesiod, http://omacl.org/Hesiod/works.html

Ishi: Kroeber, T., p. 176.

Jacques Cartier: Bakeless, J., p. 113.

'A rose is not necessarily . . .' Pittendrigh, Colin quoted in Foster, R. & Kreitzman, L., p. 10.

Carolus Linnaeus: Brian G. Gardiner, 'Linnaeus' Floral Clock', http://www.linnean.org/fileadmin/images/The_Linnean_-_Tercentenary/4-Floral_Clock.pdf

Photoperiodism: Tudge, C., p. 274.

Wheat flowers as the days get longer: Foster, R. & Kreitzman, L., p. 132.

Font de Gaume cave: Foster, R. & Kreitzman, L., p. 131.

Reindeer migration: Hoge, Warren in *New York Times*, 26 March 2001.

'The myriads of tormenting flies . . .' and 'Our enemy the polar bear . . .' Thompson, D. from Bohls, Elizabeth A. & Duncan, Ian, pp. 379–80.

'I usually rise when I hear the merry laugh . . .' Leichhardt, L., p. 107.

'Breaking suddenly into a hollow . . .' Shepherd, N., p. 50.

Cicada root experiment: Foster, R. & Kreitzman, L., p. 51.

Marco Polo observed that the Tartars: Polo, M., p. 97.

One second in 10 billion years: Aveni, A., p. 193.

'The gods confound the man who first found out . . .' Plautus, http://en.wikipedia.org/wiki/Time_discipline, accessed 20 November 2011.

Smooth grey pebble: Zalasiewicz, J., p. 40.

'brother of death'. Homer's *Iliad*. Stewart, Michael. 'Hypnos' *Greek Mythology: From the Iliad to the Fall of the Last Tyrant*. http://messagenetcommresearch.com/myths/bios/hypnos.html

Doggerland: Pryor, F., p. 27.

Henry Hudson: Bakeless, J., p. 228.

'They are a brave sight . . .' Van der Post, L., p. 110.

'The broken branches were strewed around . . .' Easton, Charlotte Anne, *Narrative of a Residence in Belgium during the Campaign of 1815*, 1817, from Bohls, Elizabeth A. & Duncan, Ian, p. 63.

Christianity is a religion that blossomed in cities: Watts, A., pp. 25–6.

Language

Menderes river: Ball, P., *H2o*, p. 38.

Brooks, gills, etc.: Barrett, Jeff, Turner, Robin & Walsh, Andrew, p. 9.

Place names ending -by or -thorp: Pryor, F., pp. 240–1.

Patrick Whitefield makes the claim: Whitefield, P., p. 7.

Latin word for grey: BBC website, accessed 12 May 2011, http://www.bbc.co.uk

Japanese word for blue: Ackerman, D., p. 253.

'The natives seemed to speak a less melodious language . . .', Kobboyakka, Nobungob: Leichhardt, L., p. 223.

'rough magic'. Solnit, R., *Wanderlust*, p. 176.

'The conversation of the Scots grows every day less unpleasing . . .' Johnson, Samuel, *A Journey to the Western Islands of Scotland*, 1775, quoted in Bohls, Elizabeth A. & Duncan, Ian, p. 161.

San Nicolas island: Kroeber, T., p. 5.

Companions

'Anywhere you go, we will go with you; anything you ask us to do . . .' Amundsen, quoted in Hanbury-Tenison, R., p. 102.

'Adieu to disappointment and spleen . . .' Austen, Jane, quoted in Solnit, R., *Wanderlust*, p. 100.

Italo Calvino: Calvino, I., p. 44.

'If you fight with each other, I will cut off these breasts . . .' Polo, M., p. 263.

'I never found the companion that . . .' Thoreau, H. D., *Walden*, quoted in Perrin, J., p. 58.

'a bubble of Englishness'; 'They don't do that in Haywards Heath!' Thubron, Colin, 'Travel and the Writer', a lecture at the Royal Geographical Society, 1 March 2011.

'Every thing around bears an air so calm and tranquil . . .' Gilpin, W., pp. 40–42.

'I am alone, sitting facing the grey expanse of the shifting sea . . .' Eberhardt, I., quoted in Kershaw, E., p. 23.

Charles Kingsley: Lubbock, J., p. 6.

Richard Nelson . . . Koyukon: Abram, D., p. 69.

'swayed by an overmastering impulse within me . . .' Battutah, Ibn, quoted in Mackintosh-Smith, T., p. 3.

Robin Hanbury-Tenison: Talk at the 'Words by the Water' Literary Festival, Keswick, 8 March 2011.

'I have been four years in the East . . .' Paton, Andrew Archibald, *Servia, the Youngest Member of the European Family: or, a Residence in Belgrade*, 1845, quoted in Roberts, J., pp. 311–12.

Customs and Habits

'Nothing so needs reforming as other people's habits.' Twain, M., http://www.gutenberg.org/files/102/old/puddn10.txt

Talmud: Van Swaaij, L. & Klare, J., p. 22.

'Look, for instance, at that Indian Moslem drinking a glass of water . . .' Burton, R., pp. 1–2.

Olaudah Equiano: Equiano, O., p. 51.

Marco Polo: Polo, M., pp. 82–83, 88, 91–2, 98, 105, 172–5.

Humboldt in Cartagena: Humboldt, A., p. 292.

Ludwig Leichhardt: Leichhardt, L., p. 112.

Religion

'In the worshipful attitude toward Nature there is a highly religious . . .' Suzuki, D. T., p. 335.

'All over the earth similarities may be found . . .' Humboldt, A., p. 105.

'It is a fact that all the Saracens in the world are agreed . . .': Polo, M., pp. 53–4.

'since Armenians, Nestorians, and Jacobites differ in certain points of doctrine . . .' Polo, M., p. 57.

the holy wells in Ireland: Solnit, R, *Wanderlust*, p. 49.

'baptising the customs': Turner, Victor & Edith, quoted in Solnit, R., *Wanderlust*, p. 49.

'When God began to create heaven and earth . . .' *Tanakh, The Holy Scriptures*, quoted in Abram, D., p. 239.

'When we die, the wind blows away our footprints and that is the end of us . . .' Minshull, D., quoted in *Vintage Book of Walking*.

'There is assuredly morality in the oxygen of the mountains.' Tyndall, J., quoted in Macfarlane, R., p. 160.

'It seemed to me that the high mountains, the rivers, lakes, trees, flowers . . .' Jung, C. G., p. 28.

'the appreciation of the beautiful is at bottom religious.' Suzuki, D. T., p. 363.

'Everybody is offended except the Explorer . . .' Schama, S., p. 375.

'Picking up blossoms doesn't seem to be a man's work at all in any kind of times . . .' Muir, J., p. 25.

El Escorial: *New York Times*, 15 March 1994, accessed online 17 April 2011.

Beauty

'Beauty, thou wild fantastic ape . . .' From Cowley, Abraham, 'Beauty', complete poem in *The Works of the English Poets, from Chaucer to Cowper*, Samuel Johnson ed., 1656, vol. 7, p. 115.

'The rose is a large flower, yet it grows upon a small shrub . . .' Burke, E., p. 86.

'The eye was lost in the profusion of objects . . .' (and all further Gilpin quotes from the same source). Gilpin, W., pp. 20 et al.

Bella donna: Ackerman, D., p. 270.

'In 1968 in New York a study found . . .' Ackerman, D., p. 272.

'Marco Polo's reports that the women of Badakshan . . .' Polo, M., p. 78.

Studies to work out the scenes we like today: Pretty, J., p. 33.

'If the world were perfect, it wouldn't be.' Van Swaaij, L. & Klare, J., p. 80.

'My work always tried to unite the truth with the beautiful . . .' Weyl, H., http://www.weylmann.com/

'Below my window in Ross . . .' Potter, D., http://www.guardian.co.uk/theguardian/2007/sep/12/greatinterviews and personal correspondence with Lord Bragg.

'What by general consent is allowed to be a more beautiful object . . .' Burke, E., p. 86.

Inner Time and Mood

'Learn to reverence night . . .' Beston, H., p. 173.

Rhythms of Life: For the facts in this section I am indebted to the excellent book *Rhythms of Life* by Russell Foster and Leon Kreitzman.

testosterone is highest in men during early afternoons in October: Ackerman, D., p. 250.

'When a woman responds to her impatient husband . . .' Lecompte du Nuoy, Pierre, quoted in Foster, R. & Kreitzman, L., p. 9.

'If something is boring after two minutes, try it for four . . .' Cage, J., quoted in Smith, K., p. 49.

'irresistible impatience to come to the end'. Leichhardt, L., p. 224.

Leichhardt savoured his first sugar: Leichhardt, L., p. 119.

Gerard Manley Hopkins: Deakin, R., *Wildwood*, p. 39.

Roger Deakin, Sylvia Plath: Barrett, J., Turner, R. & Walsh, A., p. 90.

Amondawa tribe: *When Time is not Space: The social and linguistic construction of time intervals and temporal event relations in an Amazonian culture*, Sinha, C., da Silva Sinha, V., Zinken, J. & Sampaio, W., *Language and Cognition*, 3(1): 137–169, 2011.

'utterly vanished'. Muir, J., p. 123.

Spiced apples and lavender: Ackerman, D., p. 57.

their grip strengthened by 13.5 percent: Ackerman, D., p. 254.

Musk: Ackerman, D., p. 12.

A fifteen-year study of psychiatric patients in Sweden: Pretty, J., p. 31.

'The sense of all this produc'd different . . .' Dennis, J., quoted in Macfarlane, R., p. 73.

'The air at this spot I found so soft, balmy, and exhilarating . . .' Roberts, J., p. 118.

Imagination and Wonder

'How strangely mobile is man's imagination . . .' Humboldt, A., p. 95.

Mary Ann Hathaway, 'cadence of a cascade': Bohls, Elizabeth A. & Duncan, Ian, p. 166.

'I shall never find in the wilds of Labrador any greater wildness . . .' Thoreau, H. D., *Journal*, 30 August 1856, quoted in Schama, S., p. vii.

'Already it is more difficult to find sustenance . . .' Bourdillon, F. W., quoted in Macfarlane, R., p. 193.

'a sentiment of ecstatic wonder, not unallied to madness.' Shelley, P., quoted in Schama, S., p. 475.

'If there were men whose habitations had been always underground . . .' Aristotle, quoted by Cicero, from Lubbock, J., p. 9.

Satori: Watts, A., p. 94.

'When was the last time you actually tasted a glass of water?' Puddicombe, A., *Guardian Podcast*, 24 January 2011.

'restless hearts': St Augustine, *Confessions*,
http://www.ccel.org/ccel/augustine/confessions.iv.html
'through art, through the pure, disinterested contemplation of beauty.'
Kenny, A., p. 766.

Sharing the Experience

'The beauty of nature re-forms itself in the mind . . .' Emerson, R. W.,
p. 47.
'even the cleverest and most judicious minds have neglected extensive
areas . . .' Mas' Udi, p. 4.
'concavely cylindrical, not dichotomous . . .' Clarke, W. B., quoted in
Leichhardt, L., p. 104.
We may understand the sun, sky, land, meteorology, thermodynamics:
This is a paraphrase of an expression of A. N. Whitehead's, quoted in
Watts, A., p. 83.
'only the source of their influence on our emotions . . .' Cornish, V.,
p. 21.
'But what language can reproduce the sensations . . .' de Saussure,
Horace-Benedict, http://www.archive.org/stream/
lifeofhoracebeneoofresuoft/lifeofhoracebeneoofresuoft_djvu.txt
'You paint a Big Tree and it only looks like a common tree in a cramped
coffin.' Fitz Hugh, Ludlow, 'Seven Weeks in the Great Yo-Semite',
Atlantic Monthly, 13 (June 1864), p. 745, quoted in Shama, S., p. 194.
'The landscape thinks itself in me . . . and I am its consciousness.'
Cezanne, quoted in Wylie, J., p. 2.
'As I contemplate the blue of the sky . . .' Merleau-Ponty, quoted in
Wylie, J., p. 150.
'combination of a silver tongue and iron thighs seems to be a rare one.'
Solnit, R., *Wanderlust*, p. 129.
'Sir, if a man has experienced the inexpressible, he is under no obligation
to express it.' Johnson, S., quoted in Halpern, D. & Frank, D., p. 226.
'On the summit of the precipice, and in the heart of the green woods . . .'
Roberts, J., p. 355.
'modern civilization can be characterized by how it broadens our ideas . . .'
Humboldt, A., p. 10.

Epilogue

'We shall not cease . . .' Eliot, T. S., *Four Quartets*, http://en.wikiquote.
org/wiki/T._S._Eliot

Bibliography

Abram, David, *The Spell of the Sensous*, New York: Vintage Books, 1997

Ackerman, Diane, *A Natural History of the Senses*, New York: Vintage, 1995

Adam, John A., *A Mathematical Nature Walk*, Princeton: Princeton University Press, 2009

Aldus Books Ltd, *A History of Discovery and Exploration: Eastern Islands, Southern Seas*, London: Aldus Books & Jupiter Books, 1973

Anderson, JRL, *The Ulysses Factor: The Exploring Instinct in Man*, London: Hodder & Stoughton, 1970

Archer, Jeremy, *Away at Christmas: Heroic Tales of Exploration from 1492 to the Present Day*, London: Elliott and Thompson Ltd, 2009

Aveni, Anthony, *People and the Sky: Our Ancestors and the Cosmos*, London: Thames & Hudson, 2008

Bakeless, John, *The Eyes of Discovery: America as Seen by the First Explorers*, New York: Dover Publications, 1961

Ball, Philip, *H2O: A Biography of Water*, London: Orion Books Ltd, 2000

Ball, Philip, *Bright Earth: The Invention of Colour*, London: Vintage, 2008

Ball, Philip, *Nature's Patterns: a Tapestry in Three Parts: Branches, Flow and Shapes*, Oxford: Oxford University Press, 2009

Banks, Joseph, *The Endeavour – Journal of Sir Joseph Banks*, Middlesex: The Echo Library, 2006

Barber, Lynn, *The Heyday of Natural History, 1820–1870*, London: Jonathan Cape Ltd, 1980

Barrett, Jeff, Turner, Robin & Walsh, Andrew, *Caught by the River: A Collection of Words on Water*, London: Octopus Publishing Group Ltd, 2009

Barth, Heinrich, *Travels and Discoveries in North and Central Africa (Volume 3); Being a Journal of an Expedition Undertaken Under the Auspices of H.B.M.'s Government*, Tennessee: General Books, 2010

Beston, Henry, *The Outermost House*, New York: First Owl Books, 1992

Binney, Ruth, *Wise Words & Country Ways: Weather Lore*, Cincinnati: David & Charles Ltd, 2010

Bohls, Elizabeth A. & Duncan, Ian, *Travel Writing 1700–1830: An anthology*, Oxford: Oxford University Press, 2008

Bond Head, Francis, *Rough Notes Taken During Some Rapid Journeys Across the Pampas and Among the Andes*, Cambridge: Cambridge University Press, 2009

Borrow, George, *Wild Wales*, London: Collins Clear-Type Press, 1955

Boysen, Sally, *The Smartest Animals on the Planet*, A & C Black, 2009

Bowles, Paul, *Travels: Collected Writings, 1950–93*, London: Sort of Books, 2010

Burke, Edmund, *A Philosophical Enquiry*, Oxford: Oxford University Press, 2008

Burton, Tim, *To the Holy Shrines*, London: Penguin Group, 2007

Calvino, Italo, *Invisible Cities*, London: Vintage, 1997

Carpenter, Rees, *Beyond the Pillars of Hercules: The Classical World Seen Through the Eyes of its Discoveries*, London: Universal–Tandem Publishing Co. Ltd, 1973

Conrad, Joseph, *Heart of Darkness*, London: Penguin, 1994

Cook, James, *The Journals*, London: Penguin Group, 2003

Cornish, Vaughan, *The Beauties of Scenery: A Geographical Survey*, London: Frederick Muller, 1944

Darwin, Charles, *The Voyage of the Beagle: Journal of Researches into the Natural History and Geology of the Countries Visited during the Voyage of HMS Beagle round the World, Under the Command of Captain Fitz Roy, RN*, Hertfordshire: Wordsworth Editions Ltd, 1997

Davidson, Robert (ed.), *Journeys: An Anthology*, London: Pan Macmillan Ltd, 2002

Deakin, Roger, *Wildwood: A Journey Through Trees*, London: Penguin Group, 2007

Dennis, Felix, *Tales from the Woods*, London: Ebury Press, 2010

Ellis, William, *Polynesian Researchers: Hawaii*, Rutland: Charles E. Tuttle Co, 1969

Emerson, Ralph Waldo, *Nature and Selected Essays*, London: Penguin, 2003

Equiano, Olaudah, *Sold as a Slave*, London: Penguin Group, 2007

Fortey, Richard, *The Hidden Landscape: A Journey into the Geological Past*, London: The Bodley Head, 2010

Foster, Russell & Kreitzman, Leon, *Rhythms of Life: The Biological Clocks that Control the Daily Lives of Every Living Thing*, London: Profile Books Ltd, 2005

Frazer, Sir James, *The Golden Bough*, Ware: Wordsworth Editions, 1993

Gilpin, William, *Observations on the River Wye*, London: Pallas Athene, 2005

Gooley, Tristan, *The Natural Navigator*, London: Virgin Books, 2010

Goudie, Andrew & Viles, Heather, *Landscapes and Geomorphology: A Very Short Introduction*, Oxford, Oxford University Press, 2010

Griffiths, Jay, *Wild*, London: Penguin, 2008

Halpern, Daniel & Frank, Dan (ed.), *The Nature Reader*, New Jersey: The Echo Press, 1996

Hanbury-Tenison, Robin, (selected by) *The Oxford Book of Exploration*, Oxford: Oxford University Press, 1994

Harberd, Nicholas, *Seed to Seed: The Secret Life of Plants*, London: Bloomsbury Publishing plc, 2007

Holmes, Richard, *The Age of Wonder: How the Romantic Generation Discovered the Beauty and Terror of Science*, London: HarperCollins Publishers, 2009

Hudson, WH, *Afoot in England*, Oxford: John Beaufoy Publishing, 2010

Huntford, Ronald, *Shackleton*, London: Abacus, 1996

Jamie, Kathleen, *Findings*, London: Sort of Books, 2005

Jellicoe, Geoffrey & Susan, *The Landscape of Man: Shaping the Environment from Prehistory to the Present Day*, London: Thames & Hudson, 1975

Jung, C. G., *The Earth Has a Soul: CG Jung on Nature, Technology & Modern Life*, California: North Atlantic Books, 2008

Keay, John (ed.), *History of World Exploration*, London: Reed International Books Ltd, 1991

Kenny, Anthony, *A New History of Western Philosophy*, Oxford: Oxford University Press, 2010

Kershaw, Elizabeth (ed.), *The Nomad: The Diaries of Isabelle Eberhardt*, Chichester: Summersdale Publishers Ltd, 2002

Kroeber, Theodora, *Ishi in Two Worlds: A biography of the Last Wild Indian in North America*, California, University of California Press, 2002

Lamb, F Bruce, *Wizard of the Upper Amazon: The Story of Manuel Cordova-Rios*, California: North Atlantic Books, 1986

Laws, Bill, *Fifty Plants that Changes the Course of History*, Cincinnati: Quid Publishing, 2010

Leask, Nigel, *Curiosity and the Aesthetics of Travel Writing 1770–1840*, Oxford: Oxford University Press, 2008

Leichhardt, Ludwig, *Journal of an Overland Expedition in Australia: from Moreton Bay to Port Essington, a distance of upwards of 3000 miles, during the years 1844–1845*

Levi-Strauss, Claude, *Structural Anthropology*, New York, Basic Books, 1963

Lewis, Meriwether and Clark, William, *The Journals of Lewis and Clark*, Washington, National Geographic Society, 2002

Lubbock, John, *The Beauties of Nature and the Wonders of the World We Live in*, London: Macmillan & Co, 1892

Lummis, Charles F. *A Tramp Across the Continent*, New York: Charles Scribner's Sons, 1892

Mabey, Richard, *A Brush with Nature*, BBC Books, 2010

Macfarlane, Robert, *Mountains of the Mind: A History of a Fascination*, London: Granta Publications, 2003

Mackintosh-Smith, Tim (ed.), *The Travels of Ibn Battutah*, London: Pan Macmillan, 2002

Mas' Udi, *Meadows of Gold*, London: Penguin Group, 2007

McKee, Alexander, *A World Too Vast: The Four Voyages of Columbus*, London: Souvenir Press Ltd, 1990

Meredith, George, *The Egoist*, 1879, Google Books

Merleau-Ponty, Maurice, *Sense and Non-sense*, US: Northwestern University Press, 1964

Minshull, Douglas (ed.), *The Vintage Book of Walking: An Anthology*, London: Vintage, 2000

Minshull, Douglas (ed.), *The Burning Leg*, London: Hesperus Press, 2010

Moran, Joe, *On Roads*, London: Profile Books, 2010

Morris, Desmond, *Manwatching: A Field Guide to Human Behaviour*, London: Collins Publishing Group, 1987

Muir, John, *A Thousand-Mile Walk to the Gulf*, Boston: Mariner Books, 1998

Nicholson, Geoff, *The Lost Art of Walking: The History, Science, Philosophy, Literate, Theory and Practice of Pedestriansim*, Chelmsford: Harbour Books Ltd, 2010

Oxford Dictionary of National Biography

Pallasmaa, Juhani, *The Eyes of Skin: Architecture and the Senses*, Chichester, John Wiley & Sons Ltd, 2010

Park, Mungo, *Travels in the Interior Districts of Africa*, Hertfordshire: Wordsworth Editions Ltd, 2002

Perrin, Jim, *River Map*, Ceredigion: Gomer Press, 2002

Pliny the Elder, *Natural History: A Selection*, London: Penguin Group, 2004

Polo, Marco, *The Travels*, London: Penguin Group, 1958

Pretty, Jules, *The Earth Only Endures: On Reconnecting with Nature and Our Place in it*, London: Earthscan, 2009

Pryor, Francis, *The Making of the British Landscape: How We Have Transformed the Land, from Prehistory to Today*, London: Penguin Group, 2010

Rackham, Oliver, *The History of the Countryside: The Full Fascinating Story of Britain's Landscape*, London: JM Dent & Sons, 1987

Rackham, Oliver, *Woodlands*, London: Collins, 2010

Readers' Digest Assocation Ltd, *Secrets of the Seashore: The Living Countryside*, London: Readers' Digest Association Ltd, 1984

Readers' Digest, *Joy of Nature: How to Explore and Enjoy the Fascinating World Around You*, London: Readers Digest Association Ltd, 1978

Roberts, Jason, *A Sense of the World: How a Blind Man Became History's Greatest Traveller*, London: Simon & Schuster UK Ltd, 2006

Robinson, JC, *The Walk: Notes on a Romantic Image*, Oklahoma: University of Oklahoma Press, 1989

Ruskin, John, *Modern Painters, Volume IV*, London: George Allen, 1906

Schama, Simon, *Landscape and Memory*, London: Harper Perennial, 2004

Shaw, Philip, *The Sublime*, London: Routledge, 2010

Shepherd, Nan, *The Living Mountain*, Edinburgh: Canongate Books Ltd, 2008

Smith, Keri, *How to be an Explorer of the World: Portable Art/Life Museum*, New York: Penguin Group, 2008

Solnit, Rebecca, *A Field Guide to Getting Lost*, Edinburgh: Canongate Books Ltd, 2006

Solnit, Rebecca, *Wanderlust; A History of Walking*, London: Verso, 2002

Spufford, Francis, *The Antarctic: An Anthology*, London: Granta Publications, 2008

Stewart, Ian, *Why Beauty is Truth: A History of Symmetry*, New York: Basic Books, 2008

Suzuki, Daisetz T., *Zen and Japanese Culture*, New York: Bollingen Foundation, 1959

Tanizaki, Junichiro, *In Praise of Shadows*, London: Vintage 2001

Thesiger, Wilfred, *Across the Empty Quarter*, London: Penguin Group, 2007

Thomas, Lowell, *The Untold Story of Exploration*, London: George G. Harrap & Co Ltd

Thompson, D'Arcy, *On Growth and Form*, Cambridge: Cambridge University Press, 2000

Thoreau, Henry David, *Walking*, Rockville: Arc Manor, 2007

Thoreau, Henry David, *Walden or, Life in the Woods*, New York: Dover Publications Inc, 1995

Tidmarsh, Celia, *Geography First – Mountains*, Lewes: White-Thomas Publishing Ltd, 2004

Towle, David W., Molecular Approaches to Understanding Salinity Adaptation of Estuarine Animals, American Zoology, 1997

Tudge, Colin, *The Secret Lives of Trees: How They Live and Why They Matter*, London: Penguin Group, 2006

Twain, Mark, *A Tramp Abroad*, New York: Penguin, 1997

Van der Post, Laurens, *The Lost World of the Kalahari*, London: Penguin, 1962

Van Swaaij, Louise & Klare, Jean, *The Atlas of Experience*, London: Bloomsbury Publishing plc, 2000

Vince, Ian, *The Lie of the Land: An Under-the-Field Guide to the British Isles*, London: Boxtree, 2010

Von Humboldt, Alexander, *Personal Nature of a Journey to the Equinoctial Regions of the New Continent*, London: Penguin Group, 1995

Wallace, Alfred Russell, *The Malay Archipelago*, Tennessee: General Books, 2009

Watts, Alan, *Nature, Man and Woman*, New York: Vintage Books, 1991

Wheeler, Sara, *Tips About Icebergs*, London: Slightly Foxed Ltd, 2010

Whiston Spirn, Anne, *The Language of Landscape*, New Haven: Yale University Press, 1998

White, Gilbert, *The Natural History of Selbourne*, London: Penguin Group, 1987

Whitefield, Patrick, *The Living Landscape: How to Read it and Understand it*, Hampshire: Permanent Publications, 2009

Williams, Raymond, *The Country and the City*, New York: Oxford University Press, 1973

Wylie, John, *Landscape*, London: Routledge, 2007

Yarham, Robert, *How to Read the Landscape*, Lewes: Ivy Press, 2010

Zalasiewicz, Jan, *The Planet in a Pebble: A Journey into Earth's Deep History*, Oxford: Oxford University Press, 2010

New York Times, 9 March 1912.

Index